# PhoneGap Build

## Developing Cross Platform
## Mobile Applications
## in the Cloud

# PhoneGap Build

## Developing Cross Platform Mobile Applications in the Cloud

B.M. Harwani

CRC Press
Taylor & Francis Group
Boca Raton London New York

CRC Press is an imprint of the
Taylor & Francis Group, an **informa** business

AN AUERBACH BOOK

CRC Press
Taylor & Francis Group
6000 Broken Sound Parkway NW, Suite 300
Boca Raton, FL 33487-2742

First issued in paperback 2019

ISBN-13: 978-1-4665-8974-2 (hbk)
ISBN-13: 978-1-138-37482-9 (pbk)

---

**Library of Congress Cataloging-in-Publication Data**

---

Harwani, B. M.
   PhoneGap build : developing cross platform mobile applications in the cloud / Bintu Harwani.
      pages cm
   Includes bibliographical references and index.
   ISBN 978-1-4665-8974-2 (hardback)
   1. Mobile computing. 2. PhoneGap (Application development environment) 3. Application software--Development. 4. Cloud computing. 5. Cross-platform software development. I. Title.

QA76.59.H367 2013
004.67'82--dc23
                                                   2013037623

---

# Contents

# Preface

PhoneGap is a standards-based, open-source development framework for building fast, easy, cross-platform mobile apps with HTML5, CSS3, and JavaScript for iPhone/iPad, Android, Windows Phone 8, Palm, Symbian, BlackBerry, and more. Once written, the PhoneGap application can be deployed to any mobile device without losing the features of a native app. The PhoneGap applications are able to interact with mobile device hardware, such as the accelerometer or global positioning system (GPS). In other words, PhoneGap provides access to a device's accelerometer, compass, and geolocation capabilities. In addition, you can access device contacts, the local file system, camera, and media on multiple platforms without writing a single line of code.

This book is for intermediate to advanced users. It is comprehensive and covers each topic in detail. The book teaches techniques to configure environments for different mobile platforms. It describes the use of HTML5, CSS3, and JavaScript to develop apps that run on devices of different mobile operating systems. It exploits the features provided by PhoneGap and PhoneGap Build to develop cross-platform mobile applications for the cloud.

The book begins with explaining the differences among the existing mobile platforms, the different types of browsers they support, and the programming languages and integrated development environment (IDE) required to develop apps for each of them. It then describes how PhoneGap makes the task of developing cross-platform mobile apps easier. Initially beginning with small applications, the text gradually moves toward discussing advanced concepts, exploiting different application programming interfaces (APIs) and methods in creating real-life practical applications. By the time you finish the book, you will have learned how to develop feature-rich mobile applications that can run on the cloud to support different platforms.

This book is designed to teach you how to

- Use and configure development environments for mobile platforms, including iOS, Android, BlackBerry, Windows phone, webOS, and Symbian
- Exploit PhoneGap features to develop cross-platform mobile applications
- Use PhoneGap Build to develop mobile apps in the cloud
- Exploit geolocation, compass, accelerometer, contacts, camera, media, and capture APIs and use them in real-life practical mobile applications
- Use the `Database` object to save, fetch, and maintain information for future use
- Use PhoneGap with Sencha Touch
- Use PhoneGap with jQuery Mobile

This book will be beneficial for developers and instructors who want to learn or teach mobile programming. For practical implementation, the book also explains using back-end databases for storing and fetching information. In short, it is a very useful reference book.

# About the Author

B.M. Harwani is the founder and owner of Microchip Computer Education (MCE), based in Ajmer, India, which provides computer education in all programming and Web developing platforms. He graduated with a B.E. in computer engineering from the University of Pune, and also has a C Level (master's diploma in computer technology) from DOEACC, Government of India. Having been involved in the teaching field for more than 19 years, Harwani has developed an art of explaining even the most complicated topics in a straightforward and easily understandable fashion. He has written several books that include *Foundation Joomla!* (friendsofED, 2009); *jQuery Recipes: A Problem-Solution Approach* (Apress, 2010); *Beginning Web Development for Smartphones: Developing Web Applications with PHP, MSQL, and jQTouch* (CreateSpace, 2010); *Core Data iOS Essentials* (Packt Publishing, 2011); *Introduction to Python Programming and Developing GUI Applications with PyQT* (Cengage Learning PTR, 2011); *Android Programming Unleashed* (Sams Publishing, 2012); and *The Android Tablet Developer's Cookbook* (Developer's Library) (Addison-Wesley Professional, 2013). To learn more, visit his blog at: http://bmharwani.com/blog.

# Chapter 1

## Introducing PhoneGap

In this chapter, the following topics will be covered:

- Introduction to PhoneGap
- Exploring PhoneGap's features
- Setting up an Android environment
- Creating a first PhoneGap application for Android
- Updating the Activity class
- Configuring the project metadata
- Ensuring PhoneGap is loaded

Today, there are many smartphone platforms on the market: Android, iPhone, BlackBerry, Nokia, Windows Phone 8, and Samsung's bada and MeeGo. The job of developing cross-platform mobile applications has become very critical because of the growing number of mobile operating systems (OSs). The developers have to first set up different environments for each platform. They then need a bit of expertise with each respective OS.

Not only OSs but also different programming languages are required for different mobile platforms. In addition to this, developers need to be familiar with the features supported by each mobile platform. Table 1.1 shows the list of operating systems, software, and programming languages required by various mobile platforms.

There is one more problem: different mobile platforms use different kinds of browsers. To overcome these problems, the PhoneGap framework is popularly used for cross-platform development.

## Introduction to PhoneGap

PhoneGap is a standards-based, open-source development framework for building fast, easy, cross-platform mobile apps with HTML5, CSS3, and JavaScript for iPhone/iPad, Android, Windows Phone 8, Palm, Symbian, BlackBerry, and more. Once written, the PhoneGap application can be deployed to any mobile device without losing features of a native app. PhoneGap applications are able to interact with mobile device hardware, such as the accelerometer or GPS. In other words,

1

**Table 1.1  List of Operating Systems, Software, and Programming Languages Required by Different Mobile Platforms**

| Mobile OS | Operating System | Software/IDEs | Programming Language |
|---|---|---|---|
| iOS | Mac only | Xcode | Objective C |
| Android | Windows/Mac/Linux | Eclipse/Java/Android Developer Tools (ADT) | Java |
| BlackBerry | Windows | Eclipse/Java Development Environment (JDE) | Java |
| Symbian | Windows/Mac/Linux | Carbide | C++ |
| WebOS | Windows/Mac/Linux | Eclipse/WebOS plug-in | HTML/JavaScript/C++ |
| Windows Phone 8 | Windows Visual Studio 2010 | Silverlight or Windows Presentation Foundation (WPF) | C# |

PhoneGap provides access to a device's accelerometer, compass, and geolocation capabilities. Not only this, but we can access a device's contacts, local file system, camera, and media on multiple platforms, without writing a single line of code.

PhoneGap applications are also built and packaged like native applications, meaning that they can be distributed through the Apple App Store or the Android Market. Also, we can upload our application to the PhoneGap Build service where it is compiled in the "cloud." The process produces app store-ready apps for Apple iOS, Google Android, Windows Phone 8, Palm, Symbian, BlackBerry, and other OSs.

The PhoneGap Software Development Kit (SDK) provides an application programming interface (API) that is an abstraction layer providing the developer with access to hardware- and platform-specific features. As PhoneGap abstracts the native mobile platform, the same code can be used on multiple mobile platforms with little or no change.

## Exploring PhoneGap Features

Features that PhoneGap supports are as follows:

- The Accelerometer API of PhoneGap enables the application to sense change in the device's orientation and act accordingly.
- The Camera API of PhoneGap either allows applications to retrieve a picture from the camera or fetches the images from already existing photo galleries.
- The Compass API of PhoneGap is useful for map and navigation applications, since the map rotates as the user changes the bearing of the phone. There is an option to fetch one reading of change in the device heading or to continuously receive the changes in the device heading.
- The Contacts API of PhoneGap enables us to read and write contacts.
- The File API of PhoneGap allows applications to read, write, and list directories and file systems.

- The Geolocation API helps to retrieve the device's geolocation. The API is usually used in map-based applications and in applications where the user can check into a place by using his or her GPS location.
- The Media API allows applications to control the media sensors and other applications on the device. This API allows applications to record and play back audio and video recordings.
- The Network API of PhoneGap provides the applications with the ability to see the state of the network. The API tells the applications whether the device is on a 2G/3G/4G network or a WiFi network.
- The Notification API allows applications to notify the user that something has occurred, by making a beep, vibration, or providing a visual alert.
- The Storage API of PhoneGap provides a built-in Structured Query Language (SQL) database for the applications. This enables applications to insert, retrieve, update, search, and delete data through SQL statements.

To create applications with PhoneGap, we need to first install the standard SDK for the mobile platforms we want to target for our app. This is because PhoneGap will actually use these SDKs when compiling our app for that platform.

The PhoneGap framework is primarily a JavaScript library that allows Hypertext Markup Language (HTML)/JavaScript applications to access device features. The PhoneGap framework also has a native component that works behind the scene and does the actual work on the device. Let us begin our journey of understanding PhoneGap by developing apps for an Android platform first.

## Setting Up an Android Environment

The first step toward creating a PhoneGap application is to set up a mobile development environment. We will begin with Android because the Android application development is in Java, which is based on Eclipse and supports almost all features of PhoneGap. We need to download and install the following prerequisites for Android:

1. JDK 1.6+
2. Eclipse integrated development environment (IDE)
3. Android SDK
4. Android Developer Tools (ADT) plug-in for Eclipse

Refer to Appendix A for the procedures used to install the software above.

Let us go ahead and download and install PhoneGap. Visit the URL: `http://phonegap.com/download`, and download PhoneGap. The version that is available at the time of this writing is PhoneGap 2.2.0. After downloading, extract the archive to your local disk drive.

We are now ready to create our first PhoneGap application for Android within Eclipse.

## Creating a First PhoneGap Application for Android

Let us create a simple Hello World! application. In this application, we will simply embed the PhoneGap's JavaScript file and display a `Hello World!` message. Name the newly created Android project `PGHelloWorld`.

To create an application, launch Eclipse and choose `File->New->Android Application Project`, or click the Android Project Creator icon on the Eclipse toolbar. A dialog box appears asking for information about the new Android application, as shown in Figure 1.1. In the `Application Name:` box, enter the name of the application. Let us name the application `PGHelloWorld`. The `Project Name:` box shows the name of the project automatically by default. The project name assigned is the same as the application name, that is, `PGHelloWorld`. You can change the project name if desired. The `Package Name:` box shows the default package name, `com.example.pghelloworld`. Let us enter the package name as `com.phonegap.pghelloworld`. The package name serves as a unique identifier for the application. A package name may contain uppercase or lowercase letters, numbers, and underscores. The parts of the package name may only begin with letters. The package name must be unique across all packages installed on the Android system. Next, we need to select the version of Android that represents the device most commonly used by our target audience. From the `Minimum Required SDK` select the minimum version of the Android platform that is required by the application to run. That is, the application will not run if the device's API level is lower than the API level specified through this drop-down list. Let us select `API 11: Android 3.0 (Honeycomb)` from the `Minimum Required SDK` drop-down. It also means the application will require at least API 11 to run. Let us select `Android 4.2 (API 17)` as the target platform and the platform that will be used for compiling the application. Let the theme of the application be the default, `Holo Light with Dark Action Bar`. The theme determines the foreground, background color, and font style of the application. Click the `Next` button to continue.

The next dialog determines whether we wish to create a custom launcher icon and activity. It also asks for the location on the disk where we want to keep the new project. Keeping the default selected, we will continue by selecting the `Next` button. By default, the new project is stored on our disk drive at the workspace location that was specified when opening Eclipse for the first time.

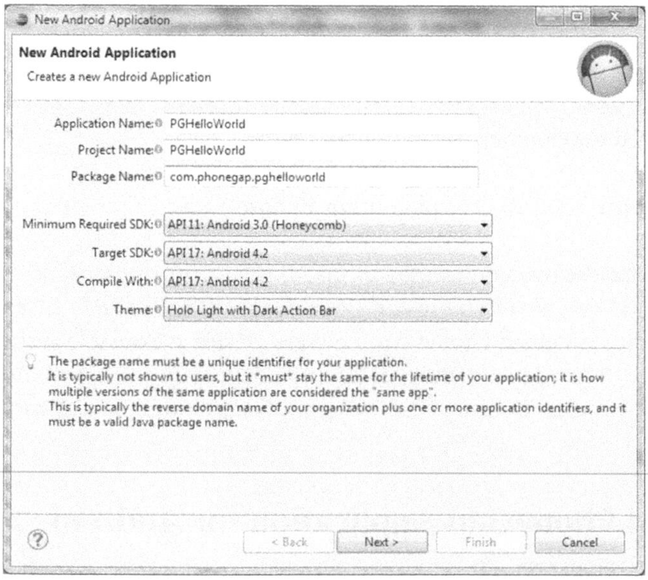

**Figure 1.1  The dialog box to specify the new project information.**

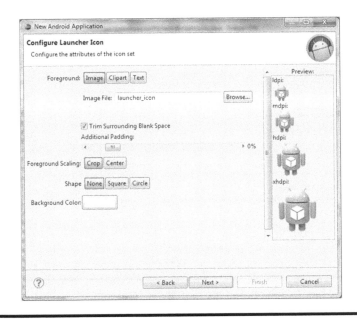

**Figure 1.2  The dialog box to configure the launcher icon.**

The next dialog, Configure Launcher Icon (see Figure 1.2), is used for configuring the icon for the application. The dialog shows three options, Image, Clipart, and Text, to define the icon for our application. The option Clipart is selected by default, showing one of the built-in clipart. We can select the Browse button to open the list of available clipart and select one of them as our application's icon. We can also select the Image option to specify the custom image to be used as our application's icon. The Text option, when selected, will display a text box where we can enter text to represent our application. We can select the Font button to change the font of the text and also to specify the font size and style. The dialog box also shows a checkbox, Trim Surrounding Blank Space, that we can select to remove the extra blank space around the chosen image, clipart, or text. A scroll bar is also provided that we can use to specify the padding around the icon. The icon can be set to appear at the center of the assigned space or can be cropped to accommodate the assigned space. The dialog also shows buttons to make the icon appear in a square or circle shape. Also, two buttons, Background Color and Foreground Scaling, are provided that display different colors to change the background colors and to scale the launcher icon, respectively. After defining the icon, click the Next button to continue.

The next dialog prompts us to select whether we wish to create an activity or not. If we wish to create an activity, the dialog box asks whether we wish to create a BlankActivity, FullscreenActivity, LoginActivity, MasterDetailFlow, or SettingsActivity (see Figure 1.3). The BlankActivity option will create a new blank activity, whereas other options will create fragments and their respective activities. To keep things simple, we will go for blank activity for this application. Because we wish to create a blank activity, let us select the Create Activity checkbox and the BlankActivity option from the list, followed by clicking Next.

The next dialog confirms the creation of the activity. The Android SDK assigns the default name MainActivity to the newly created activity. Also, the layout file is assigned the default name activity _ main. Let us name the activity PGHelloWorldActivity. The layout filename will automatically change to reflect the newly assigned activity name (see Figure 1.4). The layout name will become activity _ pghello _ world. We can always change the

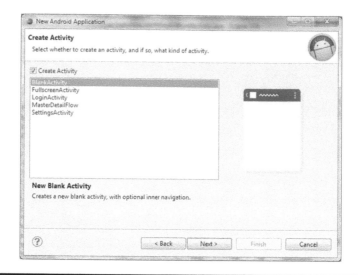

**Figure 1.3   The dialog box to select the type of activity to create.**

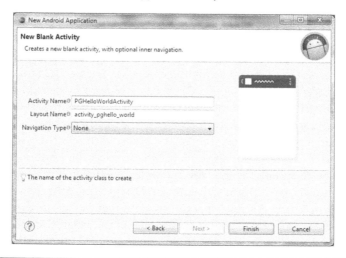

**Figure 1.4   The dialog box to specify the information of the newly created activity.**

auto-assigned layout filename. Keeping the auto-assigned layout filename, let us create the application by clicking the Finish button.

The project will be created and the ADT plug-in will automatically create all the required project files.

The newly created Android project is not yet configured to use PhoneGap. The files and directories of the usual Android project will appear as shown in Figure 1.5a. To configure the Android project to use PhoneGap, follow the steps given below:

1. Create an assets/www directory in the new Android project. The HTML and JavaScript code of the PhoneGap application reside within this assets/www folder.
2. From the downloaded PhoneGap package, navigate to the lib/android subdirectory and copy cordova-2.2.0.js to the assets/www directory of the Android project.

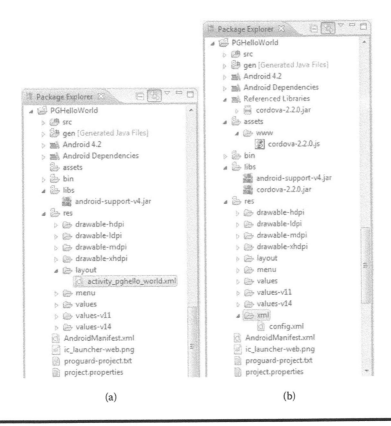

(a)                              (b)

**Figure 1.5** **(a) The** `Package Explorer` **window displaying the original files and directories of the project. (b) The** `Package Explorer` **window after adding the desired directories and files to the project.**

3. Copy `cordova-2.2.0.jar` from the PhoneGap package into the `libs` directory of our Android project.
4. We need to add the `cordova-2.2.0.jar` library to the build path for the Android project. Right-click the `cordova-2.2.0.jar` file in the `Project Explorer` window and select the `Build Path->Add To Build Path` option.
5. Copy the `xml` directory from the PhoneGap package into the `/res` directory of our Android project.

Our Android project is now configured to use PhoneGap. After performing the five steps above, the `Project Explorer` window will show the files and directories as shown in Figure 1.5b.

Now, let us add some content to the application. To do so, we need to add an `index.html` file to the `assets/www` folder. In the `Project Explorer` window, right-click the www folder and select the `New->File` option. We get a dialog box as shown in Figure 1.6. In the `Filename:` box, enter the filename as `index.html`, followed by clicking the `Finish` button.

The `index.html` file will be created and will appear in the `assets/www` folder. Like in Web applications, `index.html` is the starting file of the PhoneGap application. In this PhoneGap application, we just need to embed the PhoneGap's JavaScript file and display the `Hello World!` message. To do so, right-click the `index.html` file in the `Package Explorer` window and select the `Open With->Text Editor` option to write the code as shown in Listing 1.1.

**Figure 1.6    Adding an `index.html` file to the `assets/www` folder.**

**Listing 1.1    Code in the `index.html` File**

```
<!DOCTYPE HTML>
<html>
   <head>
      <title>PhoneGap Application</title>
      <script type = "text/javascript" charset = "utf-8"
      src = "cordova-2.2.0.js"></script>
   </head>
   <body>
      <h1>Hello World! </h1>
   </body>
</html>
```

We can see in the code above that the `Hello World!` message is set to appear in heading 1. The Android project will not invoke the `index.html` file until the main Java Activity class is asked to do so. So, let us now update the Java Activity class.

## Updating the Activity Class

The steps to update the Activity class to use PhoneGap are given below:

1. Open the main Java Activity file, `PGHelloWorldActivity.java`.
2. Add an import statement for org.apache.cordova.DroidGap:

```
import org.apache.cordova.DroidGap;
```

3. Change the base class from `Activity` to `DroidGap`:

```
public class PGHelloWorldActivity extends DroidGap {
```

Now our application can access the methods of the base class, `DroidGap`.

4. To make it accessible from anywhere in the application, change the access specifier of the `onCreate()` method from `protected` (default) to `public`.

5. Replace the call to the `setContentView()` method by the reference to load the PhoneGap interface, that is, `index.html` file from the local `assets/www` folder:

```
super.loadUrl("file:///android_asset/www/index.html");
```

The statement above will create the view from the `index.html` file instead of the traditional layout file.

**Note:** In PhoneGap projects, the files located in the `assets` directory are referenced with a URL reference, `file:///android _ asset`, followed by the path name to the file.

After performing the steps above, the Java Activity file, `PGHelloWorldActivity.java`, will appear as shown in Listing 1.2.

**Listing 1.2   Code in the `index.html` File**

```
package com.phonegap.pghelloworld;
import android.os.Bundle;
import org.apache.cordova.DroidGap;

public class PGHelloWorldActivity extends DroidGap {
    @Override
    public void onCreate(Bundle savedInstanceState) {
        super.onCreate(savedInstanceState);
        super.loadUrl("file:///android_asset/www/index.html");
    }
}
```

# Configuring the Project Metadata

After updating the Activity class to use PhoneGap, the next step is to configure the project metadata to enable PhoneGap to run. The following steps are taken to configure the project metadata:

1. Add the following `<uses-permission>` elements and paste them as children of the root `<manifest>` node in the `AndroidManifest.xml` file:

```
<uses-permission android:name =
"android.permission.ACCESS_NETWORK_STATE"/>
```

The `<uses-permission>` elements enable desired features in an application. The permission above is essentially required by all PhoneGap applications, and hence the statement above will be used in all PhoneGap applications.

2. This step is optional. A good application is one that supports screens of different sizes. An application is said to support a given screen size if it resizes to fill the entire screen. Usually, an application automatically resizes itself per different screen sizes. By using the

<supports-screens> element, we can define the types of screens supported by our application; that is, we can control whether our application should be distributed to smaller screens or scaled up to fit larger screens using the system's screen compatibility mode. A few of the most common attributes of the <supports-screens> element are given below:

- Android:resizeable—Determines whether the application is resizable for different screen sizes. This attribute is true by default. If set to false, our application will run in screen compatibility mode on large screens.
- Android:smallScreens—Determines whether the application supports a smaller screen or not. A small screen is the one with a smaller aspect ratio than the normal HVGA screen.
- Android:normalScreens—Determines whether an application supports the normal screen, that is, Half-Size Video Graphics Array (HVGA) medium-density, WQVGA low-density, and WVGA high-density screens. This attribute is true by default.
- Android:largeScreens—Determines whether the application supports a larger screen, that is, a screen larger than a normal handset screen.

In AndroidManifest.xml, we can add the following supports-screen statements as a child of the root manifest node:

```
<supports-screens
    android:largeScreens = "true"
    android:normalScreens = "true"
    android:smallScreens = "true"
    android:resizeable = "true"
    android:anyDensity = "true"/>
```

By performing the steps above, our project is configured to run as a PhoneGap project for Android.

But where are we going to run our PhoneGap project? To run our PhoneGap project, we need either a physical device or an Android Virtual Device (AVD).

## Creating Android Virtual Devices

For running applications, we need to create an Android Virtual Device and Eclipse launch configurations. Let us see how both are created. AVD represents a device configuration. To test whether an Android application is compatible with a set of Android devices, AVDs that represent their configuration are created. Thereafter, the Android emulator is set to point to each of the AVDs when testing the application. If the application runs successfully on an AVD, it means the application will also run successfully on a device with the same configuration.

To create AVDs in Eclipse, select the Window->Android Virtual Device Manager option. An Android Virtual Device Manager dialog opens that displays a list of existing AVDs (if any), letting us create new AVDs and manage existing AVDs. Select the New button to define a new AVD. A Create new Android Virtual Device (AVD) dialog box appears (see Figure 1.7a). The fields are listed below:

- AVD Name: Used to specify the name of the AVD.

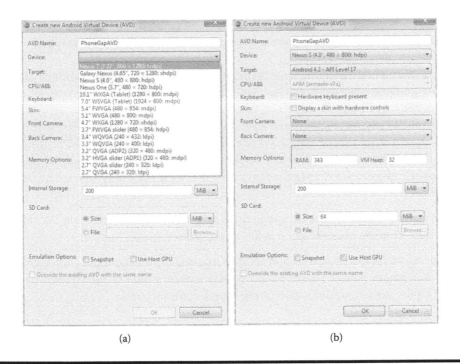

**Figure 1.7**    (a) The dialog to create a new AVD. (b) The specifications of a new AVD, PhoneGapAVD.

- **Device:** Used for selecting the device for which we want to test our application.
- **Target:** Used to specify the target API level. Our application will be tested against the specified API level.
- **CPU/ABI:** Determines the processor that we want to emulate on our device.
- **Keyboard:** If the device has a physical keyboard, the Hardware keyboard present checkbox is checked. If the device does not have a physical keyboard and we want a virtual keyboard to appear while interacting with the applications, clear the Hardware keyboard present checkbox.
- **Skin:** Used for setting the screen size. Each built-in skin represents a specific screen size. We can try multiple skins to see if your application works across different devices.
- **Front Camera/Back Camera:** The drop-down lists show the following three options:
  - **None**—Used when our app does not require a camera.
  - **Webcam0**—Used if our app requires a camera and a Web cam is attached to our computer.
  - **Emulated**—Used if our app requires a camera but a Web cam is not present on our computer.
- **Memory Options:** Enable us to specify the Random Access Memory (RAM) and Virtual Machine (VM) Heap required to run our application.
- **Internal Storage:** Used to specify the internal storage of the device to run the application and save its data (if any).
- **SD Card:** Used for extending the storage capacity of the device. Large data files, such as audio and video for which the internal memory is insufficient, are stored on the secure digital (SD) card.
- **Snapshot:** Enable this option to avoid booting of the emulator and start it from the last saved snapshot. Hence, this option is used to start the Android emulator quickly.

■ Use Host GPU: Enable this option to improve the emulation experience. GPU stands for graphics processing unit and is popularly used in rendering 2D and 3D graphics optimally.

In the AVD Name box, enter the name of the AVD as PhoneGapAVD. Assuming most of the clients that are going to use our PhoneGap application use a Nexus S device, let us choose the same from the Device drop-down list. Choose Android 4.2—API Level 17 for the Target, set the SD card to 64 MiB, and leave all the options in the dialog box at their default values. Click the OK button (see Figure 1.7b) to create the virtual device called PhoneGapAVD.

The new AVD, PhoneGapAVD, will be created and will be displayed in the list of existing AVDs, as shown in Figure 1.8. Select the Refresh button if the newly created AVD does not appear in the list.

**Note:** The larger the allocated SD card space, the longer it will take to create the AVD. Unless it really is required, keep the SD card space as low as possible.

After creating an AVD, the next important step required to run the application is to create an Eclipse launch configuration and specify the virtual device on which to run the application. The Android ADT provides two options for creating launch configurations:

■ Run configuration: Used to run an application on a given device.
■ Debug configuration: Used to debug an application while it is running on a given device.

To create an Eclipse launch configuration, select the Run->Debug Configurations option. A Debug Configurations dialog box opens. Double-click the Android application in the left pane. The wizard inserts a new configuration named New _ configuration. Let us rename the configuration to PGHelloWorld _ configuration. We need to specify the project name that we want to launch in the Project box. So, click the Browse button and choose our PhoneGap project, PGHelloWorld. From the Launch drop-down list in the Launch Action section, select the Activity file com.phonegap.pghelloworld.PGHelloWorldActivity option, followed by the Apply button (see Figure 1.9a). Next, we need to define a device on which to run the

**Figure 1.8   The newly created AVD listed in the AVD Manager.**

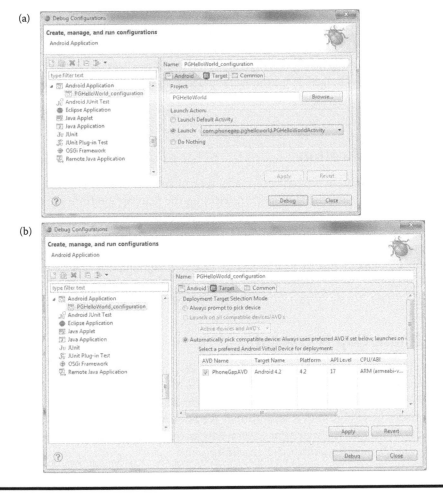

**Figure 1.9** **(a) Creating a new configuration called** PGHelloWorld_configuration. **(b) Defining the target AVD for the new configuration.**

application. Select the Target tab in the same dialog box. You get the screen shown in Figure 1.9b. The Deployment Target Selection Mode displays the following three options:

- Always prompt to pick device: Allows us to choose the device or AVD to connect to while running the application.
- Launch on all compatible devices/AVD's: Will deploy the application automatically on all the compatible AVDs or devices available.
- Automatically pick compatible device: Will deploy the application on the AVDs that are selected. If none of the AVDs are selected, the application will be launched on the compatible AVDs or devices available.

Let us select the third option, Automatically pick compatible device, followed by selecting the PhoneGapAVD that we created earlier, to deploy the application automatically on this virtual device (see Figure 1.9b). We select the PhoneGapAVD checkbox because we want to test the application against the Android 4.2 target. We can create more AVDs targeting other platforms from the AVD Manager window, and all the defined AVDs will automatically appear in this dialog box, allowing us to select the desired target to test the application. After selecting the AVD, select the Apply button, followed by the Close button, to save the launch configuration file.

You now have everything ready for developing Android applications—the Android SDK, the Android platform, the Eclipse IDE, the ADT plug-in, and an AVD for testing the Android application.

## Running the Application

Once the launch configuration file has been made, we can run the Android application by selecting the Run icon from the Eclipse IDE toolbar, selecting the Run option from the Run menu, or pressing the Ctrl+F11 keys. The window's title bar contains the port number of our computer on which the emulator is running (5554) and the AVD name (PhoneGapAVD). Upon running the application, a Hello World! message will be displayed as shown in Figure 1.10.

Recall that we defined the Hello World! message through the <H1> element in the index.html file.

## Ensuring PhoneGap Is Loaded

In every PhoneGap application, we need to ensure that PhoneGap is loaded before any PhoneGap JavaScript function is called. This is essential because it might take time to load JavaScript. To know when PhoneGap is loaded, we use the help of the deviceready event. The deviceready event fires when PhoneGap is fully loaded. We associate an event listener to the deviceready event. For example, the statement given below associates a listener to the deviceready event and fires the PhonegapLoaded() function:

```
document.addEventListener("deviceready", PhonegapLoaded(), false);
```

To add the deviceready event to our index.html file, it is modified to appear as shown in Listing 1.3.

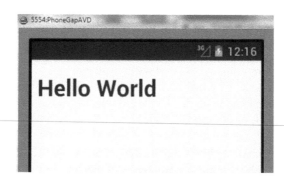

**Figure 1.10   The** Hello World! **message displayed upon running the PhoneGap application.**

**Listing 1.3   Code Written in the `index.html` File**

```
<!DOCTYPE HTML>
<html>
   <head>
   <title>PhoneGap Application</title>
   <script type = "text/javascript" charset = "utf-8" src = "cordova-2.2.0.js">
   </script>
   <script type = "text/javascript">
      function onBodyLoad() {
         document.addEventListener("deviceready", PhonegapLoaded, false);
      }
      function PhonegapLoaded(){
         alert("PhoneGap is Loaded");
      }
   </script>
   </head>
   <body onload = "onBodyLoad()">
      <h1>Hello World!</h1>
   </body>
</html>
```

In the code above, the `onload` event is used in the `<body>` element of the HTML code. The `onload` event occurs immediately after a page is loaded, which in turn will fire the `onBody-Load()` function. In the `onBodyLoad()` function, an event listener is associated to the `deviceready` event, which will fire the `PhonegapLoaded()` function when PhoneGap is fully loaded. The `PhonegapLoaded()` function displays an alert dialog informing that `PhoneGap is Loaded`, as shown in Figure 1.11.

**Figure 1.11   The alert dialog box informing us that PhoneGap is loaded.**

## Summary

In this chapter, we learned about PhoneGap and explored its features. We also learned how to set up an environment for developing Android apps using PhoneGap. We learned to update the Activity class and configure the project metadata. In the Android applications that we learned to develop, we saw the measures for ensuring that PhoneGap is loaded before any of the JavaScript code is executed.

In Chapter 2, we will learn how to create user interaction and introduce debugging capabilities. We will also learn how to configure BlackBerry to use with PhoneGap, and the procedure of developing apps for different platforms using PhoneGap Build.

# Chapter 2

# Creating a User Interface

In this chapter, we cover mainly two things: creating a user interface and the procedure of digitally signing applications and subsequently installing them on emulators and Android devices. A brief outline of the topics covered in this chapter is given below:

- Getting data through a text box
- Getting user's choice through checkboxes and radio buttons
- Displaying options through drop-down lists
- Implementing navigation
- Introducing debugging capabilities
- Creating a keystore and digitally signing the Android application
- Installing applications on the emulator and device

Before we explore PhoneGap's capability to access and interact with mobile device hardware, let us first learn to create applications that interact with the user. User interaction is required to get feedback from the user and to fetch the data to process. We will also learn how event listeners can be associated with Hypertext Markup Language (HTML) elements.

All the Android applications that we will be creating in this chapter will first require being configured for PhoneGap. In Chapter 1, we learned the steps to configure Android Development Environment for PhoneGap. The steps are given below for reference:

1. Create a www folder in the /assets folder of the Android project.
2. Copy cordova-2.3.0.js from the /lib/android subdirectory of the downloaded PhoneGap package into the /assets/www directory of the Android project.
3. Copy cordova-2.3.0.jar from the /lib/android subdirectory of the PhoneGap package into the libs directory of our Android project.
4. Add the cordova-2.3.0.jar library to the build path of the Android project by right-clicking the cordova-2.3.0.jar file in the Project Explorer window and selecting Build Path->Add To Build Path option.
5. Copy the xml directory from the /lib/android subdirectory of the PhoneGap package into the /res directory of our Android project.

6. Add an `index.html` file to the `assets/www` folder by right-clicking the www folder in the `Project Explorer` window and selecting New->File option.
7. Open the Java Activity file and replace the `setContentView()` method with the following line in the `onCreate()` method:

```
super.loadUrl("file:///android_asset/www/index.html");
```

Also import the following library file in the Java Activity file:

```
import org.apache.cordova.DroidGap;
```

Let the Java Activity class extend `DroidGap` instead of `Activity` class.
Change the access specifier of the `onCreate()` method from `protected` to `public`.
8. Add the following permission statement as a child of `<manifest>` node in the `AndroidManifest.xml` file:

```
<uses-permission android:name = "android.permission.ACCESS_NETWORK_
STATE"/>
```

Performing the steps above on an Android application will configure it for PhoneGap.

## Getting Data through a Text Box

We will begin our journey of creating a user interaction by creating a PhoneGap application that asks the user to enter some data through a text box. More specifically, this application will prompt a user to enter a name followed by clicking a `Submit` button. After entering a name, when the user clicks the button, a welcome message along with the entered name will be displayed on the screen. So, let us begin.

Launch Eclipse and create a new Android application project called `PGWelcomeMsg`. Using the steps shown above, configure the newly created Android application for PhoneGap. In the `index.html` file, we will write the code to do the following tasks:

■ Display a text box and a `Submit` button
■ Associate a `click` event listener with the `Submit` button so that the desired processing is initiated when the user clicks on the `Submit` button
■ Define a `<div>` element in the HTML body to display the response of the application, that is, to display a welcome message on the screen
■ Ensure that PhoneGap is loaded before any of the JavaScript function is called
■ Write JavaScript code that listens for the occurrence of a `click` event on the `Submit` button
■ Access the name entered in the text box and display it through the `<div>` element when a `click` event occurs on the `Submit` button

For doing the above-mentioned tasks, the code shown in Listing 2.1 is written in the `index.html` file.

**Listing 2.1   Code Written in the `index.html` File**

```html
<!DOCTYPE HTML>
<html>
   <head>
   <title>PhoneGap Application</title>
   <script type = "text/javascript" charset = "utf-8" src = "cordova-2.3.0.js">
   </script>
   <script type = "text/javascript">
   function onBodyLoad() {
      document.addEventListener("deviceready", PhonegapLoaded, false);
   }
   function PhonegapLoaded(){

document.getElementById("submitButton").addEventListener("click", dispMessage);
   }
   function dispMessage(){
      var nameOfUser = document.getElementById("name").value;
      document.getElementById("welcomemsg").innerHTML = "Welcome "+nameOfUser +
      " !";
   }
   </script>
   </head>
   <body onload = "onBodyLoad()">
      <form>
          Enter your name <input type = "text" id = "name"><br/>
          <input type = "button" id = "submitButton" value = "Submit">
          <div id = "welcomemsg"></div>
      </form>
   </body>
</html>
```

We can see that the `onload` event is used in the `<body>` element, which fires the `onBody-Load()` function immediately after the page is loaded. In the `onBodyLoad()` function, an event listener is associated to the `deviceready` event that fires the `PhonegapLoaded()` function when PhoneGap is fully loaded. In the `PhonegapLoaded()` function, a `click` event listener is added to the `Submit` button so that when it is clicked, the `dispMessage()` function is called. In the `dispMessage()` function, the name entered by the user in the input text box is accessed. To access and identify the input text box, button, and `<div>` elements in the JavaScript code, they are assigned the IDs `name`, `submitButton`, and `welcomemsg`, respectively. The name entered in the input text box is accessed and assigned to the `nameOfUser` variable, which is then displayed along with the welcome message through the `<div>` element of ID `welcomemsg`. Upon running the application, the application prompts for the username. When the user clicks the `Submit` button after entering the name, a welcome message is displayed on the screen along with the username, as shown in Figure 2.1.

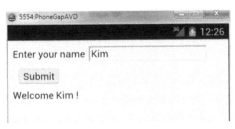

**Figure 2.1   The welcome message is displayed upon selecting the `Submit` button.**

**Note:** The innerHTML property of an HTML element can be used to modify its HTML code as well as its text content. The getElementById() method works on all browsers and is used to access any HTML element through its ID. The addEventListener() method is used to register an event handler to the specified HTML element. The addEventListener() method takes the three parameters as shown in the syntax given below:

```
object.addEventListener (eventName, functionName, capturePhase)
```

where eventName represents an event (click, change, mouseup, mousedown, etc.) that the method has to wait for. The functionName is the function that will be invoked to handle the event if it occurs. The capturePhase is a Boolean value that is set to true to indicate that the event handler has to be called during the capture, that is, the listening phase. The capture-Phase value is set to false to call the event handler during the "bubble" phase, that is, when the event propagates up and is dispatched to the ancestor elements of the original target element. The removeEventListener() method can be used to remove an event listener from a given HTML element.

## Getting User's Choice through Checkboxes and Radio Buttons

Checkboxes are used to display the options when the user can select more than one. That is, the user can select any number of options that are displayed through checkboxes. The radio buttons, on the other hand, are used to display options that are mutually exclusive; that is, only one of the options can be selected from a group. Upon selecting a radio button, the previously selected radio button (if any) will be deselected. Let us learn how to use checkboxes and radio buttons through a running example.

So, create a new Android application project called PGCheckboxRadioApp and configure it for PhoneGap. In this application, we will display certain templates and contact names. Templates like "Happy birthday to you," "Have a nice day," and "It's time to take backup" will be displayed through radio buttons so that the user can select only one of them. The contact names will represent the person names in the form of checkboxes so that the user can select any number of them. After selecting the desired template and contacts, when the user clicks the Send button, the chosen template and contacts will be displayed on the screen. At the moment, the application will simply display the options that are selected by the user. In later chapters, we will learn how to e-mail the selected template to the chosen contacts.

In the index.html file, we need to write the code to do the following tasks:

- Display templates and contact names through radio buttons and checkboxes, respectively. Also display a Send button that when clicked will display the options that are chosen by the user.
- Associate a click event listener with the Send button.
- Define a <div> element in the HTML body to display the response of the application, that is, to display which of the radio buttons and checkboxes are selected by the user.
- Ensure that PhoneGap is loaded before any of the JavaScript function is called.
- Write JavaScript code that listens for the occurrence of a click event on the Send button.

■ Access all the `input` elements in the `index.html` file, use the `for` loop to access each of the checkboxes and radio buttons defined in the file, and check if any of them are checked. The `value` property of the chosen template (radio button) and contacts (checkboxes) is accessed and displayed through the `<div>` element when a `click` event occurs on the `Send` button.

For doing the above-mentioned tasks, the code shown in Listing 2.2 is written in the `index.html` file.

**Listing 2.2 Code Written in the `index.html` File**

```html
<!DOCTYPE HTML>
<html>
    <head>
    <title>CheckBox and Radio Buttons App</title>
    <script type = "text/javascript" charset = "utf-8" src = "cordova-2.3.0.js">
    </script>
    <script type = "text/javascript">
    function onBodyLoad() {
        document.addEventListener("deviceready", PhonegapLoaded, false);
    }
    function PhonegapLoaded(){

document.getElementById("sendButton").addEventListener("click", dispMessage);
    }
    function dispMessage(){
        ElementsArray = document.getElementsByTagName('input');
        var selectedContact = "";
        var selectedTemplate = "";
        for(var i = 0; i< ElementsArray.length; i++){
            if(ElementsArray[i].type = ="checkbox" && ElementsArray[i].checked){
                selectedContact+ = ElementsArray[i].value + " ";
            }
            if(ElementsArray[i].type = ="radio" && ElementsArray[i].checked){
                selectedTemplate+ = ElementsArray[i].value;
            }
        }
        document.getElementById("info").innerHTML = "Template selected is: " +
        selectedTemplate +"<br>Contacts selected are : "+selectedContact;
    }
    </script>
    </head>
    <body onload = "onBodyLoad()">
        <form>
            Choose a template <br>
            <input type = "radio" name = "template" value = "Happy Birthday to You">
            Happy Birthday to You <br>
            <input type = "radio" name = "template" value = "Have a nice day"> Have a
            nice day <br>
            <input type = "radio" name = "template" value = "Its time to take
            backup"> Its time to take backup <br><br>
            Choose the contacts to send the selected template: <br>
            <input type = "checkbox" name = "contact" value = "Bintu"> Bintu <br>
            <input type = "checkbox" name = "contact" value = "Naman">Naman <br>
            <input type = "checkbox" name = "contact" value = "Chirag">Chirag <br>
            <input type = "checkbox" name = "contact" value = "Kim">Kim <br><br>
```

```
      <input type = "button" id = "sendButton" value = "Send">
      <div id = info></div>
    </form>
  </body>
</html>
```

We can see that the getElementsByTagName() method is used to access all the HTML elements with the input tag name. The method returns an HTMLCollection object that is assigned to the ElementsArray. It means that the ElementsArray contains all the HTML elements of the index.html file. Two strings, selectedContact and selectedTemplate, are defined to store the selected template and the contact names, respectively. Using a for loop, each HTML element in the ElementsArray is accessed and tested. If the HTML element is a checkbox and is checked, its value property is appended to the selectedContact string. Similarly, if the HTML element is a radio button and is found checked, its value property is appended to the selectedTemplate string. The text, that is, the selected template and contact names in the selectedContact and selectedTemplate, respectively, is displayed on the screen via the <div> element, info. Upon running the application, it will display a few templates and contact names. When a user, after selecting the desired template and contact names, clicks the Send button, the chosen template and contacts will be displayed on the screen as shown in Figure 2.2.

When it is required to display a lot of options to the user in a small space, a drop-down list is the best way to do so.

## Displaying Options through Drop-Down Lists

The drop-down list not only takes up a minimum amount of space for displaying a large number of options, but it also can be configured for single as well as multiple selections. First, we will learn to display a drop-down list that enables the user to choose a single option. Let us create an

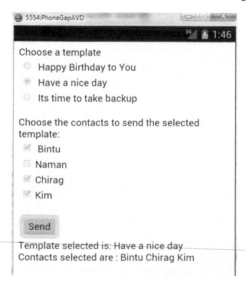

**Figure 2.2** **The chosen template and contact names are displayed through the <div> element upon selecting the Send button.**

application that displays a list of phone numbers in the form of a drop-down list. The phone number that is selected from the drop-down list is then displayed on the screen. The drop-down list is initially configured for single selection; that is, the user will be able to select just a single phone number from the drop-down list. After understanding the concept of single selection, we will modify this application for multiple selections—allowing the user to select more than one phone number from the drop-down list.

So, create a new Android application project called PGListApp and configure it for PhoneGap. In the index.html file, we need to write the code to do the following tasks:

- Display phone numbers through a drop-down list
- Associate a change event listener with the drop-down list so that whenever any part of the option is changed (i.e., whenever a new phone number is selected), the respective event handling function is invoked
- Define a <div> element in the HTML body to display the response of the application, that is, to display the chosen phone number
- Ensure that PhoneGap is loaded before any of the JavaScript function is called
- Write JavaScript code that listens for the occurrence of a change event on the drop-down list and that invokes the event handling function to display the phone number that is selected by the user through the <div> element

For doing the above-mentioned tasks, the code shown in Listing 2.3 is written in the index. html file.

**Listing 2.3    Code Written in the index.html File**

```
<!DOCTYPE HTML>
<html>
    <head>
    <title>List App</title>
    <script type = "text/javascript" charset = "utf-8" src = "cordova-2.3.0.js"></
script>
    <script type = "text/javascript">
    function onBodyLoad() {
        document.addEventListener("deviceready", PhonegapLoaded, false);
        }
    function PhonegapLoaded(){
        document.getElementById("PhoneNo").addEventListener("change", dispMessage);
        }
    function dispMessage(){
        var selectedPhone = document.getElementById("PhoneNo").value;
        document.getElementById("info").innerHTML = "Phone Number selected is: " +
        selectedPhone;
    }
    </script>
    </head>
    <body onload = "onBodyLoad()">
        <select id = "PhoneNo" >
            <option value = "none">Select a Phone Number</option>
            <option value = "1111111111">1111111111</option>
            <option value = "2222222222">2222222222</option>
            <option value = "3333333333">3333333333</option>
            <option value = "4444444444">4444444444</option>
            <option value = "5555555555">5555555555</option>
```

```
    </select><br><br>
    <div id = "info"></div>
  </body>
</html>
```

We can see that the `<select>` element is defined along with the `<option>` tags to display phone numbers in the form of a drop-down list. To access in the JavaScript code, the `<select>` element is assigned `PhoneNo` ID. The `<div>` element with ID `info` is defined to display the chosen phone number. When a user selects any phone number from the drop-down list, the `change` event will be fired, and consequently, the `dispMessage()` function will be invoked. In the `dispMessage()` function, the `value` property of the `<select>` element is used to access the chosen phone number and is displayed through the `info` `<div>` element.

Upon running the application, the drop-down will initially appear in collapsed form, as shown in Figure 2.3a. Upon clicking the drop-down list, it will expand, showing all the phone numbers defined in it (see Figure 2.3b). The text `Select a Phone Number` at the top in the drop-down list directs the user to select a phone number from the list. Upon selecting a phone number, it will be displayed through the `<div>` element (see Figure 2.3c).

To configure the `<select>` element, the following attributes can be used:

- **Autofocus**—If set to the Boolean value `true`, this attribute will make the drop-down list automatically focus when the page is loaded.
- **Disabled**—If set to `true`, this attribute will disable the drop-down list.
- **Multiple**—Enables multiple selections in a drop-down list.
- **Name**—Used to define the name for the drop-down list that can be used to access and identify it in JavaScript code.
- **Size**—Defines the number of visible options in a drop-down list.

For example, the following statement will display a drop-down list that initially displays four elements along with the scroll buttons if the `<select>` element has more than four options. Also,

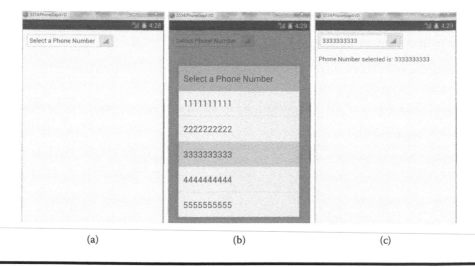

(a)　　　　　　　　(b)　　　　　　　　(c)

**Figure 2.3 (a) The collapsed drop-down list is displayed upon application start-up. (b) The drop-down list expands upon clicking it, showing all the options. (c) The chosen option is displayed on the screen.**

the drop-down list is assigned the Phone No name, configured to select more than one option, and gains focus automatically when the page is loaded:

```
<select name = "PhoneNo" size = "4" autofocus = "true" multiple = "multiple">
```

To enable a user to select more than one phone number from the drop-down list, the index. html file is modified to appear as shown in Listing 2.4. Only the code in bold is modified; the rest is the same as we saw in Listing 2.3.

**Listing 2.4   Code Written in the `index.html` File**

```
<!DOCTYPE HTML>
<html>
   <head>
   <title>List App</title>
   <script type = "text/javascript" charset = "utf-8" src = "cordova-2.3.0.js">
   </script>
   <script type = "text/javascript">
   function onBodyLoad() {
      document.addEventListener("deviceready", PhonegapLoaded, false);
   }
   function PhonegapLoaded(){ document.getElementById("PhoneNo").
   addEventListener("change", dispMessage);
   }
   function dispMessage(){
      Phones = document.getElementById("PhoneNo");
      var selectedNumbers = "";
      for(var i = 0; i< Phones.options.length; i++){
         if (Phones.options[i].selected) {
            selectedNumbers + = Phones.options[i].value + " ";
         }
      }
      document.getElementById("info").innerHTML = "Phone Numbers selected are : "
      +selectedNumbers;
   }
   </script>
   </head>
   <body onload = "onBodyLoad()">
      <select name = "PhoneNo" id = "PhoneNo" multiple = "multiple">
         <option value = "none">Select Phone Numbers</option>
         <option value = "1111111111">1111111111</option>
         <option value = "2222222222">2222222222</option>
         <option value = "3333333333">3333333333</option>
         <option value = "4444444444">4444444444</option>
         <option value = "5555555555">5555555555</option>
         <option value = "6666666666">6666666666</option>
         <option value = "7777777777">7777777777</option>
         <option value = "8888888888">8888888888</option>
         <option value = "9999999999">9999999999</option>
         <option value = "1111122222">1111122222</option>
      </select><br><br>
      <div id = "info"></div>
   </body>
</html>
```

We can see that a few more `<option>` tags are added to the `<select>` element to increase the number of phone numbers displayed. The `multiple` attribute is added to the `<select>`

element to enable us to select more than one phone number from the drop-down list. In the dispMessage() function, a for loop is used to access and check each option of the <select> element. A string selectedNumbers is defined and the value property of each of the selected options is appended to the selectedNumbers string; that is, all the phone numbers that are selected from the drop-down list are appended to the selectedNumbers string. The phone numbers in the selectedNumbers string are thereafter displayed on the screen through the <div> element, info.

Upon running the application, the phone numbers are displayed in the drop-down list. Each option, that is, phone number, has a checkbox on its right. The checkboxes (see Figure 2.4a) indicate that more than one phone number can be selected from the drop-down list. The selected phone numbers are displayed on the screen as shown in Figure 2.4b.

It is quite obvious that an application comprises several Web pages. To navigate among Web pages hyperlinks are used. Let us understand how navigation is performed among the Web pages.

## Implementing Navigation

In this section, we will learn how forward navigation is performed in an application and how the Back button of the device can be used to implement backward navigation. For forward navigation, we will make use of the traditional HTML hyperlinks, and for backward navigation, we will use the backbutton event. Let us learn the concept practically through a running example.

So, let us create an Android project called PGNavigation and configure it for PhoneGap. In this application, we will create two hyperlinks by the names, About and Contact. Upon clicking on a hyperlink, we will navigate to the associated Web page. To define two hyperlinks, the code shown in Listing 2.5 is written in the index.html file.

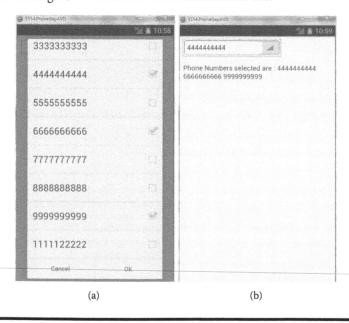

(a)                    (b)

**Figure 2.4   The drop-down list displaying phone numbers with the checkboxes on their right (a) and the selected phone numbers displayed on the screen (b).**

**Note:** Traditionally, when the Back button on the device is selected, it exits from the application and opens the previous screen, which may be the Home screen or application lists screen—from where the application is invoked.

**Listing 2.5    Code Written in the `index.html` File**

```
<!DOCTYPE HTML>
<html>
    <head>
    <title>PhoneGap Application</title>
    <script type = "text/javascript" charset = "utf-8" src = "cordova-2.3.0.js">
    </script>
    </head>
    <body>
        <a href = "about.html">About</a>
        <a href = "contact.html">Contact</a><br/>
        <b> Welcome to our PhoneGap App </b>
    </body>
</html>
```

In the code above, we can see that two hyperlinks, About and Contact, are defined, which when clicked will navigate us to the about.html and contact.html Web pages, respectively. So, let us add two HTML files by the names about.html and contact.html to the assets/www folder of our Android application.

In the about.html, write the code shown in Listing 2.6.

**Listing 2.6    Code Written in the `about.html` File**

```
<!DOCTYPE HTML>
<html>
    <head>
    <title>About Us</title>
    <script type = "text/javascript" charset = "utf-8" src = "cordova-2.3.0.js">
    </script>
    <script type = "text/javascript">
    function onBodyLoad() {
       document.addEventListener("deviceready", PhonegapLoaded, false);
    }
    function PhonegapLoaded(){
       document.addEventListener("backbutton", function(e){
       e.preventDefault();
       alert("Back Button Pressed");
       navigator.app.backHistory();
       }, true);
    }
    </script>
    </head>
    <body onload = "onBodyLoad()">
        <b> We are dealing with Smartphone Apps </b>
    </body>
</html>
```

Just to differentiate the about.html file from index.html and contact.html, a small text, We are dealing with Smartphone Apps, is displayed in the body of the about.

html file. In addition, the onBodyLoad() function is used to ensure that PhoneGap is loaded before any of the JavaScript function is called. The PhonegapLoaded() function will be called only after the PhoneGap is loaded. In the PhonegapLoaded() function, an event listener is registered for the backbutton event. The backbutton event is fired when the Back button on the device is pressed. The event handling function calls the preventDefault() method to override the traditional Back button behavior; that is, we will not be navigated out of the application to the Home or other device screen, but will remain in the application. An alert dialog is invoked to inform us that the Back button in the device has been pressed. Finally, the navigator.app.backHistory() method is called to move back to the previous page in the history.

The code in the contact.html file will be the same as in the about.html file. The only difference between the two HTML files is in the text that is displayed in the body of each. The code shown in Listing 2.7 is written in the contact.html file.

**Listing 2.7   Code Written in the contact.html File**

```
<!DOCTYPE HTML>
<html>
    <head>
    <title>Contact Us</title>
    <script type = "text/javascript" charset = "utf-8" src = "cordova-2.3.0.js">
    </script>
    <script type = "text/javascript">
    function onBodyLoad() {
        document.addEventListener("deviceready", PhonegapLoaded, false);
    }
    function PhonegapLoaded(){
        document.addEventListener("backbutton", function(e){
            e.preventDefault();
            alert("Back Button Pressed");
            navigator.app.backHistory();
            }, true);
        }
    </script>
    </head>
    <body onload = "onBodyLoad()">
       <b>For details, contact us at XYZ address </b>
    </body>
</html>
```

Upon running the application, the index.html file will open displaying the two hyperlinks, About and Contact (see Figure 2.5a). Upon selecting the About hyperlink, the about. html Web page will open displaying the text We are dealing with Smartphone Apps (see Figure 2.5b). Upon selecting the Back button on the device, an alert dialog opens up confirming that the backbutton event is fired (see Figure 2.5c). On closing the alert dialog, we will be navigated to the previous Web page in the history, that is, to the index.html file.

The two hyperlinks used in the application above look very simple and do not appear like the attractive navigation bars that we usually see in professional applications. We will learn how to create dynamic and better navigation bars using jQuery Mobile in later chapters, but for the time being, we will learn how to use Cascading Style Sheets (CSS) to make the hyperlinks appear better. So, add a CSS style sheet by the name style.css to the assets/www folder of our Android application and write in it the code shown in Listing 2.8.

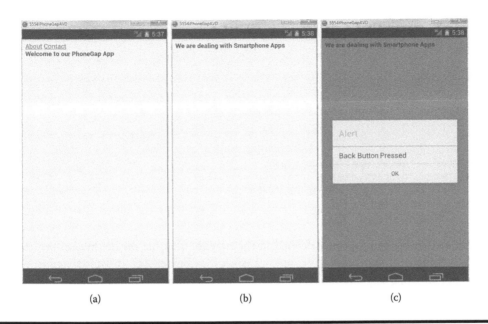

**Figure 2.5** **(a) Two hyperlinks,** About **and** Contact, **are displayed in the** index.html **file. (b)** About.html **opens upon selecting the** About **hyperlink. (c) The** Alert **dialog opens when the** Back **button on the device is clicked.**

**Listing 2.8** **Code Written in the** style.css **File**

```
a{
    margin:0;
    padding:5px;
    font-family:arial;
    font-weight:bold;
    border: 1px solid black;
    background-color:#00f;
    color:#fff;
    text-decoration:none;
}
```

The code above indicates that the style will be applied to all the <a> elements of the HTML file. Because the two hyperlinks are created through the <a> element, the said style will be applied to both of them. The properties font-family and font-weight will make the hyperlink text appear in Arial font and in bold appearance. The value of the text-decoration property is set to none to remove the traditional underlines that appear in hyperlink text. The background-color and color properties will make the hyperlink text appear in white over a blue background. The padding property will make the hyperlinks appear to be 5 pixels apart.

To include the external defined CSS style sheet in the index.html, we need to use the rel attribute of the <link> element. So, modify the index.html file to include the style.css file (see Listing 2.9). Only the code in bold is the newly added code; the rest is the same as we saw in Listing 2.5.

**Listing 2.9  Code Written in the `index.html` File**

```
<!DOCTYPE HTML>
<html>
   <head>
   <title>PhoneGap Application</title>
   <link rel = "stylesheet" href = "style.css" type = "text/css"/>
   <script type = "text/javascript" charset = "utf-8" src = "cordova-2.3.0.js">
   </script>
   </head>
   <body>
      <a href = "about.html">About</a>
      <a href = "contact.html">Contact</a><br/><br/>
      <b> Welcome to our PhoneGap App </b>
   </body>
</html>
```

On application of the properties defined in the `style.css` file on the hyperlinks, the two hyperlinks `About` and `Contact` will appear as shown in Figure 2.6. In later chapters, we will learn to make use of jQuery Mobile to make attractive and dynamic navigation bars.

## Introducing Debugging Capabilities

One of the best ways to debug an application is to display the values of the intermediate results. Comparing the intermediate results with the expected values will certainly help in isolating the statement(s) resulting in bugs. To debug an application, we can make use of the `console` object

**Figure 2.6  Two hyperlinks, `About` and `Contact`, after application of styles.**

that displays messages to the browser's console. The `console` object can be used in the JavaScript code of the application. Several methods can be used with the `console` object for implementing debugging. The most common methods are `log()`, `warn()`, and `error()`. The method name itself depicts the purpose of the method. For example, the `log()` method is for log messages, `warn()` is for displaying warnings, and `error()`is meant for showing error messages. Let us apply the `log()`, `warn()`, and `error()` methods to the `PGWelcomeMsg` application that we created at the beginning of the chapter.

So, launch Eclipse and open the Android application project `PGWelcomeMsg`. From the `assets/www` folder, open the `index.html` file. After adding the debugging methods, (`log()`, `warn()`, and `error()`), the `index.html` will appear as shown in Listing 2.10. Only the code in bold is the newly added code; the rest is the same as we saw in Listing 2.1.

**Listing 2.10   Code in the `index.html` File**

```html
<!DOCTYPE HTML>
<html>
    <head>
        <title>PhoneGap Application</title>
        <script type = "text/javascript" charset = "utf-8" src = "cordova-2.3.0.js">
        </script>
        <script type = "text/javascript">
            function onBodyLoad() {
                document.addEventListener("deviceready", PhonegapLoaded, false);
            }
            function PhonegapLoaded(){
            document.getElementById("submitButton").addEventListener("click",
            dispMessage);
                console.warn("This is a warning message!");
                console.log("This is a log message!");
            }
            function dispMessage(){
                var nameOfUser = document.getElementById("name").value;
            document.getElementById("welcomemsg").innerHTML = "Welcome "+nameOfUser + "
            !";
                try {
                    var nameOfUser = document.getElementById("nme").value;
                } catch (e) {
                    console.error("Error occurred : " + e.message);
                }
            }
        </script>
    </head>
    <body onload = "onBodyLoad()">
        <form>
            Enter your name <input type = "text" id = "name"><br/>
            <input type = "button" id = "submitButton" value = "Submit">
            <div id = "welcomemsg"></div>
        </form>
    </body>
</html>
```

We can see that a warning message, `This is a warning message!`, is displayed followed by a log message, `This is a log message!`. Also, an error message, `Error occurred: Cannot read property 'value' of null...`, is displayed as shown in Figure 2.7.

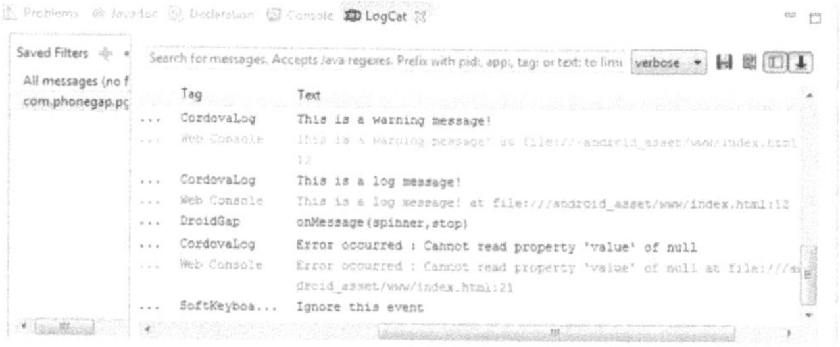

**Figure 2.7  The messages displayed through a `console` object.**

Now that we have learned how to create a user interface in PhoneGap applications and the technique of finding bugs while developing applications, let us learn how the applications are prepared for installing on emulators and devices.

## Creating a Keystore and Digitally Signing the Android Application

Several of the mobile platforms require that applications must be digitally signed before they can be loaded on devices or deployed to different application stores. More specifically, the applications need to be digitally signed with a certificate whose private keys belong to the owner of the application. But why is this? It is because the digital signature declares our ownership on the application and hence helps in preventing fraud when distributed on app stores.

As far as the Android platform is concerned, no application can be installed on an emulator or device until it is digitally signed. A question that may occur to you is: How is it possible that we have created and run so many Android applications before on the emulator without signing them? The answer is that for installing and running our applications on the emulator, the Android Software Development Kit (SDK) automatically signs the applications with a special `debug` key that is created by its build tools. The `debug` key is stored in `debug.keystore`, and Android uses the default digital certificate in this `debug.keystore` to sign our applications. The `debug.keystore` is suitable only for debugging and testing applications. For releasing and distributing an application to the market, it must be signed with a proper private key.

**Note:** There are two modes for building Android applications: `debug` mode and `release` mode. Debug mode is used while developing and testing applications, whereas `release` mode is for building a `release` version of our application for public distribution.

Let us learn how applications are digitally signed. There are two ways of creating private keys and digitally signing the Android applications:

- **Manually**—Using `keytool` and `jarsigner` tools for creating a private key and signing the application with the generated key. The generated keys are kept in keystores.
- **Using Export wizard**—The `Export` wizard of Eclipse Android Developer Tools (ADT) automatically creates a keystore and digitally signs the applications.

## Manually Creating a Keystore and Signing the Application

It is quite evident that it is a three-step approach. First, a private key has to be created, followed by creating an unsigned application, and finally signing the unsigned application with the keys.

### Creating a Private Keystore

For creating a private key, it is essential that Java is installed on our machine and a path for the Java bin directory is set. The tool used for creating private keys is `keytool`. The `keytool` generates private keys and stores them in a keystore.

The syntax for using keytool is given below:

```
keytool -genkey -v -keystore private_key.keystore -alias alias_name
-keyalg encryption_algorithm -keysize size_of_key -validity period_days
```

where:

- `-genkey` is for generating keys.
- `-v` is for verbose output.
- `-keystore` is for specifying the filename to store the generated key.
- `-alias` is for specifying the alias for the generated key.
- `-keyalg` is for specifying the encryption algorithm to be used for generating the key. The `keytool` supports both algorithms, RSA as well as DSA. RSA stands for Ron Rivest, Adi Shamir, and Leonard Adleman, the people who designed this encryption algorithm. DSA, on the other hand, stands for Digital Signature Algorithm.
- `-keysize` is for specifying the size of the generated key in bits. The default size of the generated key is 1024 bits.
- `-validity` is for specifying the validity period of the generated key in days.

**Example**

```
keytool -genkey -v -keystore AndroidApp.keystore -alias WelcomeApp
-keyalg RSA -keysize 2048 -validity 10000.
```

The command above will generate a private key and store it in the `AndroidApp.keystore`. The `alias` for the generated key will be `WelcomeApp`, and the key will be of 2048 bits, encrypted with the RSA algorithm and with the validity period of 10,000 days. The output generated upon using `keytool` is shown in Figure 2.8.

We can see that upon using `keytool`, we will be prompted for a password; reenter the password and other information to identify the application's owner. This information is stored in the private keystore, for example, first and last name of the developer, name of the organizational unit, name of the organization, name of the city or locality, name of the state or province, and the two-letter country code. The tool will also ask for the password for creating the self-signed certificate. To keep the same password that we used for the keystore, just press the `Enter` key. The private keystore `AndroidApp.keystore` will be created for us.

To understand how the private key is used for signing an application, let us first create an unsigned Android application.

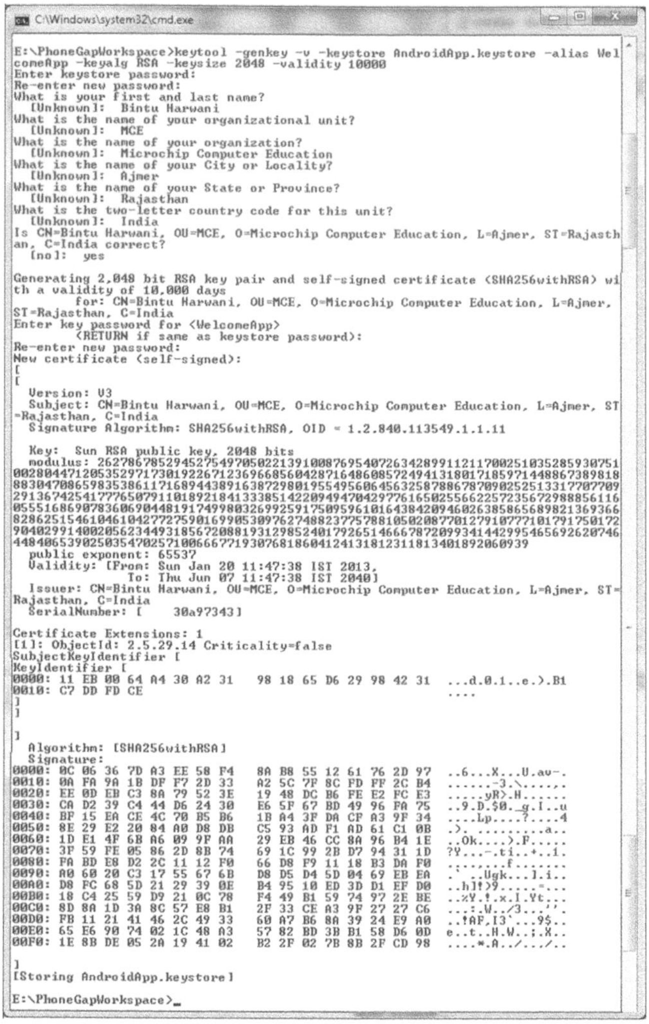

**Figure 2.8** Messages generated upon creating a private key with keytool.

## Creating an Unsigned Android Application

In this section, we will learn to create an unsigned Android application and subsequently sign it with the private key. We will make use of the PGWelcomeMsg application that we created in the beginning of this chapter for creating an unsigned application. So, launch Eclipse, right-click the PGWelcomeMsg project in the Package Explorer window, and select the Android Tools > Export Unsigned Application Package option. We will be prompted to specify the location and filename by which we want to export or create the unsigned application. Let us create the unsigned application by its same original name. So, let us assign the filename as PGWelcomeMsg, followed by clicking the Save button. A dialog will appear to inform the user that the application needs to be signed with the key before publishing it. Click the OK button to close the dialog box. The unsigned Android application will be created by the name PGWelcomeMsg.apk.

**Note:** Android applications are represented by an .apk extension. The term *APK* stands for Application Package file and usually represents a single application.

## Signing the Application with a Private Key

To sign the unsigned application that we created above with the private keystore, we will make use of the jarsigner tool. The jarsigner tool uses the application's APK and the keystore containing the private key and signs the application's APK. The syntax for using the jarsigner tool is as given below:

```
jarsigner -verbose -sigalg MD5withRSA -digestalg SHA1 -keystore private_
key.keystore application_to_sign.apk alias_name
```

where:

- ■ -verbose is for verbose output.
- ■ -sigalg is to specify the signature algorithm to be used for signing the application. Preferably, the MD5withRSA algorithm is used.
- ■ -digestalg is to specify the message digest algorithm to be used for processing the application's entries. Preferably, the SHA1 algorithm is used.
- ■ -keystore is to specify the keystore, that is, the filename where the private key is kept.
- ■ -alias is to specify the alias of the private key.

### Example

```
jarsigner -verbose -sigalg MD5withRSA -digestalg SHA1 -keystore
AndroidApp.keystore PGWelcomeMsg.apk WelcomeApp
```

The statement above will sign the PGWelcomeMsg.apk application with the AndroidApp. keystore. The signing will be done with the MD5withRSA algorithm, and to process the application's entries, the SHA1 algorithm is used. To ensure that our application is signed successfully, we can use the -verify option with jarsigner. The following statement verifies if the PGWelcomeMsg.apk application is successfully signed with the private key or not:

```
jarsigner -verify PGWelcomeMsg.apk
```

If the statement above displays a message, jar verified, it means the application is successfully signed. On signing the application with the jarsigner tool, output as shown in Figure 2.9 is generated.

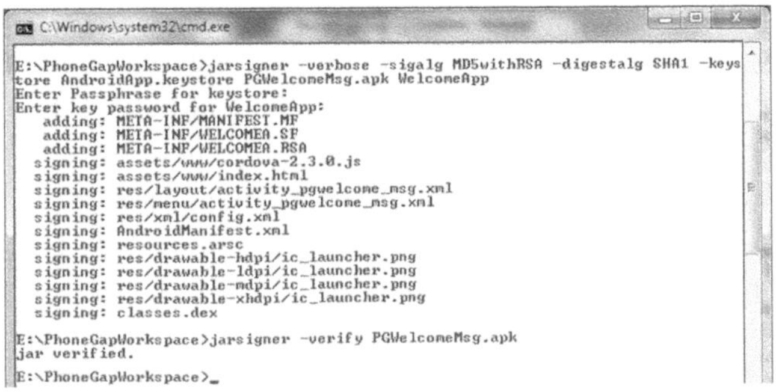

**Figure 2.9    Messages generated upon signing an application with a private key using** jarsigner.

**Note:** While installing the upgraded versions of the application, it must be signed with the same certificate that was used for the older version(s) because certificates in older and newer versions are compared. If the two certificates match, then only the application being installed is considered as the upgraded version; otherwise, it will be considered to be a completely new application.

Eclipse with the ADT plug-in provides the `Export` wizard that can be used to automatically generate a private key, a certificate, and also sign an application with the generated certificate. Let us learn more.

### Using Export Wizard for Creating a Keystore and Signing the Application

The `Export` wizard provided by Eclipse with ADT plug-in makes the task of creating a keystore (with a private key) and signing the application quite easy. The wizard provides a graphical user interface (GUI) that asks information regarding the keys and the application from the user and internally uses the `keytool` and `jarsigner` tools to generate a private key and sign the application. Assume that we want to sign the Android project `PGWelcomeMsg` that we created earlier, using the `Export` wizard. Below are the steps to do so:

1. Launch Eclipse and select the Android project `PGWelcomeMsg` in the `Package Explorer` window and select the `File->Export` option or right-click the project in the `Package Explorer` window and select the `Export` option.
2. In the `Export` dialog, expand the Android item and select `Export Android Application`. Click the `Next` button.
3. We will be prompted to specify the project to export. Our Android project name, `PGWelcomeMsg`, will be displayed in the `Project` box by default. Click the `Next` button.
4. The next dialog window will prompt you to either select an existing keystore or create a new one. Let us select the `Create new keystore` option to create a new keystore for our application. In the `Location` box, specify the name and path of the new keystore. Let us generate the keystore by the name of the application, and so, assign the keystore name as `PGWelcomeMsg`. In the `Password` and `Confirm` boxes, enter the passwords to protect the keystore. After entering the passwords (see Figure 2.10), click `Next`.
5. Provide an `Alias` for the private key and fill in the `Password` and `Confirm` boxes to provide a password to protect the private key (see Figure 2.11). Provide the period of `Validity` as 25 years. The validity period of the generated key is recommended to be 25 years or more for the simple reason that developers get enough time to upgrade their applications. Also fill the `First and Last Name` box in with the developer's name and click `Next`.
6. We will be prompted to specify the path and name of the signed application. Let us generate the signed application by its original name, and so assign the name `PGWelcomeMsg` in the `Destination APK file` box along with the path as shown in Figure 2.12. Click the `Finish` button.

The signed application by the name `PGWelcomeMsg.apk` will now be generated in the specified folder. The signed application is now ready for distribution. Before installing our application on a physical device, let us first ensure that it installs and runs correctly on the emulator.

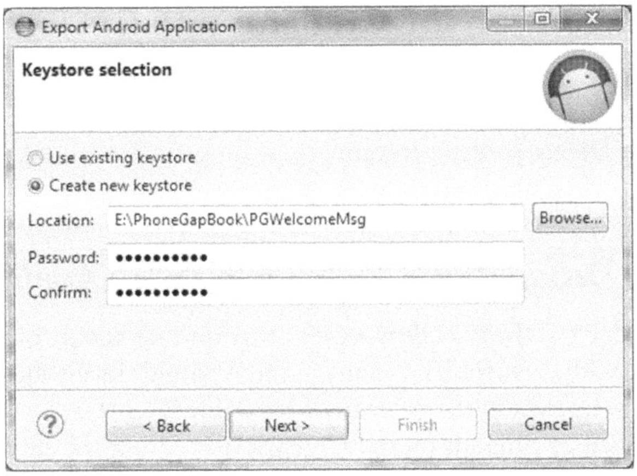

**Figure 2.10** The `Export Android Application` dialog box prompting for keystore information.

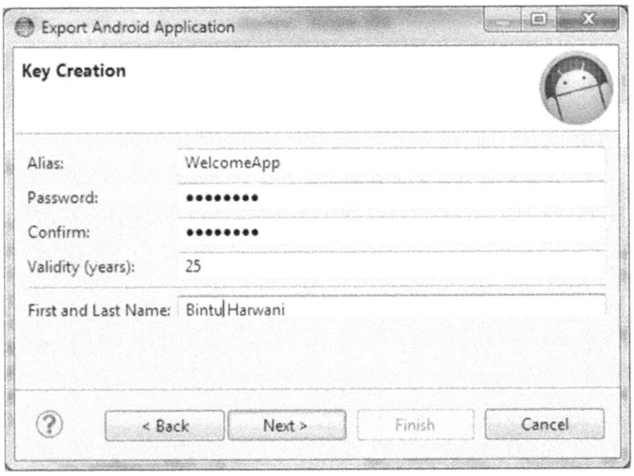

**Figure 2.11** The dialog prompting for information for key creation.

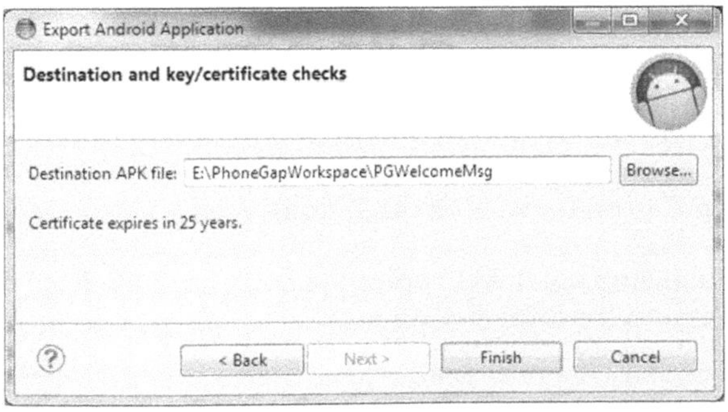

**Figure 2.12** The dialog prompting for the name and path of the signed application.

# Installing Applications on the Emulator and Device

There are two ways to install applications on an emulator and device:

- Using the Android Debug Bridge program
- Using Eclipse with ADT plug-in

## *Using the Android Debug Bridge Program to Install Applications*

The Android Debug Bridge (ADB) is a client-server program that is part of the Android SDK. It is used to communicate with, control, and manage the Android device and emulator. The adb commands can be used to interact with one or more emulator instances, install applications, push and pull files, and run shell commands on the target device. Using the shell commands, we can perform several tasks, such as listing existing applications, deleting applications, and querying or modifying content on the device/emulator.

To access ADB through Windows, open the command prompt and navigate to the folder where adb.exe is located by using the cd command. By default, adb.exe is installed in the C:\ Program Files (x86)\Android\android-sdk\platform-tools folder. Table 2.1 shows a brief description of the adb commands that are used to interact with the device or emulator.

**Table 2.1  A Brief Description of the adb Commands**

| Command | Description |
|---------|-------------|
| adb devices | Displays the list of devices attached to the computer. The command also shows the currently running emulator on our computer. |
| adb push | Copies files from a computer to the device/emulator.<br><br>Syntax:<br><br>`adb push source destination`<br><br>where source refers to the file along with its path that we want to copy, and destination refers to the place in the device or emulator where we want to copy the file. The following statement copies the song.mp3 file from the C:\ drive to the sdcard folder of the running emulator.<br><br>`C:\Program Files (x86)\Android\android-sdk\platform-tools>adb push C:\song.mp3/sdcard` |
| adb pull | Copies files from the device/emulator to our computer.<br><br>Syntax:<br><br>`adb pull source [destination]`<br><br>The following statement copies the song.mp3 file from the sdcard of the emulator to the local disk drive D:<br><br>`C:\Program Files (x86)\Android\android-sdk\platform-tools>adb pull/sdcard/song.mp3 D:\` |

*(Continued)*

**Table 2.1    A Brief Description of the** `adb` **Commands (Continued)**

| Command | Description |
|---------|-------------|
| `adb shell` | Displays the shell prompt where we can give different Unix commands like `ls`, `cd`, `cp`, `rm`, etc., to do normal file operations. For example, the following statements delete the `song.mp3` file that we pushed into the emulator:<br><br>`C:\Program Files (x86)\Android\android-sdk\platform-tools> adb shell`<br>`# cd sdcard`<br>`rm song.mp3`<br><br>To quit from the shell, press the `Ctrl+D` keys. |
| `adb install` | Installs an application from our computer to the device/emulator.<br><br>Syntax:<br><br>`adb install appname.apk`<br><br>The following statement installs the application `PGWelcomeMsg.apk` from the `E:\PhoneGapWorkspace` folder to the currently running emulator instance (see Figure 2.13):<br><br>`C:\Program Files (x86)\Android\android-sdk\platform-tools>adb install E:\PhoneGapWorkspace\PGWelcomeMsg.apk` |

Figure 2.13 shows the `adb` commands to display the list of currently running emulator instances and to install the signed application `PGWelcomeMsg.apk` on the emulator.

Figure 2.14 shows the list of applications in the emulator. Among the list of applications, we find our `PGWelcomeMsg` application, which confirms that our application `PGWelcomeMsg.apk` is successfully installed on the emulator.

The `adb install` command can be used to install the application on the physical device too. To do so, connect an Android device to the computer via the USB. Thereafter, go to the `C:\Program Files (x86)\Android\android-sdk\platform-tools` folder, as `adb.exe` is present in this folder by default. First, run the `adb devices` command to see if the Android device is recognized by the computer and is visible. If the device is not recognized by the PC, click on the `Settings` option on the device and choose the `Developer options`. From the `Developer options`, enable the `USB debugging` option. It will enable the Android device to plug in to our PC through the USB cable. Figure 2.15 displays the device name, and hence ensures that the Android device is recognized by the computer. Now we give the following

**Figure 2.13    Screenshot of installing the** `PGWelcomeMsg.apk` **application on the emulator instance.**

**Figure 2.14    The installed application appears in the Apps list on the emulator.**

**Figure 2.15    Screenshot of installing the** `PGWelcomeMsg.apk` **application on the connected physical device.**

`adb install` command to install our signed `PGWelcomeMsg.apk` application on the current visible device:

```
C:\Program Files (x86)\Android\android-sdk\platform-tools>adb install E:\
PhoneGapWorkspace\PGWelcomeMsg.apk
```

On the device, among the list of applications, we find our `PGWelcomMsg` application (see Figure 2.16), which confirms that the `adb install` command has successfully installed our application on the device.

If there is more than one emulator or device connected to the computer and we want to install an application to a particular device, we specify that device/emulator by using the `-s` option with the `adb` command. For example, the following statement installs the `PGWelcomeMsg.apk` application on the emulator with ID `emulator-5556`:

```
C:\Program Files (x86)\Android\android-sdk\platform-tools>adb -s
emulator-5556 install PGWelcomeMsg.apk
```

**Figure 2.16    The installed application appears in the Apps list on the device.**

In addition to ADB, the Eclipse integrated development environment (IDE) that has the ADT plug-in installed can also be used to install applications on the emulator/device. Let us see how.

## Installing Applications to the Device Using Eclipse ADT

To install an application to the physical Android device, we connect the device to the computer via the USB. To make the device recognizable by the computer, perform the steps given below on the device:

- Unlock the device and press the Home button.
- Go to Settings (see Figure 2.17a) in the Android device.
- You might see several Settings options (see Figure 2.17b). Select Developer options.
- Check the USB debugging option (see Figure 2.17c).

The device that is connected with the USB cable will now be recognized by the PC.

Upon running the application on Eclipse, we want it to prompt to choose the device/emulator to run the application on. To do so, perform the steps given below in Eclipse IDE:

- Select the Run->Debug Configurations option.
- Select the application that we want to install from the list of Android applications, that is, select the PGWelcomeMsg application.
- Select the Target tab, and set the Deployment Target Selection Mode to Always prompt to pick device to enable us to choose the device or Android Virtual Device (AVD) on which we want to install and run the application (see Figure 2.18).
- Apply the changes to the configuration file by clicking the Apply button.

If we do not perform the steps above, then while running the application, it will not run on the connected device, but an AVD that is compatible to the application will be invoked and the application will run on it.

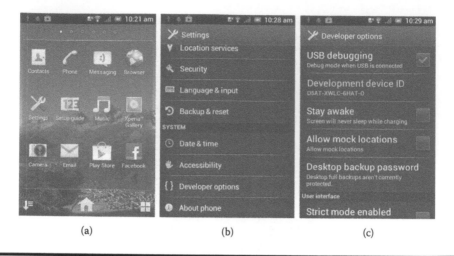

(a)  (b)  (c)

**Figure 2.17** **(a) The different options are displayed upon clicking the** `Home` **button on the device. (b) The settings option is displayed upon selecting the** `Settings` **button. (c) The developer options are displayed upon selecting** `Developer options` **from** `Settings`.

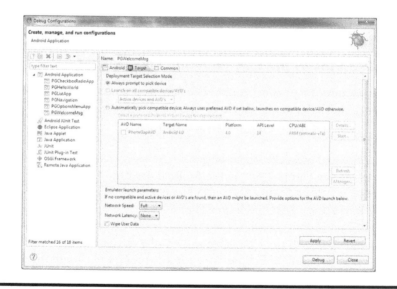

**Figure 2.18** **Configuring the application to prompt for the device/emulator to run on.**

**Note:** Because Eclipse runs an application in the `debug` mode by default, we need to ensure that our application is debuggable. This is done by assigning a `true` value to the `android:debuggable` attribute in the `<application>` element of the `AndroidManifest.xml` file of our application. We did not do this step above because as of ADT 8.0, this is done by default.

Now, we are all set to run and install the application on the physical device. So, select the Run->Run option or select the Run icon from the toolbar, or right-click on the application in the `Package Explorer` window and select the `Run As->Android Application` option. We will get the `Android Device Chooser` dialog (see Figure 2.19a) showing the connected device and running AVDs (if any). Select the device followed by clicking the OK button to install

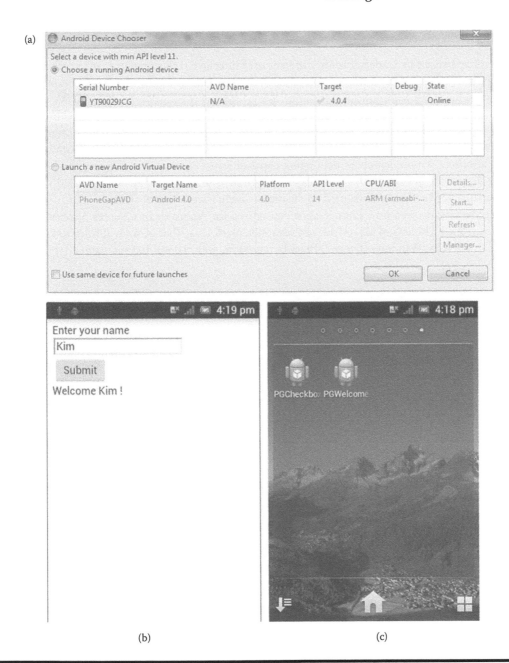

**Figure 2.19** **(a) The** `Android Device Chooser` **prompting to select the device/emulator to run the application. (b) The application runs on the selected device. (c) The installed application appears in the Apps list of the device.**

and run the selected application on the device (see Figure 2.19b). The fact is that when we run an application, the Eclipse invokes ADB internally and installs that application to the device.

After running the application, we can see that the application name appears in the applications list (see Figure 2.19c) on the device, which confirms that the application has been successfully installed on it.

## Summary

This chapter focused on understanding different user interface (UI) controls that are required for creating a user interface in various applications. We saw the usage of the text box in fetching data from the user and the technique of associating event listeners with different controls. We saw how to get mutually exclusive input using radio buttons and multiple inputs using checkboxes. We learned to use the drop-down list for displaying options, and also learned how to configure it for single as well as multiple selections. We saw the usage of hyperlinks in navigating from one Web page to another. We implemented debugging capabilities in applications. We saw the procedure for creating private keys and using these keys for digitally signing the applications. Finally, we saw the procedure for installing the signed applications on emulators and devices.

We have already seen how PhoneGap is configured for Android. In Chapter 3, we will learn how to configure PhoneGap for the rest of the mobile platforms. That is, we will learn to configure PhoneGap for iOS, Windows Phone 7, BlackBerry, bada, and HP webOS platforms.

# *Chapter 3*

# Configuring PhoneGap

In Chapter 1, we learned the procedure to configure PhoneGap for the Android environment. In this chapter, we will learn to explore the rest of the mobile platforms. That is, we will learn to configure PhoneGap for mobile platforms like iOS, Windows Phone 7, BlackBerry, bada, and webOS. The topics covered in this chapter include:

- Configuring PhoneGap for iOS
- Configuring PhoneGap for Windows Phone 7
- Configuring PhoneGap for the BlackBerry
- Configuring PhoneGap for bada
- Configuring PhoneGap for webOS

## Configuring PhoneGap for iOS

iOS is an operating system that was developed by Apple and is successfully applied to the iPhone, iPod Touch, iPad, Apple TV, and other Apple products. A few of its features are given below:

- **Enables multitouch operation**—Includes swiping, tapping, pinching, and reverse pinching.
- **Supports iCloud**—Stores music, photos, apps, mail, contacts, and documents, and can push to all devices wirelessly. That is, our content can be pushed on the Mac, iPhone, and iPod Touch, too.
- **Secure**—iOS secures the data by encrypting it.
- **Supports developers**—Apple provides a rich set of tools and application programming interfaces (APIs) to create different varieties of sophisticated apps and games. It is because of this that in addition to built-in apps, there are over 700,000 more apps and games available in the App Store.
- **Hardware advantage**—iOS enables developers to take full advantage of the iOS device hardware, such as the retina display, multitouch interface, sensors, front and back cameras, microphone, and so forth.

- **Free updates**—iOS updates are free. Whenever new updates are available, the device alerts of the latest version and the upgraded version can be easily downloaded on the iPhone, iPad, or iPod Touch wirelessly.
- **Supports different languages**—iOS supports over 30 languages and has built-in dictionary support for over 50 languages, making it a popular mobile platform all over the world.
- **Supports voice recognition**—Enables users to send messages, schedule meetings, and perform other tasks just by speaking.

To develop the PhoneGap application for iOS, we require the following things:

- An Intel-based computer running Mac OS X Snow Leopard (10.6) or later.
- Latest version of Xcode (version 4 or above). Xcode is a developer tool that is used for iOS development. I used Xcode 4.4.1 in this book. I assume Xcode is already installed on our machine.
- Next, we need to install the Xcode Command Line Tools. So, select the `Xcode Preferences->Downloads->Components->Command Line Tools->Install` option (see Figure 3.1).
- Download the latest version of PhoneGap from `http://phonegap.com/`. The latest version of PhoneGap at the time of this writing is 2.3.0. On unzipping the downloaded PhoneGap file, we find numerous subfolders, each labeled with the targeted OS inside the `lib` folder. For configuring PhoneGap for iOS, we will need the `/lib/iOS` subfolder that contains several files, as shown in Figure 3.2.

**Note:** We also need to register as an Apple developer in Apple's developer program. It is an essential requirement to deploy any iOS applications on the devices or through Apple's App Store. There is a yearly membership fee for different development programs. For more information, visit: `http://developer.apple.com`.

We launch `Terminal.app` by dragging the `bin` subfolder from the `iOS` folder (which was provided in the PhoneGap package) shown in Figure 3.2 and dropping it into the `Terminal.app`

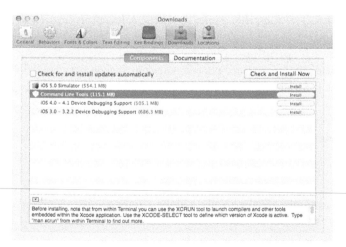

**Figure 3.1  Installing Command Line Tools.**

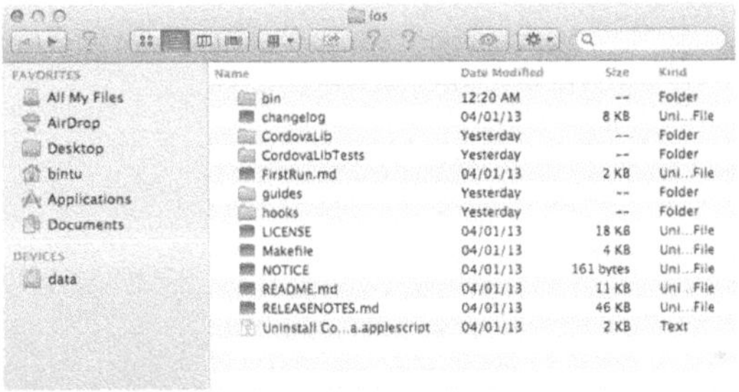


**Figure 3.2 Library, tools, and source code for configuring PhoneGap for iOS.**

icon in the dock. It will not only launch a new terminal window, but also change directory to the `bin` subfolder of the `iOS` folder.

In the `bin` subfolder, we will create our PhoneGap-based iOS project by using the `create` command in the following syntax in the Terminal window:

```
./create <project_folder_path> <package_name> <project_name>
```

where:

- <project_folder_path> is the path to the PhoneGap-based iOS project that we want to create. This folder must be empty if it exists.
- <package_name> is the package name of the project (to give it a unique identity).
- <project_name> is the filename by which we want to create our new project.

**Example**

The statement shown in Figure 3.3a will create a PhoneGap-based iOS project named `HelloWorldApp` in the `iosphoneapps` folder on the desktop. The package name of the project will be `com.phonegap.HelloWorldApp` (see Figure 3.3a).

The `create` command will automatically create files and folders of our iOS project, `HelloWorldApp`, in the `iosphoneapps` folder (see Figure 3.3b).

Double-click the `HelloWorldApp.xcodeproj` file in the `iosphoneapps` folder to open the project in the Xcode project window. We can see that the Xcode project window consists of multiple panes and a toolbar (see Figure 3.4). The leftmost pane is called the `navigator area`. It provides an outline view of the project contents. If we click the little triangle to the left of any item (the disclosure triangle) in the `navigator pane`, it will be expanded to show the subitems

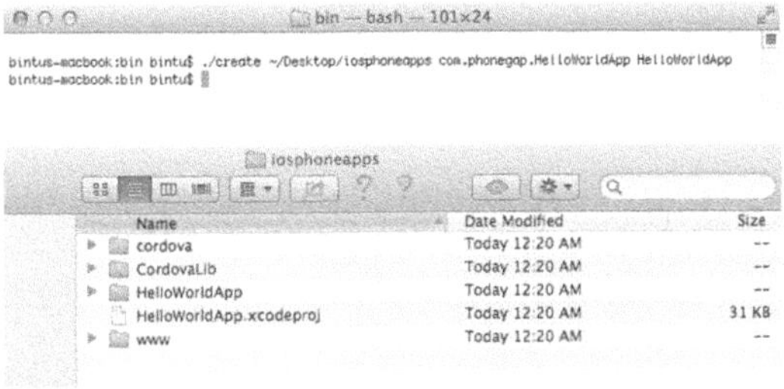


**Figure 3.3 (a) Creating an iPhone application using the files provided in the PhoneGap package. (b) The list of files and folders that are automatically generated.**

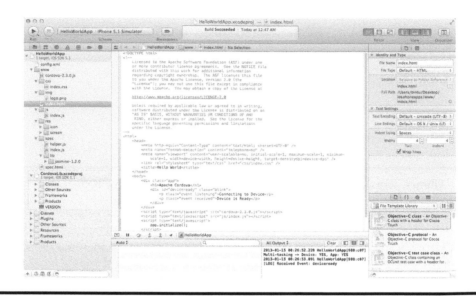

**Figure 3.4  iOS application opened in Xcode IDE.**

in it. We can click the triangle again to hide the subitems. On the right is the Editor pane that opens the selected file for editing.

All the project files are organized into different folders or groups in the navigator pane on the left side of the Xcode project window. At the bottom is a footer that shows messages related to our builds. Double-click the index.html file in the www folder to display its code in the Editor pane. Original content in the index.html file (provided by the PhoneGap package) is shown in Listing 3.1.

**Listing 3.1  Original Content in the index.html File**

```
<!DOCTYPE html>
<html>
    <head>
        <meta http-equiv = "Content-Type" content = "text/html; charset = UTF-8"/>
        <meta name = "format-detection" content = "telephone = no"/>
        <meta name = "viewport" content = "user-scalable = no, initial-scale = 1,
        maximum-scale = 1, minimum-scale = 1, width = device-width, height = device-
        height, target-densitydpi = device-dpi"/>
        <link rel = "stylesheet" type = "text/css" href = "css/index.css"/>
        <title>Hello World</title>
    </head>
    <body>
        <div class = "app">
            <h1>Apache Cordova</h1>
            <div id = "deviceready" class = "blink">
                <p class = "event listening">Connecting to Device</p>
                <p class = "event received">Device is Ready</p>
            </div>
        </div>
        <script type = "text/javascript" src = "cordova-2.3.0.js"></script>
        <script type = "text/javascript" src = "js/index.js"></script>
        <script type = "text/javascript">
```

```
        app.initialize();
    </script>
  </body>
</html>
```

Select the `Product->Run` option to run the application or click the Run icon shown in the toolbar at the top. But before running the application, select the simulator on which we want to see the output. By default, the `iPad 5.1 Simulator` is selected in the simulator's drop-down list. Because the application is for the iPhone, select the `iPhone 5.1 Simulator` option from the list of simulators. Upon clicking the Run icon, Xcode will build the application, launch the selected simulator, load the application into the simulator, and start the application. We can see that the default `index.html` file displays the text `Apache Cordova` in heading 1 style and the message `Device is Ready`, which confirms that the `deviceready` event has occurred (see Figure 3.5a). The `deviceready` event also confirms that PhoneGap is successfully loaded.

To modify the `index.html` file into a welcome application as we did in the Android application in Chapter 1, we need to modify the `index.html` file. Recall, in Chapter 1, we created a PhoneGap-based Android application that prompts the user to enter a name followed by clicking a button. After entering a name, when the user clicks a button, a welcome message is displayed on the screen. To convert the current application into a welcome application, modify the `index.html` file to appear as shown in Listing 3.2.

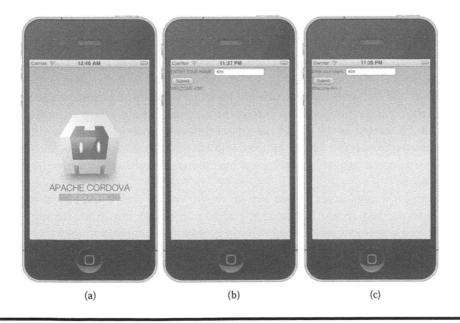

(a)      (b)      (c)

**Figure 3.5  (a) The output displayed by the default index.html. (b) All text, including the welcome message, appears in uppercase. (c) The welcome message is displayed after removing the** `text-transform` **attribute from the** `index.css` **file.**

**Listing 3.2   Code Written in the `index.html` File**

```
<!DOCTYPE html>
<html>
   <head>
      <title>Welcome Message App</title>
      <meta http-equiv = "Content-Type" content = "text/html; charset = UTF-8"/>
      <meta name = "format-detection" content = "telephone = no"/>
      <meta name = "viewport" content = "user-scalable = no, initial-scale = 1,
      maximum-scale = 1, minimum-scale = 1, width = device-width, height = device-
      height, target-densitydpi = device-dpi"/>
      <link rel = "stylesheet" type = "text/css" href = "css/index.css"/>
      <script type = "text/javascript" src = "cordova-2.3.0.js"></script>
      <script type = "text/javascript" src = "js/index.js"></script>
      <script type = "text/javascript">
         document.addEventListener("deviceready", PhonegapLoaded, false);
         function PhonegapLoaded() {
         document.getElementById("submitButton").addEventListener("click",
         dispMessage);
         }
         function dispMessage() {
            var nameOfUser = document.getElementById("name").value;
            message = document.getElementById("welcomemsg");
            message.innerHTML = "Welcome " + nameOfUser + " !";
         }
      </script>
   </head>
   <body>
      Enter your name <input type = "text" id = "name"><br/>
      <input type = "button" id = "submitButton" value = "Submit">
      <div id = "welcomemsg"> </div>
   </body>
</html>
```

In the code above, we see that an event listener is registered with the `deviceready` event. The `deviceready` event is related to loading of PhoneGap. It also means that when PhoneGap is loaded, the `deviceready` event will fire and the event handler function, that is, `PhonegapLoaded()`,will be invoked. In the `PhonegapLoaded()` function, a `click` event is associated with the `Submit` button. An event handling function, `dispMessage()`, is set to execute when the `click` event occurs or fires on the `Submit` button. In the `dispMessage()` function, the name entered by the user in the input text box is retrieved and displayed along with a welcome message through the `<div>` element with ID `welcomemsg`. That is, the `<div>` element with ID `welcomemsg` will display a welcome message on the screen when the user clicks the `Submit` button.

Upon running the application, we see that an input text box and a button with the caption `Submit` appears on the screen. After entering a name in the input box, when the user clicks the `Submit` button, a welcome message along with the entered name appears on the screen, as shown in Figure 3.5b.

One thing that might surprise you is that though the entered name is in normal case (only the first character is in uppercase and the rest of the characters are in lowercase), the welcome message and the entered name appear all in uppercase. The reason for this happening is that the Cascading Style Sheets (CSS) file `index.css`, which is available in www/css folder and is linked to our `index.html` file, applies certain styles to the `<body>` element of the `index.html` file. A part of the `index.css` file in the www/css folder that applies style to the `<body>` element of the Hypertext Markup Language (HTML) file is shown in Listing 3.3.

**Listing 3.3  Style Properties in the `index.css` File**

```
body {
    background-color:#E4E4E4;
    background-image:linear-gradient(top, #A7A7A7 0%, #E4E4E4 51%);
    background-image:-webkit-linear-gradient(top, #A7A7A7 0%, #E4E4E4 51%);
    background-image:-ms-linear-gradient(top, #A7A7A7 0%, #E4E4E4 51%);
    background-image:-webkit-gradient(
        linear,
        left top,
        left bottom,
        color-stop(0, #A7A7A7),
        color-stop(0.51, #E4E4E4)
    );
    background-attachment:fixed;
    font-family:'HelveticaNeue-Light', 'HelveticaNeue', Helvetica, Arial, sans-serif;
    font-size:12px;
    height:100%;
    margin:0px;
    padding:0px;
    text-transform:uppercase;
    width:100%;
}
```

The `text-transform` property defined in the `index.css` file is assigned an `upper-case` value, as a result of which the text in the `<body>` element of the `index.html` file is automatically converted to uppercase. To make the text in the `<body>` element appear in normal case, let us delete the following line from the `index.css` file:

```
text-transform:uppercase;
```

Now, when we run the application, we observe that the entered name as well as the welcome message appears in normal case, as shown in Figure 3.5c.

# Configuring PhoneGap for Windows Phone 7

Windows Phone 7 is Microsoft's mobile operating system. A few of the features of this mobile platform are given below:

- **Supports multitasking**—Enables switching among recently used applications by pressing and holding the back button.
- **Organized**—Several features of Windows Phone are organized into "hubs." For example, there is a People hub, Pictures hub, Games hub, Marketplace hub, and so on. Each hub provides special facilities. For example, the People hub connects with Facebook, Twitter, Outlook, LinkedIn, and Windows Live messenger.
- **Supports visual search**—In addition to text, a picture can also be used to search. Information related to the picture that is being used for the search is displayed.
- **Supports music search**—Music that is being played can be searched; that is, the track, artist, song, and other information about the music are displayed.
- **Hardware access**—Supports WiFi, sensors, camera, GPS, multitouch technology, and other features, allowing developers to develop sophisticated applications.

- **Supports security and privacy**—Uses 128-bit to 256-bit Secure Sockets Layer (SSL) encryption to secure information.

For configuring PhoneGap for Windows Phone 7, the operating system required is either Windows 7 or Windows Vista with Service Pack 2 (SP2). On either operating system, follow the steps below to configure PhoneGap for Windows Phone 7:

1. Download the Windows Phone Software Development Kit (SDK) from `http://www.microsoft.com/en-us/download` and install it. At the time of this writing, Windows Phone SDK 7.1 is available to download.
2. Download the last version of the PhoneGap package and unzip it. For developing Windows Phone 7 applications, we require the `windows-phone-7` directory present in the `lib` folder of the PhoneGap package.

Assuming that Visual Studio is installed on your machine, let us begin with our task of configuring PhoneGap for Windows Phone 7.

## Creating a Project Template

For creating a PhoneGap-based application on Windows Phone 7, we first need to set up a new template. Templates or project templates provide a structure to an application and also automatically create files and folders for the application on the basis of the selected template.

To create a template for PhoneGap, open the `CordovaExample.sln` that is present in the `\lib\windows-phone-7\example` folder of PhoneGap's package in Visual Studio. We will get the screen shown in Figure 3.6.

Choose the `File->Export Template` option. We will be prompted to choose the type of template that we want to create. Because we want to create a project, select the `Project`

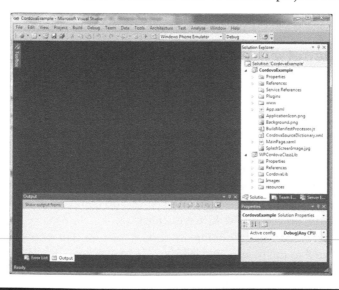

**Figure 3.6** `CordovaExample.sln` **is provided in the PhoneGap package and opened in Visual Studio 2010.**

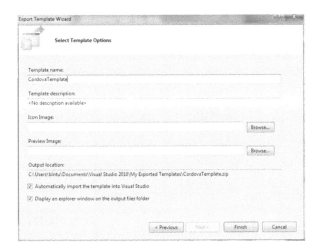

**Figure 3.7    Creating a project template using the Export Template Wizard.**

`template` option. A dialog window will appear asking information for the new project template. We need to specify the name of the new template, a small description, icon image, and so on. Let us assign the name `CordovaTemplate` to the project template. After filling in the details as shown in Figure 3.7, click the `Finish` button to create the project template.

## Creating a Windows Phone 7 Project

Once the project template is created, we can go ahead and create our PhoneGap-based Windows Phone 7 project. Start Visual Studio and select the `File->New Project` option. From the dialog that opens, select the `Visual C#` category in the navigator on the left side. We will see a new type of project template named `CordovaTemplate` among the existing list of project templates. Select the `CordovaTemplate` and provide a name and destination for the application. Let us assign the application name `PGWinPhoneApp` and click the `OK` button (see Figure 3.8).

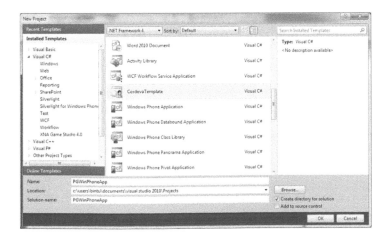

**Figure 3.8    Creating a Windows 7 project using the newly created `CordovaTemplate`.**

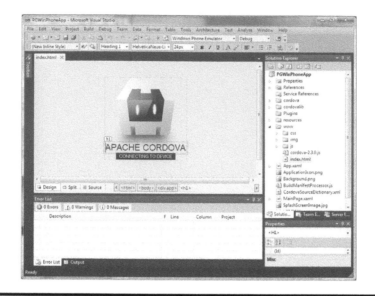

**Figure 3.9** **The `index.html` file content in the `Design` window.**

Visual Studio will create the application `PGWinPhoneApp` along with a default `index.html` and style sheet. In the `Solution Explorer` shown on the right side, expand the www folder, and then double-click the `index.html` file to open it in the editor. The `index.html` file in the `Design` window will appear as shown in Figure 3.9.

The default source code in the `index.html` file is shown in Listing 3.4.

**Listing 3.4** **Code in the Original `index.html` File Provided with the PhoneGap Package**

```html
<!DOCTYPE html>
<html>
    <head>
        <meta http-equiv = "Content-Type" content = "text/html; charset = UTF-8"/>
        <meta name = "format-detection" content = "telephone = no"/>
        <meta name = "viewport" content = "user-scalable = no, initial-scale = 1,
        maximum-scale = 1, minimum-scale = 1, width = device-width, height = device-
        height, target-densitydpi = device-dpi"/>
        <link rel = "stylesheet" type = "text/css" href = "css/index.css"/>
        <title>Hello World</title>
    </head>
    <body>
        <div class = "app">
            <h1>Apache Cordova</h1>
            <div id = "deviceready" class = "blink">
                <p class = "event listening">Connecting to Device</p>
                <p class = "event received">Device is Ready</p>
            </div>
        </div>
        <script type = "text/javascript" src = "cordova-2.3.0.js"></script>
        <script type = "text/javascript" src = "js/index.js"></script>
        <script type = "text/javascript">
            app.initialize();
        </script>
    </body>
</html>
```

For testing the Window Phone applications, Visual Studio supports Windows Phone emulator. We can choose the execution target from the toolbar. The drop-down list in the toolbar displays options (execution targets) to test the application on `Windows Phone Emulator` as well as on `Windows Phone Device`. Let us select the option `Windows Phone Emulator` to test the application on the emulator. Run the application by selecting the `Debug->Start Debugging` option; press the F5 key or click the `Start Debugging` icon from the toolbar. Visual Studio will build the application, launch the emulator (if it is selected as the execution target), and deploy and run the application on the emulator. The default `index.html` file that is provided in the PhoneGap package will display the output as shown in Figure 3.10a.

Again, let us modify the application into a welcome application; that is, we want the application to prompt for the username, and when the user clicks the button after entering a name, a welcome message is displayed on the screen. To do so, let us modify the `index.html` file to appear as shown in Listing 3.2.

Upon running the application, an input box along with a `Submit` button will appear on the screen. After entering a name in the input text box, when the user clicks the `Submit` button, a welcome message along with the entered name will appear on the screen, as shown in Figure 3.10b. As expected, the text will appear in uppercase. Recall, the style property `text-transform` is set to `uppercase` in the `index.css` file that is linked to the `index.html` file. On deleting the said style property from the `index.css` file, the welcome message and the entered name will appear in normal case, as shown in Figure 3.10c.

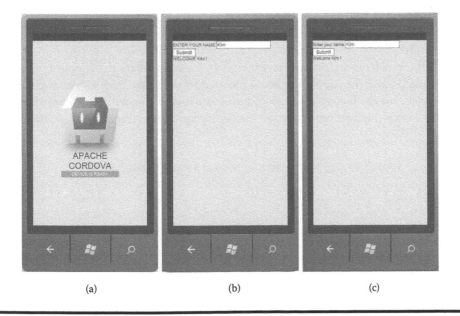

(a)  (b)  (c)

**Figure 3.10** (a) The output of the `default index.html` file. (b) The welcome message is displayed by the modified `index.html` file in uppercase. (c) The welcome message is displayed in normal case after modifying the style sheet file.

## Configuring PhoneGap for the BlackBerry

BlackBerry is a brand of smartphone devices developed by the Canadian telecommunications company Research In Motion (RIM). The operating system used by BlackBerry devices supports several features. A few of them are listed below:

- Uses HTML5 for best browsing experience
- Supports touch screen keyboard
- Supports a high level of security by implementing message encryption
- Supports Near Field Communication (NFC) to share data among NFC-enabled BlackBerry devices wirelessly
- Supports a new mobile user interface called Flow that enables communication between the applications
- Supports BlackBerry Hub, a master inbox that collects the entire user's communications, across e-mail, Facebook, messages, and so on, in one place

I assume that Java and BlackBerry WebWorks SDK are already installed on your computer. The version of BlackBerry SDK that is available at the time of this writing is BlackBerry 10 WebWorks SDK 1.0.4.7.

The steps for configuring PhoneGap for BlackBerry are as follows:

- Download the Ripple emulator from `https://developer.blackberry.com/html5/download/`. The Web application for BlackBerry platform can be compiled from the Ripple emulator.
- Start the Google Chrome browser. If you do not have Google Chrome, download it from `https://www.google.com/intl/en/chrome/browser/`.
- In the address bar of Google Chrome, paste `chrome://chrome/extensions/` and then press the `Enter` key. The Google Chrome Extensions window will open, as shown in Figure 3.11.
- Open a file explorer window and navigate to the location where the Ripple emulator file is downloaded. Click the Ripple emulator's file, that is, the `ripple _ ui.crx` file, and drag and drop it into the Google Chrome Extensions window. We will be prompted to add the extension; click the `Add` button to add the Ripple emulator extension to Google Chrome.

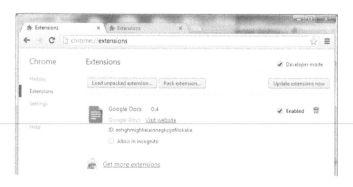

**Figure 3.11   A list of extensions enabled in Google Chrome.**

**Figure 3.12    Enabling the Ripple emulator in Google Chrome.**

- A `Ripple` button will be added to our Google Chrome toolbar. The PhoneGap-based BlackBerry project that we are going to create will consist of an `index.html` file and a few CSS and JavaScript files. So, copy the `css`, `img`, and `js` folders along with the `config.xml`, `cordova-2.3.0.js`, and `index.html` files from the `\lib\blackberry\sample\www` folder of the PhoneGap package into a separate folder. Let us name this folder `bbapp`.
- In the browser's address bar, type the URL or path of the `index.html` file of our application—`file:///E:/bbapp/index.html`.
- After typing the URL of the `index.html` file, click the `Ripple` button on the right side of the Google Chrome toolbar and click the `Enable` button, as shown in Figure 3.12.
- On starting the Ripple emulator for the first time, it displays the license agreement that we need to read and accept for using the Ripple emulator. After accepting the license agreement, if the Ripple emulator is invoked for the first time, the next screen prompts us to select the platform for which we want to develop and test applications. The available options are as shown in Figure 3.13. Because we are going to run PhoneGap-based applications, we will select the `Apache Cordova (2.0.0)` option.

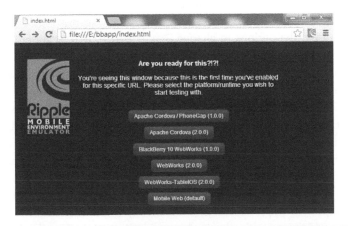

**Figure 3.13    The Web page prompting us to select the platform for testing and running applications.**

■ We need to select the platform only once, as the Ripple emulator remembers the selection and loads it automatically when the application is loaded the next time. The index.html file provided in the PhoneGap package contains the default code shown in Listing 3.5.

**Listing 3.5    Code Provided in the `index.html` File Provided with the PhoneGap Package**

```
<!DOCTYPE html>
<html>
    <head>
        <meta http-equiv = "Content-Type" content = "text/html; charset = UTF-8"/>
        <meta name = "format-detection" content = "telephone = no"/>
        <meta name = "viewport" content = "user-scalable = no, initial-scale = 1,
        maximum-scale = 1, minimum-scale = 1, width = device-width, height = device-
        height, target-densitydpi = device-dpi"/>
        <link rel = "stylesheet" type = "text/css" href = "css/index.css"/>
        <title>Hello World</title>
    </head>
    <body>
        <div class = "app">
        <h1>Apache Cordova</h1>
        <div id = "deviceready" class = "blink">
            <p class = "event listening">Connecting to Device</p>
            <p class = "event received">Device is Ready</p>
        </div>
        </div>
        <script type = "text/javascript" src = "cordova-2.3.0.js"></script>
        <script type = "text/javascript" src = "js/index.js"></script>
        <script type = "text/javascript">
        app.initialize();
        </script>
    </body>
</html>
```

We can see that the code displays an image and text, Apache  Cordova, in heading 1 style. The two texts, Connecting  to  Device and Device  is  Ready, are related to the deviceready event and inform us whether PhoneGap is loaded or not.

To load the application in Google Chrome, we specify the URL of the index.html file of our BlackBerry application stored in the E:\bbapp folder, as shown in Figure 3.14. On the left-side panel, we can see the options to change Devices, Platforms, and their respective versions. Not only this, but we can change the orientation of the device in the output from land-scape to portrait and vice versa. On the right-side panel, we see the options to change Device  & Network  Settings, configuration settings, GeoLocation, and so forth. The right panel also contains a Build section that can be used to build and deploy applications on the device.

As we did with the mobile platforms above, let us modify the index.html file to convert it into a welcome application. The index.html file is modified to appear as shown in Listing 3.2.

Upon running the application, we see that the application asks the user to enter a name. After entering a name in the input text box, when the user clicks the Submit button, a welcome mes-sage along with the entered name will be displayed on the screen. All the text that will appear on the screen will appear in uppercase. Why? We already know the reason behind it: the style property text-transform used in the index.css file is linked to the index.html file. As we did in previous mobile applications, let us delete this style property from the index.css

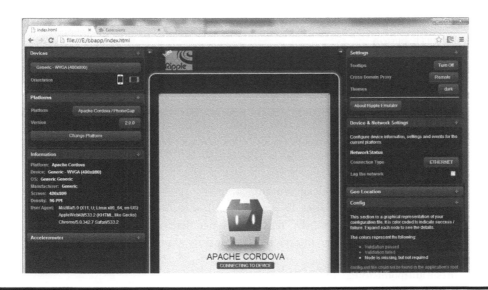

**Figure 3.14    The output of the default `index.html` file in Google Chrome with the Ripple emulator.**

file from the `css` folder of the application. After doing this, when we run the application, both the welcome message and the entered name will appear in normal case, as shown in Figure 3.15.

If you do not get the welcome message upon clicking the `Submit` button, it means the `deviceready` event has not fired. To fire the `deviceready` event, select the `device-ready` button followed by clicking the `Fire  Event` button from the right-side panel. The

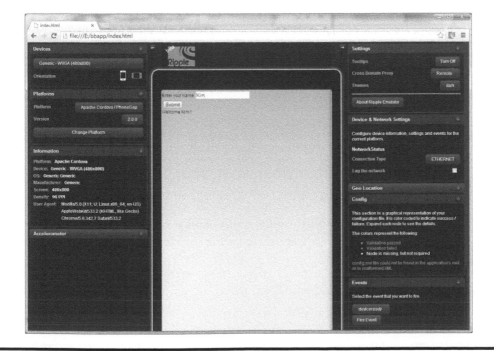

**Figure 3.15    The welcome message is displayed upon clicking the `Submit` button.**

`deviceready` event will fire and now the welcome message will appear whenever the user clicks the `Submit` button.

## Configuring PhoneGap for bada

Samsung bada is a smartphone platform that supports a wide range of devices. The idea behind developing the bada platform is to provide a wider choice of cost-effective smartphones to consumers. A few of the features of Samsung bada are as follows:

- Supports WiFi Direct for wireless communication.
- Includes Speech To Text and Text To Speech features.
- Allows reading and writing on NFC tags, mobile payments, file sharing, etc.
- Provides a large range of user interface (UI) controls along with sensors to make highly interactive applications.
- Supports multipoint touch and 3D graphics.
- Provides continuous support to the developers. Samsung supports bada developers in making and marketing high-quality applications.
- Utilizes and explores the device hardware to deliver high performance. Today, bada is deployed in many successful handsets, like Wave II and Wave.

For configuring bada for PhoneGap, we need to install bada SDK. So, download it from `http://developer.bada.com/devtools/sdk`. The bada SDK version that I use in this book is 2.0.0. On double-clicking the downloaded file, `bada SDK 2.0.0.exe`, it will begin downloading and installing bada through a setup wizard.

The first screen in the setup wizard is a welcome screen (see Figure 3.16a). Click the `Next` button to continue. The next dialog displays the license agreement and other terms for using bada SDK. Click the `I Agree` button if you agree with the terms of agreement and to continue. Next, the dialog prompts us to choose the components or features that we want to install. Let us select the two binary platforms, `Wave (WVGA)` and `Wave (HVGA)`, followed by clicking the `Next` button (see Figure 3.16b).

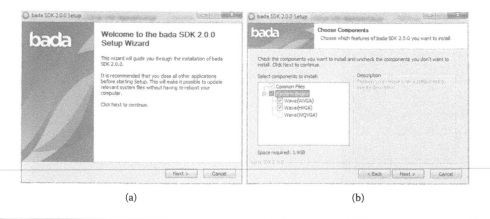

(a)  (b)

**Figure 3.16  (a) The welcome screen is displayed upon installing bada SDK. (b) The dialog prompting us to choose the components to install.**

Next, the dialog asks for the location where we want to install bada SDK. The dialog displays the default location, C:\bada\2.0.0, in the Destination Folder box (see Figure 3.17a). We can select the Browse button to install bada SDK at some other location if desired. Click the Next button to continue. Next, the dialog asks to choose the Start Menu folder where we want to create the shortcut for bada SDK 2.0.0 (see Figure 3.17b). Keeping the defaults selected, click the Install button to initiate installing of bada SDK.

After all the files are copied successfully, a dialog will appear informing us of completion of the bada SDK 2.0.0 setup wizard. Click the Finish button to exit from the wizard.

Let us now configure bada for PhoneGap. Invoke the bada integrated development environment (IDE). The bada IDE starts by displaying its logo, followed by a Workspace Launcher dialog box, as shown in Figure 3.18. The Workspace Launcher dialog prompts for the location of the workspace folder where the bada project files will be stored (see Figure 3.18). A default location is displayed that we can change by selecting the Browse button. The checkbox Use this as the default and do not ask again can be checked if we do not want the bada IDE to prompt for the workspace every time it is launched. Select the OK button to continue.

When bada IDE finishes loading, a welcome screen is displayed, as shown in Figure 3.19. The welcome screen shows the links to get started: beginning bada C++ programming, flash programming, Web programming, and Workbench. The links when clicked will display respective material to guide developers. Let us select the Workbench icon to open the bada IDE Workbench.

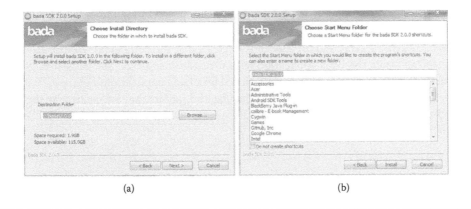

     (a)              (b)

**Figure 3.17** **(a) The dialog to specify the location to install bada SDK. (b) The dialog prompting us to choose the Start Menu folder for the bada shortcut.**

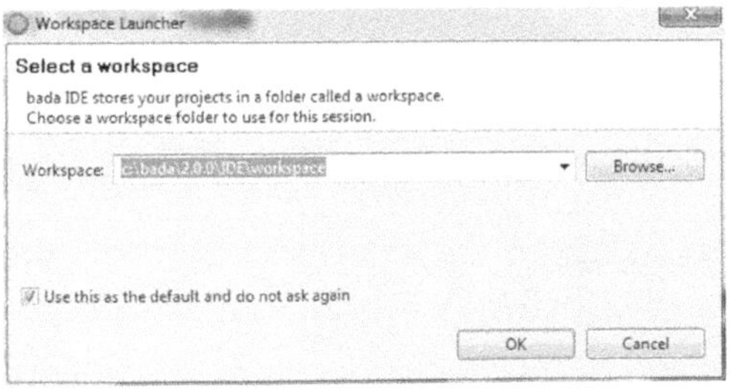

**Figure 3.18** **The dialog to specify the workspace to store bada applications.**

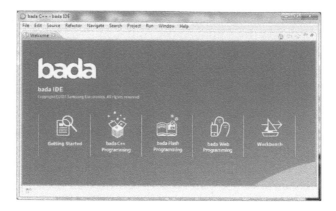

**Figure 3.19  The welcome page appears upon invoking bada IDE for the first time, showing links for the different programming options.**

We can see that all the windows in the Workbench (Package  Explorer, Editor window, Debug window, and Task List) are blank at the moment (see Figure 3.20). These windows will update their content as we develop bada applications.

To create a new bada application and configure it for PhoneGap, select the File->bada Web Application  Project option. A dialog appears that prompts for the project name and the location where we want to create it. Let us name the application BadaWelcomeMsgApp and select the Use default location checkbox to create it at the designated workspace. Click the Finish button to create the bada application with the default settings. The bada IDE will create all the files and folders automatically that are required by a bada application. Figure 3.21 shows the Project Explorer window displaying all the files and folders that are created by the IDE.

The index.html file will have the default content shown in Listing 3.6. The content is autodeveloped by the bada IDE.

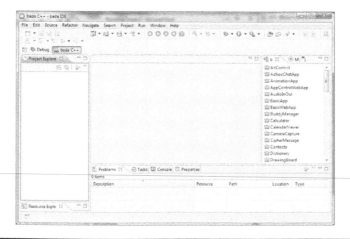

**Figure 3.20  The bada IDE Workbench showing different windows.**

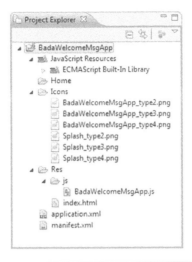

**Figure 3.21 The Project Explorer window showing the files and folders that are automatically created by bada IDE.**

**Listing 3.6 Default Code in the `index.html` File in the bada Application**

```html
<!DOCTYPE html>
<html xmlns = "http://www.w3.org/1999/xhtml" dir = "ltr" lang = "en">
<head>
<meta http-equiv = "Content-Type" content = "text/html; charset = ISO-8859-1">
<meta name = "viewport" content = "target-densitydpi = high-dpi, user-scalable = no"/>
<title>Class1</title>
<link href = "osp://webapp/css/style.css" rel = "stylesheet" type = "text/css"/>
<script type = "text/javascript" src = "osp://webapp/js/webapp_core.js"> </script>
<script type = "text/javascript" src = "osp://webapp/js/webapp_ui.js"> </script>
<script type = "text/javascript" src = "./js/BadaWelcomeMsgApp.js"> </script>
<script>
    Osp.App.Application.addEventListener("initializing", function()
    {
        Osp.Ui.init();
        appObj = new BadaWelcomeMsgApp();
        appObj.launch();
    }, this);
</script>
</head>
<body>
</body>
</html>
```

Let us run the application with the autocreated content. To run the application, either select `Run->Run As->bada Emulator Web Application` or right-click the application in the `Project Explorer` window and select `Run As->bada Emulator Web Application` or the Run icon shown in the toolbar. Upon running an application, the bada logo appears along with other splash screens as shown in Figure 3.22a. When the application is completely loaded in the emulator, a button with the caption `Click Here!` appears (see Figure 3.22b). Upon clicking the `Click Here!` button, a dialog appears informing us that the button is clicked. The title of

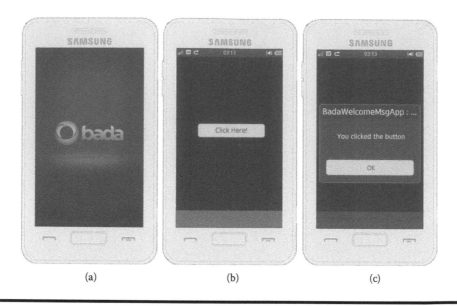

(a)          (b)          (c)

**Figure 3.22    (a) The bada logo is displayed upon running an application. (b) The button is displayed asking the user to click on it. (c) The dialog pops up informing us that the** `Click Here!` **button is clicked.**

the dialog is set to our application's name, that is, `BadaWelcomeMsgApp` (see Figure 3.22c). Click the `OK` button to close the application and exit.

Now let us configure the bada project for PhoneGap. To do so, we need to import the PhoneGap files into the bada project. Because we have already downloaded and unzipped PhoneGap, just open its `lib` subfolder. We find two more folders inside the `lib` subfolder: `bada` and `badaWac`. The `bada` folder is used with bada IDE 1.2, whereas the `badaWac` folder is used with bada IDE 2.0.0.

In bada IDE, select the `File->Import` option. Select the `General->File System` option followed by clicking the `Next` button. In the `Import` dialog that opens up, select the `Browse` button to select the `badaWac` folder in PhoneGap's lib folder. Check the `badaWac` node and its subnodes to import the complete file system into our bada application (see Figure 3.23).

After importing PhoneGap's `badaWac` files, the bada application will now have the combination of its original files and PhoneGap's files. The `Project Explorer` window shows the files and folders of the bada application after it is combined with the PhoneGap files, as shown in Figure 3.24.

To link the CSS and JavaScript files provided by bada IDE into our application, add the following two lines into the `index.html` file:

```
<link href = "osp://webapp/css/style.css" rel = "stylesheet" type =
"text/css"/>
<script type = "text/javascript" src = "osp://webapp/js/webapp_core.
js"></script>
```

After adding the two lines above, the `index.html` file will appear as shown in Listing 3.7.

**Figure 3.23 Importing the files of the** `badaWac` **folder which are provided with the PhoneGap package in the bada application.**

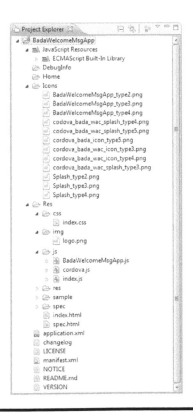

**Figure 3.24 The Project Explorer window after importing the files of the** `badaWac` **folder.**

**Listing 3.7    Code in the** `index.html` **File**

```
<!DOCTYPE html>
<html>
   <head>
      <meta http-equiv = "Content-Type" content = "text/html; charset = UTF-8"/>
      <meta name = "format-detection" content = "telephone = no"/>
      <meta name = "viewport" content = "user-scalable = no, initial-scale = 1,
      maximum-scale = 1, minimum-scale = 1, width = device-width, height = device-
      height, target-densitydpi = device-dpi"/>
      <link rel = "stylesheet" type = "text/css" href = "css/index.css"/>
      <link href = "osp://webapp/css/style.css" rel = "stylesheet" type = "text/
      css"/>
      <script type = "text/javascript" src = "osp://webapp/js/webapp_core.js">
      </script>
      <title>Hello World</title>
   </head>
   <body>
      <div class = "app">
         <h1>Apache Cordova</h1>
         <div id = "deviceready" class = "blink">
            <p class = "event listening">Connecting to Device</p>
            <p class = "event received">Device is Ready</p>
         </div>
      </div>
      <script type = "text/javascript" src = "js/cordova.js"></script>
      <script type = "text/javascript" src = "js/index.js"></script>
      <script type = "text/javascript">
      app.initialize();
      </script>
   </body>
</html>
```

Upon running the application, we will get the output as shown in Figure 3.25a.

(a)                                (b)

**Figure 3.25    (a) The output displayed by the default** `index.html` **file provided in the PhoneGap package. (b) The welcome message is displayed upon clicking the** `Submit` **button.**

Again, let us modify the default bada application into a welcome application, that is, display a welcome message to the user when the user clicks the Submit button. In order to accept input from the user, associate the event listener to the Submit button, and display a welcome message, modify the index.html file to appear as shown in Listing 3.8.

**Listing 3.8    Code Written in the index.html File**

```html
<!DOCTYPE html>
<html>
    <head>
        <title>Welcome Message App</title>
        <meta http-equiv = "Content-Type" content = "text/html; charset = UTF-8"/>
        <meta name = "format-detection" content = "telephone = no"/>
        <meta name = "viewport" content = "user-scalable = no, initial-scale = 1,
        maximum-scale = 1, minimum-scale = 1, width = device-width, height = device-
        height, target-densitydpi = device-dpi"/>
        <link href = "osp://webapp/css/style.css" rel = "stylesheet" type = "text/
        css"/>
        <script type = "text/javascript" src = "osp://webapp/js/webapp_core.js">
        </script>
        <script type = "text/javascript" src = "js/cordova.js"></script>
        <script type = "text/javascript" src = "js/index.js"></script>
        <script type = "text/javascript">
            function onBodyLoad() {
            document.getElementById("submitButton").addEventListener("click",
            dispMessage);
            }
            function dispMessage() {
                var nameOfUser = document.getElementById("name").value;
                message = document.getElementById("welcomemsg");
                message.innerHTML = "Welcome " + nameOfUser + " !";
            }
        </script>
    </head>
    <body onload = "onBodyLoad()">
        Enter your name <input type = "text" id = "name"><br/>
        <input type = "button" id = "submitButton" value = "Submit">
        <div id = "welcomemsg"> </div>
    </body>
</html>
```

Upon running the application, the user will be asked to enter a name in the input text box, followed by clicking the Submit button. When the user clicks the Submit button, a welcome message along with the user's name will appear on the screen, as shown in Figure 3.25b.

# Configuring PhoneGap for webOS

HP webOS is a very friendly as well as sophisticated mobile development platform. Based on simple Web languages like HTML, JavaScript, and CSS, webOS is very easy to develop apps for. It also includes the Plug-In Development Kit (PDK), which enables developers to include their C/C++ code in their apps. In addition to other features, the webOS platform also supports multitasking, notifications, and integration with popular cloud services and apps.

Assuming Java is already installed on our machine, we will follow the steps given below for configuring PhoneGap for webOS:

- Installing HP webOS SDK
- Installing Oracle VM VirtualBox
- Installing webOS plug-in in Eclipse IDE
- Creating a webOS application
- Importing the PhoneGap package

Let us begin with the first step.

### *Installing HP webOS SDK*

Download the HP webOS SDK from the site `https://developer.palm.com/`. I use HP webOS SDK version 3.0.5.676 in this book. Double-click on the downloaded file to begin installation. The setup wizard will start, and the first screen that appears is as usual, a welcome screen. Click the `Next` button to continue. Next, the dialog displays the license agreement and other terms (see Figure 3.26a). Read the agreement and select the `I accept the terms in the license agreement` option, followed by clicking the `Next` button to continue. Next, the dialog prompts us to choose the `setup type`, as shown in Figure 3.26b. Two setup type options will be provided, `Complete` and `Custom`. Let us select the `Complete` setup type option, as we want to install complete SDK. Click the `Next` button. Next, the dialog indicates that the setup wizard is ready to begin installation. Click the `Install` button to initiate the installation procedure. After installing all the files, a dialog appears informing us that HP webOS has been successfully installed. Click the `Finish` button to exit the wizard.

The HP webOS emulator is built on VirtualBox and is invoked through a virtual machine file. So, the next step is to install Oracle VM VirtualBox.

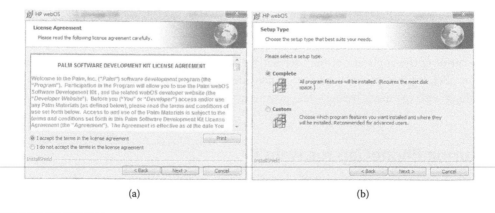

(a)                                              (b)

**Figure 3.26** **(a) The License Agreement for using HP webOS SDK. (b) The dialog prompting us to select the Setup Type.**

## Installing Oracle VM VirtualBox

The HP webOS emulator is built on VirtualBox and simulates a webOS device on all three operating systems: Linux, Mac, and Windows. The virtual machine file for the HP webOS emulator is provided along with the HP webOS SDK. Download Oracle VM VirtualBox from the `https://www.virtualbox.org/wiki/Downloads` site. I use the Oracle VM VirtualBox 4.1.22 version in this book. Double-click the downloaded file to invoke the setup wizard to begin installation. The first screen of the setup wizard is a welcome screen. Click the `Next` button to continue. Next, the dialog prompts us to select the features we want to install. The dialog also asks for the location on our disk drive where we want to install VirtualBox. The dialog displays the default features and location of installing VirtualBox, as shown in Figure 3.27a. Keeping the default selections, click the `Next` button to continue. Next, the dialog prompts whether we want to create a shortcut of VirtualBox on the desktop and in the Quick Launch Bar. Select the option where we want to create the shortcuts, followed by clicking the `Next` button. Next, the dialog displays a warning message informing that the network connection (if any) will be temporarily disconnected (see Figure 3.27b). The dialog also prompts us as to whether we want to proceed with the installation. Click the `Yes` button to continue with the installation procedure. Next, the dialog informs us that setup wizard is ready to begin installation. Click the `Install` button to begin installation. The Oracle VM VirtualBox files will be copied onto our machine, and finally a dialog appears informing us that the installation of Oracle VM VirtualBox is successful. A checkbox `Start Oracle VM VirtualBox 4.1.22 after installation` is found checked by default in the dialog box. Click the `Finish` button to complete the installation and invoke VirtualBox.

The Oracle VM VirtualBox Manager will be invoked automatically and appear as shown in Figure 3.28. The VirtualBox Manager will automatically detect the virtual machine file named `SDK 3.0.5.676 (1024 x 768)` on our machine that was created by HP webOS SDK and will not only load the virtual machine file, but also run the related virtual box, as shown in Figure 3.28. If your VirtualBox Manager could not detect the virtual machine file, select the `Machine->Add` option from the VirtualBox Manager. From the dialog that pops up, select the virtual machine file, `SDK 3.0.5.676 (1024 x 768)`, followed by clicking the `Open` button. The virtual machine file will be loaded and the related virtual box activated.

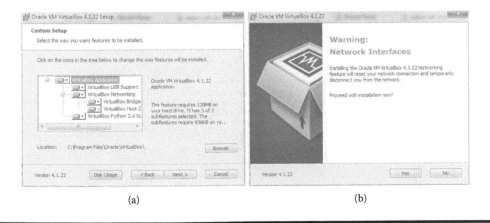

(a)                                                   (b)

**Figure 3.27** **(a) The dialog for choosing the features and location for installing VirtualBox. (b) The dialog showing the warning message of temporarily disconnecting you from the network connection.**

**Figure 3.28   The VirtualBox Manager showing the virtual box settings.**

The default settings of the virtual box will be displayed on the right, along with a preview of the virtual box at the top. We can change the settings of the virtual box if desired. We can always `pause` and `run` the virtual box by right-clicking the SDK icon on the left and selecting the desired option from the shortcut menu that pops up.

To see the virtual box, click the `Show` icon found in the toolbar at the top in the VirtualBox Manager. The virtual box will appear as shown in Figure 3.29.

Because we are creating a webOS application using the Eclipse IDE, the next step is to install the webOS plug-in in the Eclipse IDE.

**Figure 3.29   A running virtual box.**

## *Installing webOS Plug-In in Eclipse IDE*

To install the webOS plug-in, follow the steps given below:

- Launch Eclipse and select the `Help->Install New Software` option.
- In the `Available Software` dialog, click the `Add...` button.
- In the `Add Repository` dialog that pops up, enter `webOS plugin` (any text to identify) in the `Name` box and `https://cdn.downloads.palm.com/sdkdownloads/eclipse/update-site/site.xml` in the `Location` box (see Figure 3.30a), followed by clicking the OK button.
- The `Install` dialog opens up showing the `Available Software`. Expand the `Palm webOS SDK` node and check the `Palm webOS SDK` checkbox, followed by clicking the `Next` button (see Figure 3.30b).
- The next dialog shows the checked or selected software(s) to review (to correct or change the options). Click the `Next` button to continue.
- The next dialog shows the `License` terms to review. Select the option `I accept the terms of the license agreement`, followed by the `Finish` button to install the webOS plug-in.
- Restart `Eclipse` when prompted to load the installed plug-in.

Now, we are all set to create a webOS application.

## *Creating a webOS Application*

To create a webOS application, launch Eclipse and select the `File->New Project` option. A dialog opens prompting us to select a wizard for the new project. Expand the `Palm webOS` node from the list of wizards and select the `Basic Application` wizard, followed by clicking the `Next` button. The next dialog asks for information on the new project. Assign the project

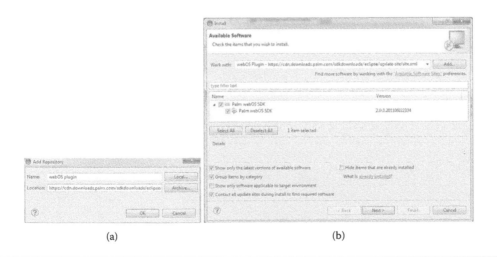

(a)         (b)

**Figure 3.30** **(a) The** `Add Repository` **dialog for adding webOS plug-in. (b) The dialog for selecting the plug-in software(s) to install.**

the name webOSWelcomeMsg. After entering the project's information, like title, vendor, package, and version, click the Finish button to create the application (see Figure 3.31).

The necessary files and folders of the project will be automatically created by the Eclipse webOS plug-in. Because it is a webOS project, we will be prompted to switch to the webOS perspective from the default Java perspective in Eclipse. Select the Yes button to open our application in the webOS perspective, as shown in Figure 3.32.

The default code in the index.html file created by the webOS plug-in is shown in Listing 3.9.

**Figure 3.31    Entering information for the new webOS application.**

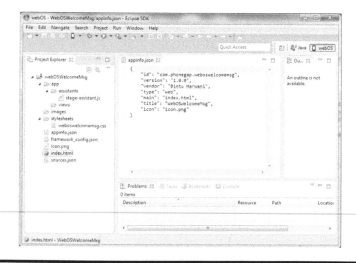

**Figure 3.32    The Eclipse IDE showing the newly created webOS application in the webOS perspective.**

**Listing 3.9  Default Code in the `index.html` File Created by the webOS Plug-In**

```
<!DOCTYPE html>
<html>
<head>
    <title>WebOSWelcomeMsg</title>
    <script src = "/usr/palm/frameworks/mojo/mojo.js" type = "text/javascript"
    x-mojo-version = "1"></script>
    <!—application stylesheet should come in after the one loaded by the
    framework—>
    <link href = "stylesheets/weboswelcomemsg.css" media = "screen" rel =
    "stylesheet" type = "text/css">
</head>
</html>
```

Let us run the application and see the output of the default `index.html` file that is generated by the Eclipse IDE and webOS plug-in. So, right-click the project in the Eclipse IDE and select the `Run As->webOS Application` option. Before running the application, ensure that the virtual box is in running mode. The application will run in the webOS emulator running inside the virtual box, as shown in Figure 3.33. No text will appear in the webOS emulator as the `index.html` file contains no text to display.

To configure PhoneGap for webOS, we need to import the PhoneGap package in our webOS application.

## Importing the PhoneGap Package

Now, it is time to import the webOS files provided by the PhoneGap package. We require the `/lib/webos` folder found in the PhoneGap package. To import the PhoneGap files into the current webOS application, right-click the application in the `Package Explorer` window and select the `Import` option. From the `Import` dialog that pops up, expand the `General` node and select the `File System` node under it. Click the Next button. From the next dialog, click the `Browse` button and navigate to the `/lib/webos/framework` folder of the PhoneGap package. Check the `framework` checkbox to select and merge all the subfolders and files found

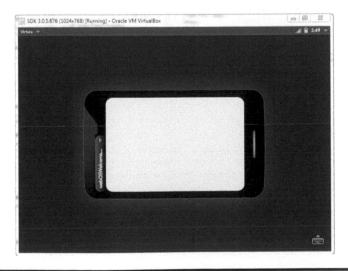

**Figure 3.33  The webOS emulator running in virtual box.**

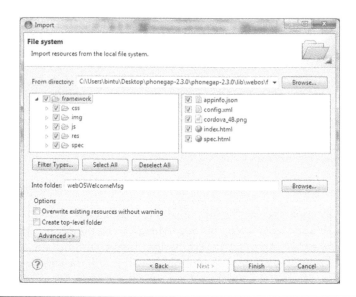

**Figure 3.34 The dialog for importing PhoneGap package's webOS files in the current application.**

in the `framework` folder (see Figure 3.34) into our webOS application. Click the `Finish` button to complete the merging process.

The `index.html` file provided by the PhoneGap package will have the default code shown in Listing 3.10.

**Listing 3.10 Default Code Written in the `index.html` File Provided in the PhoneGap Package**

```
<!DOCTYPE html>
<html>
    <head>
        <meta http-equiv = "Content-Type" content = "text/html; charset = UTF-8"/>
        <meta name = "format-detection" content = "telephone = no"/>
        <meta name = "viewport" content = "user-scalable = no, initial-scale = 1,
        maximum-scale = 1, minimum-scale = 1, width = device-width, height = device-
        height, target-densitydpi = device-dpi"/>
        <link rel = "stylesheet" type = "text/css" href = "css/index.css"/>
        <title>Hello World</title>
    </head>
    <body>
        <div class = "app">
            <h1>Apache Cordova</h1>
            <div id = "deviceready" class = "blink">
                <p class = "event listening">Connecting to Device</p>
                <p class = "event received">Device is Ready</p>
            </div>
        </div>
        <script type = "text/javascript" src = "cordova.webos.js"></script>
        <script type = "text/javascript" src = "js/index.js"></script>
        <script type = "text/javascript">
            app.initialize();
        </script>
    </body>
</html>
```

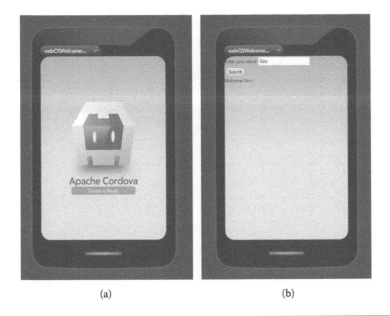

(a)                                    (b)

**Figure 3.35   (a) The output displayed by the default index.html file provided in the PhoneGap package. (b) The welcome message is displayed upon clicking the Submit button.**

Let us run the application to see if the PhoneGap files are properly merged in our webOS application and the PhoneGap is loading properly. So, right-click the application in the Package Explorer window and select the Run As->webOS Application option. The webOS emulator in the virtual box will show the Cordova icon along with the texts Apache Cordova and Device is Ready (see Figure 3.35a) to confirm that the PhoneGap files are properly merged into our webOS application.

As we did with other mobile platforms, we will modify the index.html file to convert it into a welcome message application. That is, the user will be prompted to enter a name followed by clicking the Submit button. After entering a name, when the user clicks the Submit button, a welcome message will be displayed to the user. So, modify the index.html file to appear as shown in Listing 3.11.

**Listing 3.11   Code Written in the index.html File**

```
<!DOCTYPE html>
<html>
    <head>
        <title>Welcome Message App</title>
        <meta http-equiv = "Content-Type" content = "text/html; charset = UTF-8"/>
        <meta name = "format-detection" content = "telephone = no"/>
        <meta name = "viewport" content = "user-scalable = no, initial-scale = 1,
        maximum-scale = 1, minimum-scale = 1, width = device-width, height = device-
        height, target-densitydpi = device-dpi"/>
        <link rel = "stylesheet" type = "text/css" href = "css/index.css"/>
        <script type = "text/javascript" src = "cordova.webos.js"></script>
        <script type = "text/javascript" src = "js/index.js"></script>
        <script type = "text/javascript">
```

```
        document.addEventListener("deviceready", PhonegapLoaded, false);
        function PhonegapLoaded() {
        document.getElementById("submitButton").addEventListener("click",
        dispMessage);
        }
        function dispMessage() {
            var nameOfUser = document.getElementById("name").value;
            message = document.getElementById("welcomemsg");
            message.innerHTML = "Welcome " + nameOfUser + " !";
        }
    </script>
  </head>
  <body>
  Enter your name <input type = "text" id = "name"><br/>
      <input type = "button" id = "submitButton" value = "Submit">
      <div id = "welcomemsg"> </div>
  </body>
</html>
```

After modifying the `index.html` file, when we run the application, we get a screen asking for a name. After entering a name, when we press the Submit button, a welcome message along with the entered name appears, as shown in Figure 3.35b.

## Summary

In this chapter, we learned how to configure PhoneGap to develop applications for iOS, Windows Phone 7, BlackBerry, bada, and webOS. We learned how to download and install the IDEs required for different platforms. We also saw different emulators that are invoked and used by each platform, as well as different files and folders required for each mobile platform to work with PhoneGap.

In Chapter 4, we will explore PhoneGap Build, a cloud build service that relieves us from developing applications for different platforms, as it develops code from different mobile platforms automatically.

# *Chapter 4*

# Using PhoneGap Build

In this chapter, we cover:

- Beginning with PhoneGap Build
- Defining the structure of the application to upload
- Creating builds for different mobile platforms
- Loading private keys
- Installing the builds on the emulator
- Downloading apps directly to the device
- Debugging the apps

## Beginning with PhoneGap Build

In Chapter 3, we saw that developing PhoneGap applications for multiple mobile platforms is a critical task. We need to install and configure the Software Development Kit (SDK), tools, and simulators for each platform. Because each mobile platform is based on different environments, the technique of accessing the hardware and using it in the applications is also quite different. PhoneGap Build relieves us from all this overhead.

PhoneGap Build is a cloud build service that makes the task of building PhoneGap applications in the cloud quite easy. What we are supposed to do is just create the Web content and upload it to the Build service. Thereafter, it is the task of PhoneGap Build to develop the code that supports different mobile platforms, including Android, Windows Phone, BlackBerry, iOS, Symbian, and webOS. It also means that we, as developers, just need to develop a single application (in any platform of our choice), and when that application is loaded to the Build service, PhoneGap Build will generate applications for the other platforms for us.

For using PhoneGap Build, we first need to create an account on the PhoneGap Build Web site. So, visit the URL `http://build.phonegap.com` and sign up. When we sign in to the PhoneGap Build site, we are provided with two options to upload our application: we can upload to the Build service either an open-source public app or a private app. A private app, as the name suggests, is the app that is kept on our local disk drive and is meant to be accessed and used solely by us and no one else. A public app means the application is created through the public Github account and is available for public use. An application can be as simple as a single `index.html` file or a combination of several files. If the application is a combination of several files, it can be compressed into a zip file. The `index.html` file or the compressed zip file can then be uploaded to the PhoneGap Build service.

We prefer to upload a public app that is available on a Github account into the PhoneGap Build service. That is, we will create a Git repository, push our app files into it, and then pull it into the Build service. Refer to Appendix B to create a public repository on Github. We can copy the Git repository into the box shown in Figure 4.1 to upload it to the PhoneGap Build service. But before that, let us connect PhoneGap Build with our Github account. Why?

The benefit of connecting our Github account with PhoneGap Build is that any updating done in the Github repository can be directly applied to the app that is uploaded in the PhoneGap Build service. So, to connect the PhoneGap Build account with the Github account, let us click the `Connect your Github account` link that appears below the box.

Upon clicking the `Connect your Github account` link, the `Edit account` page opens as shown in Figure 4.2. We find a link `Connect a GitHub ID` inside the `Linked`

**Figure 4.1    The first page that appears upon loading the PhoneGap Build site.**

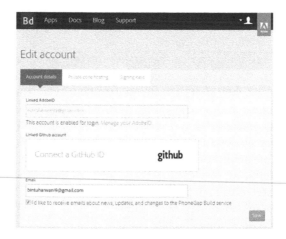

**Figure 4.2    The Edit account page showing the link to connect with the Github account.**

**Figure 4.3  The Github repository is being fetched into the PhoneGap Build service.**

Github account box. It is this link that is used for connecting a PhoneGap Build account with a Github account.

Upon clicking the link Connect a GitHub ID, a dialog will open asking whether we want to authorize PhoneGap:Build to read our public information, update our user profile, and update our private and public repositories. Click the Authorize app button to enable our PhoneGap Build account to access and modify our Github repositories.

When a connection with the Github account is established, our Github ID will appear in the Linked Github account box of the Edit account page, which confirms that our PhoneGap Build and Github accounts are successfully linked.

Now, we can enter our Github repository URI in the box (see Figure 4.1). On entering our Git repository Uniform Resource Identifier (URI), https://github.com/bmharwani/PhoneGapApps, in the box, the PhoneGap Build service will begin fetching the repository from the Github account, as shown in Figure 4.3.

## Defining the Structure of the Application to Upload

A PhoneGap application may be either a simple index.html file or a combination of several files, including JavaScript, Cascading Style Sheets (CSS), and media files, if required by the application. For example, the application that we have uploaded to the PhoneGap Build service above comprises the following three files:

- index.html—To display Web content.
- config.xml—To specify application configuration settings.
- icon.png—Image file to represent an application's icon.

In addition to the files above, we can always include JavaScript, CSS, video, and audio files in an application.

The application that we have uploaded on PhoneGap Build is the simple welcome application that we created in earlier chapters. The application prompts for a username, and when the user clicks the Submit button after entering a name, a welcome message is displayed on the screen. The index.html file is shown in Listing 4.1 for reference.

**Listing 4.1    Code Written in the `index.html` File**

```html
<!DOCTYPE HTML>
<html>
    <head>
    <title>Welcome Message App</title>
    <script type = "text/javascript" charset = "utf-8" src = "cordova-2.2.0.js">
    </script>
    <script type = "text/javascript">
    function onBodyLoad() {
        document.addEventListener("deviceready", PhonegapLoaded, false);
    }
    function PhonegapLoaded(){
    document.getElementById("submitButton").addEventListener("click", dispMessage);
    }
    function dispMessage(){
        var nameOfUser = document.getElementById("name").value;
        document.getElementById("welcomemsg").innerHTML = "Welcome "+nameOfUser + " !";
    }
    </script>
    </head>
    <body onload = "onBodyLoad()">
        <form>
            Enter your name <input type = "text" id = "name"><br/>
            <input type = "button" id = "submitButton" value = "Submit">
            <div id = "welcomemsg"></div>
        </form>
    </body>
</html>
```

One thing to remember is that we do not have to supply a copy of the PhoneGap/Cordova JavaScript with the application that we upload on the Build service, because it is automatically included by PhoneGap Build. But we do have to include its reference in the documents.

The configuration file, `config.xml`, is used to store details of our application. That is, information like application name, its description, author info, e-mail, application icon, and other settings is supplied in the form of a `config.xml` file. A sample `config.xml` file that we have used in our application appears as shown in Listing 4.2.

**Listing 4.2    Code Written in the `config.xml` File**

```xml
<?xml version = "1.0" encoding = "UTF-8"?>
<widget xmlns = "http://www.w3.org/ns/widgets"
xmlns:gap = "http://phonegap.com/ns/1.0"
id = "com.phonegap.pgwelcomemsg"
version = "1.0.0">
<name>Welcome App</name>
<description>
App that displays welcome message to the user.
</description>
<author href = "http://bmharwani.com" email = "bmharwani@yahoo.com">
Bintu Harwani
</author>
<feature name = "http://api.phonegap.com/1.0/device"/>
<preference name = "phonegap-version" value = "2.2.0"/>
<preference name = "orientation" value = "default"/>
<preference name = "target-device" value = "universal"/>
<preference name = "fullscreen" value = "false"/>
<icon src = "icon.png"/>
</widget>
```

The meanings of different elements used in `config.xml` are briefly described in Table 4.1.

If the `config.xml` file is not used in an application, PhoneGap Build will build the application using the default settings.

**Table 4.1 A Brief Description of the Elements Used in `config.xml`**

| Element | Description |
|---|---|
| `<widget>` | The `<widget>` element must be the root of our XML document. It confirms that we are following the World Wide Web Consortium (W3C) specification. The following two attributes are usually used with the `<widget>` element:<br><br>• **ID**—Used to identify our application uniquely. To support all mobile platforms, the ID is assigned in a reverse-domain name format: `com.company/category.appname`.<br><br>• **Version**—Defines the version of our application. It comprises three numbers that represent the major, minor, and patch numbers of our application. |
| `<name>` | Represents the name of the application. |
| `<description>` | Represents a small description of our application. |
| `<author>` | Specifies the author name and customer support contacts. |
| `<feature>` | Used to specify the features we want to use in our application. For example, the feature statement used in the `config.xml` file above indicates that we want to access the device application programming interface (API). |
| `<preference>` | Comprises the `name` and `value` pair and is used for defining different properties of the application. There can be zero or more `<preference>` elements in a `config.xml` file. If no `<preference>` element is used in the `config.xml` file, PhoneGap Build will apply default properties to our application. A few of the preference elements are explained below:<br><br>• The `phonegap-version` preference ensures that our application is built with the specific version of PhoneGap. The statement used in the `config.xml` above will build our application with PhoneGap version 2.2.0.<br><br>• The `orientation` preference is for enabling `landscape` and `portrait` orientations of our device. Possible values of this element are `default`, `landscape`, or `portrait`, where `default` value means that both `landscape` and `portrait` orientations are enabled.<br><br>• The `target-device` preference is for informing the target device of our application. Possible values are `handset`, `tablet`, or `universal`, where the `universal` value means that our application is compatible with all devices. |

*(Continued)*

**Table 4.1   A Brief Description of the Elements Used in `config.xml` (Continued)**

| Element | Description |
|---|---|
|  | • The `fullscreen` preference determines whether to hide the status bar at the top of the screen. Possible values are `true` and `false`, where the `true` value will hide the status bar. The default value is `false`.<br><br>• The `<icon>` element is for defining the icon image of the application. If no icon image is specified, the PhoneGap logo is considered our application's icon. The icon file must be named `icon.png` because each platform by default uses this filename for its icon. The icon image file must reside in the root of our application folder. We can also define different icons for each platform and screen type. The following statement defines an icon for the `mdpi` screen of an Android platform:<br><br>`<icon src = "icons/android/mdpi.png" gap:platform = "android" gap:density = "mdpi"/>`<br><br>Similarly, we can define icons for `ldpi`, `hdpi`, and `xhdpi` displays too. |

**Note:** You might be wondering why I have referenced PhoneGap version 2.2.0 in the config.xml file above when the recent PhoneGap version available is 2.3.0. The reason is that PhoneGap Build at the time of this writing supports up to 2.2.0 version only. The currently supported PhoneGap versions are 1.1.0, 1.2.0, 1.3.0, 1.4.1, 1.5.0, 1.6.1, 1.7.0, 1.8.1, 1.9.0, 2.0.0, 2.1.0, and 2.2.0. If we specify an unsupported version number, the app will not be built by the PhoneGap Build service.

## Creating Builds for Different Mobile Platforms

When the application is retrieved in PhoneGap Build, it will appear under the Your apps section along with its icon, title, and other information, as shown in Figure 4.4.

**Figure 4.4   The application is retrieved and visible in PhoneGap Build.**

Figure 4.4 shows the three buttons +new app, delete, and Ready to build, along with two checkboxes, enable debugging and enable hydration. The usage of the buttons and checkboxes is given below:

- enable hydration—Enables hydration in our application. Hydration is a tool that not only improves an application's compilation time but also enables us to update the application that is installed on a device. That is, whenever we upload a new build of the application, the user of the application is notified about the same upon restarting the application. If the user wants to run the new code, the hydrated app will automatically fetch and run the new build. At the time of this writing, the hydration feature is available only for iOS and Android platforms and supports PhoneGap versions 1.8.1, 1.9.0, and 2.0.0. The procedure of installing hydrated applications on the device is the same as for nonhydrated applications. To disable hydration, select an application by clicking its title or icon. From the detail page, open the Settings panel. You will see a checkbox enable hydration; just uncheck it and click the Save button.
- enable debugging—Check this checkbox to enable debugging in an application. This feature helps in modifying the application in real time, that is, when it is installed on a device. Small modifications and fixing bugs in an application can be interactively done in this debug mode. Debugging is explained at the end of this chapter.
- +new apps—Found at the top right of the page, this button is used to upload a new application. It opens a dialog to enter information for the new application. Enter the title of the application, provide its source code (either a single index.html file, .zip file, or a Git repository), and after selecting the desired settings, click the Create button to upload it to the PhoneGap Build service. The application's title, description, and icon will be fetched from the config.xml file (if it is supplied with the application files).
- Delete—This button will delete the selected application.
- Ready to build—This button, when clicked, initiates PhoneGap Build to begin the building process—creating apps for different mobile platforms. If the key is not configured for the iOS platform, PhoneGap Build will display an error while creating a build for the iOS application.

**Note:** For iOS applications, it is essential to have a developer account to get the certificate. More specifically, the iOS application needs to be signed by a developer certificate and a provisioning profile. The provisioning profile is linked to an Apple developer account. To test the application on an iOS device, the device has to be registered with this provisioning profile.

Upon selecting the Ready to build button, the builds of all the mobile platforms except the iOS platform will be made as shown in Figure 4.5. The text No key selected with iOS, Android, and BlackBerry platforms indicates that a private key has to be uploaded for these three platforms to generate their release builds. That is, until a private key is uploaded for these three platforms, PhoneGap Build will generate debug builds for them. Recall from Chapter 3 that debug builds are meant for testing purposes and cannot be installed on the devices. It also means that to develop release builds of these three mobile platforms, we need to load their respective private keys on the PhoneGap Build site.

We can press the Update code button to update our application from the Git repository and rebuild the application. On making any changes in the application, whether in terms of code or in adding or removing of keys, we can use the Rebuild button that appears on the right of

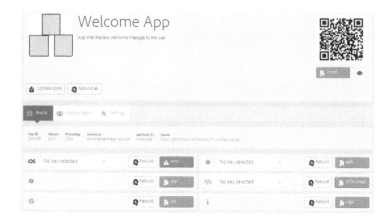

**Figure 4.5    The builds for five successfully created mobile platforms.**

each platform to develop their respective build. We can also use the `Rebuild all` button to develop the builds (cross-platform apps) for all the platforms: Android, BlackBerry, iOS, Windows Phone, Symbian, and webOS.

PhoneGap Build provides buttons to download individual builds of mobile platforms. To download the build of any platform, we can click the button on the right of the `Rebuild` button that is associated with each platform. For example, to download the build of Windows Phone 7, we can click the button with the caption `xap` found on the right of the `Rebuild` button in the Windows row. Similarly, clicking the button with the caption `apk` in the Android row will download the build for the Android platform.

## Loading Private Keys

One thing is for sure: the `apk` file of the Android platform that we will download from PhoneGap Build cannot be installed on a device. Why?

The reason is quite simple. Because we have not loaded the private key for the Android platform, the build version developed by PhoneGap Build will be a `debug` version and not a `release` version. So, let us load the private key for the Android platform. In Chapter 3, we learned to create a private keystore using `keytool`. We will use the same `AndroidApp.keystore` that we developed in Chapter 3 for building our Android app. So, click the `No key selected` text found in the Android row. A small dialog will pop up prompting us to enter the title, alias, and filename of keystore. Let us assign `AndroidApp` and `WelcomeApp` as the `Title` and `Alias` for the keystore and browse, and select the `AndroidApp.keystore` file on our local disk drive (see Figure 4.6). Finally, click the `submit key` button to upload the specified keystore on the PhoneGap Build service.

Upon clicking the `submit key` button, the key in the `AndroidApp.keystore` will be uploaded for the Android application. The title of the keystore along with a lock symbol will appear in the Android row that indicates that the key is successfully uploaded. Next, we rebuild the Android application by clicking the `Rebuild` button available in the Android row. But, we will not be able to do so, because the key needs to be unlocked while building the application. To unlock the key, click the lock symbol that appears adjacent to the keystore title. A dialog will

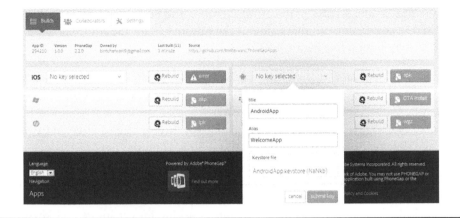

**Figure 4.6    The loading key for the Android platform.**

pop up asking for the certificate and keystore password that we used while creating the keystore through `keytool`. Enter the two passwords correctly, followed by clicking the `submit key` button to unlock the key (see Figure 4.7).

For safety purposes, PhoneGap Build will keep the keys unlocked for an hour. After an hour, the keys will be automatically locked again. While the keys are unlocked, we can click the `Rebuild` button (found on the right side of the lock symbol) to build the `release` version of our Android app.

A question that may occur to you is: Do we have to upload keys for every individual app uploaded on PhoneGap Build? Can we not upload the keys once and use the same key for all the apps?

Of course, yes! The steps to upload the Android private keys that can be universally applied to all Android apps are as follows:

■ Click your account ID link at the bottom of the page.
■ Click the `Signing keys` tab found at the top in the `Edit account` page that opens up.
■ Click the `add a key` button that appears below the Android logo.

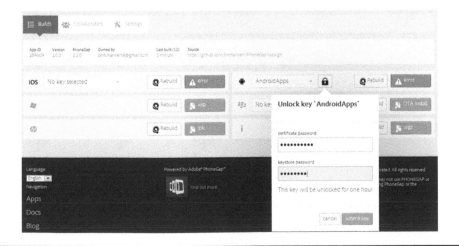

**Figure 4.7    Unlocking the Android key to prepare for its build.**

- Enter the `Title` and `Alias` of the private keystore and browse and select the keystore file, `AndroidApp.keystore`, that contains the private key for the Android apps. Click the `submit key` button (see Figure 4.8).

Upon clicking the `submit key` button, the private key for the Android apps will be stored. The private keystore filename, `AndroidApp`, appears below the Android logo to confirm that key is successfully loaded on PhoneGap Build. As stated earlier, the key will be locked by default; the lock symbol (see Figure 4.9) informs us that the key is in a locked state and needs to be unlocked before developing the Android build. The trash icon on the right of the lock symbol is meant for deleting the uploaded keystore.

Unlocking of the key can be done for individual apps, as we saw earlier or in this `Edit account` page to unlock the key for all the Android apps. To unlock the key for all Android apps, let us click the lock symbol. A dialog will appear asking for certificate and keystore passwords, similar to the one we saw in Figure 4.7. Upon entering the correct certificate and keystore passwords, the key will be unlocked.

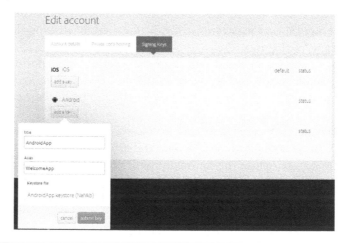

**Figure 4.8   Assigning a private key for the Android apps.**

**Figure 4.9   Keystore is uploaded and the keys are in a locked state.**

**Figure 4.10  Applying the earlier stored keys to the Android app.**

The key uploaded in the `Edit account` page, whether in a locked or unlocked state, can be applied to all the Android apps that are available in the current PhoneGap Build account. For example, to apply the key to our current `Welcome App`, click the application and click the `No key selected` text in the Android row. A drop-down list will appear showing the uploaded key, `AndroidApp`. Above the `AndroidApp` key, the text `unlocked` appears to declare that the key is currently in an unlocked state (see Figure 4.10). Whether in a locked or unlocked state, the `AndroidApp` key, when selected, will be applied to our `Welcome App` application. Unlock the key if it is in a locked state, and click the `Rebuild` button to create the `release` build of the Android app.

## Installing the Builds on the Emulator

When we feel that all updates are applied to the application and are ready to be released and distributed, click the `Install` button found on the right side of the application's title. Upon clicking the `Install` button, the builds of all the platforms will be rebuild and appear as shown in Figure 4.11. The icon below each platform title, the one with a document icon and a down arrow, represents a download link. We can download the build of any platform by clicking the download link of the respective platform. Upon clicking the download link of the Android platform, its build file, `WelcomeApp-release.apk`, will be downloaded onto our computer. The term `release` with the downloaded filename confirms that the build is a `release` version and can be installed on the devices and is ready to distribute.

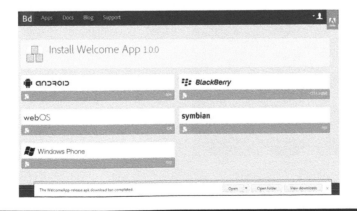

**Figure 4.11  Saving the Android build on a local machine.**

**Figure 4.12    Installing the Android build, which was retrieved from the PhoneGap Build service on the Android emulator.**

Let us check the downloaded Android build on an Android emulator. To start an Android emulator, launch Eclipse integrated development environment (IDE), open the Android Virtual Device (AVD) Manager by clicking the `Window->Android Virtual Device Manager` option, select the `PhoneGap AVD` that we created in Chapter 1, and click the `Start` button. We will make use of the `ADB` to install the downloaded Android build, `WelcomeApp-release.apk`, upon the running AVD instance. So, open the command prompt and navigate to the folder where Android Debug Bridge (ADB) exists, that is, the `C:\Program Files (x86)\Android\android-sdk\platform-tools` folder, and run the `adb devices` command to confirm if the AVD is running (see Figure 4.12). Assuming the downloaded Android build `WelcomeApp-release.apk` is available in the `E:\PhoneGapWorkspace` folder, execute the following statement to install the Android build on the running AVD instance:

```
C:\Program Files (x86)\Android\android-sdk\platform-tools> adb install
E:\PhoneGapWorkspace\WelcomeApp-release.apk
```

The message `Success` that appears upon executing the `adb install` command confirms that the Android build is successfully installed on the currently running AVD instance. `WelcomeApp` appears among the Apps list in the AVD; we can see its icon in Figure 4.13a. Upon clicking the icon, the application runs successfully. It asks for a name, and when the user clicks the `Submit` button after entering a name, a welcome message appears on the screen, as shown in Figure 4.13b.

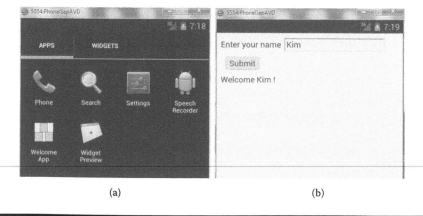

(a)                                                      (b)

**Figure 4.13    (a) The installed application appears among the Apps list. (b) The output on the screen upon running the application in the emulator.**

# Downloading Apps Directly to the Device

We have just seen the procedure of installing an app on the Android emulator. Now let us see how an app can be directly downloaded to an Android device. The first thing to do is to ensure that our Android device is enabled to install `apk` files from "unknown sources," that is, from sources other than the Google Play Store. So, select the `Settings->Security` option on the device and check the `Unknown  sources` checkbox to allow installation of non-Market apps (see Figure 4.14a). We might get a security warning and be prompted for confirmation (see Figure 4.14b). Click the `OK` button to enable our device to install apps from sources other than the Android Market.

Also, switch on `WiFi` on the device to establish a network connection. Next, we need to download a Quick Response (QR) code reader. I used the QR Droid app that is available for free from the Google Play Store. The link for the QR Droid is `https://play.google.com/store/apps/details?id = la.droid.qr&hl = en`. Download and install the QR Droid app on the device. Upon successful installation of the QR Droid, we will see its icon in the Apps list in the device. Click the QR Droid icon in the device to launch it. Bring the device closer to the QR code of our app on the PhoneGap Build site (see Figure 4.15a). The QR Droid app will read the QR code of our app and display its Web address in the form of a link (see Figure 4.15b). Click the Web address link to download our Android app on our device. The Android app will be downloaded on our device and listed in its `Download` section. Click the downloaded app in the `Download` section of the device to install it. We will be prompted for confirmation of whether we want to install the application on our device (see Figure 4.15c). Click the `Install` button and the Android application will be installed on our device. The application's icon and title appear in the Apps list of the device (see Figure 4.15d) to confirm this.

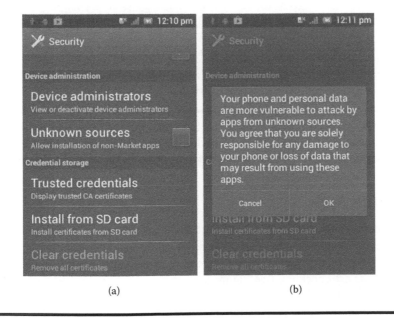

(a)                          (b)

**Figure 4.14** **(a) The security options on the device. (b) The warning that is displayed upon checking the** `Unknown  sources` **checkbox.**

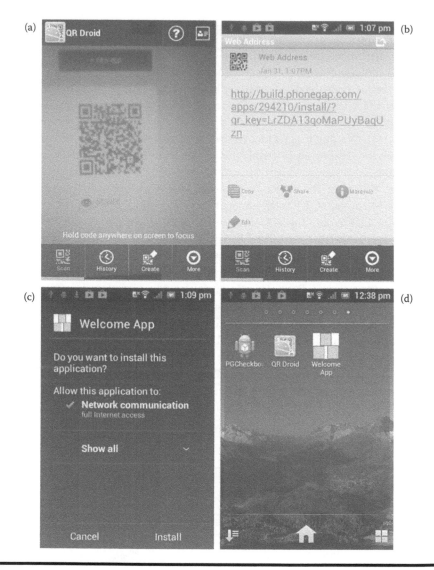

**Figure 4.15** **(a) The Android phone reading the QR code. (b) The Web address encoded in the QR code appears when read by the QR code reader. (c) The dialog prompting whether we want to install the downloaded app. (d) The installed app appears in the Apps list in the device.**

## Debugging the Apps

For debugging applications that are built and installed on a device, PhoneGap Build makes use of the Weinre debug server. To debug an application, make sure debugging is enabled in your application. You can enable debugging at the time of creating a new application by checking the `enable debugging` checkbox (see Figure 4.4) or by selecting the `Settings` button (see Figure 4.5). To enable the debugging feature in an application, PhoneGap includes the Weinre JavaScript library, `target-script-min.js`, into our application and invokes a debug server. The debug server debugs the application online and shows the results of the applied modifications on the spot. The debug server begins debugging when a device containing the debug-enabled version of the application is connected to it. This means that the application that we want to debug has to first be installed on a device, and the device must be connected to the debug server.

Below are the steps for debugging an application:

- Enable the Android device to install `apk` files from unknown sources. Select the `Settings->` `Security` option and check the `Unknown sources` checkbox to allow installation of non-Market apps.
- Switch on the WiFi on the device.
- Open the browser on the device and navigate to the PhoneGap Build Web site. Sign in and click on the application that we want to debug.
- Because we will be learning to debug an Android application, click the download link of the Android app (see Figure 4.16a).
- The Android app will be downloaded on our device and will appear in the `Download` section of the device.
- Click the downloaded app to install it on the device. A message `Application installed` appears upon successful installation of the application on the device (see Figure 4.16b).
- Launch the application by clicking its icon in the Apps list in the device.
- Next, we need to open the application on the computer. So, open the PhoneGap Build site, sign into it, click the application (that we want to debug), and click the `Debug` button (found below the application name) to begin a debug session on the server.
- A new window will open upon the browser displaying the Weinre debug server console. The device on which we launched the application will be automatically connected to the debug server. The debug console displays the information of the device that is connected to the debug server (see Figure 4.17a).

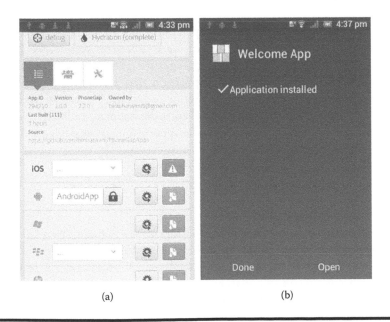

(a)                    (b)

**Figure 4.16** **(a) Downloading the Android app on the device. (b) The installed app appears in the Apps list in the device.**

(a)

(b)

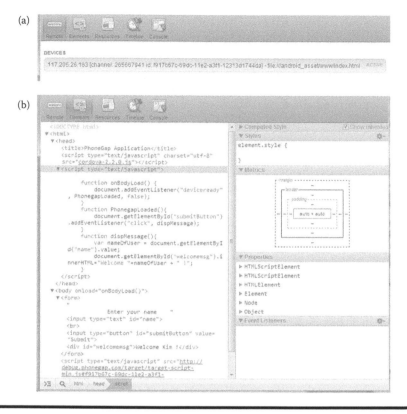

**Figure 4.17** **(a) The connected device appears in the debug console. (b) The Elements tab displaying the code for debugging.**

■ Click the Elements icon at the top to display the application on the left and its different properties on the right (see Figure 4.17b). In the Elements section, we can modify the application in real time; that is, whatever changes we do to the application's code on the left side, their impact will appear on the application that is running on the device. Hence, we can easily fix bugs on the fly, edit JavaScript code, edit Hypertext Markup Language (HTML) code, and apply CSS styles—and everything happens interactively. Not only this, but the impact of the interaction done with the application on the device can be viewed and analyzed on the debug console, too.

## Summary

In this chapter, we learned how to use the PhoneGap Build service in building cross-platform mobile applications. We saw how the structure of the application used in PhoneGap Build is defined. We learned how to upload the app through the Github repository. We also saw how to load the private keys of the apps to generate release builds. Finally, we tested the generated build on the emulator and the device. Also, we had a brief introduction to the procedure used to debug applications.

Chapter 5 focuses on understanding and using contacts. That is, we will learn how to create and save contacts on devices. We will also learn how to find, list, and remove contacts. While doing operations on contacts, we will learn how to handle errors (if any) generated.

# Chapter 5

# Using Contacts

In this chapter, we will cover:

- Understanding the PhoneGap Contacts Application Programming Interface (API)
- Creating Contacts manually
- Reading Contacts
- Adding Contacts
- Adding detailed information of the Contacts
- Deleting and updating Contacts

All mobile devices, whether an iPhone, Android, BlackBerry, Windows Phone, or Palm webOS, each has a built-in Contacts database that is used for keeping information of desired people. That is, the name, address, phone number, e-mail address, and so on, of the desired people can be kept in the Contacts database. These contacts are then used for sending e-mails, sending SMS, and remembering phone numbers, addresses, and so on. Different phone manufacturers may use different contact fields to store contact information. To resolve this difference and develop code that can be uniformly applied to access and manage contacts on different mobile devices, the PhoneGap Contacts API is used.

The PhoneGap Contacts API provides an interface to create, list, edit, copy, and delete contact rows from the device's Contacts database. When we create a contact, its information, that is, its name, e-mail addresses, phone numbers, photos, and so forth, are maintained in the form of properties. The properties that describe a contact are shown in Table 5.1.

Contacts can be created, saved, searched, and removed from the device Contacts database. The methods used for this purpose are given below:

- **Clone**—Returns a new Contact object that is a copy of the calling object. The `id` property of the returned Contact object is set to `null`.
- **Remove**—Removes the specified contact from the device Contacts database.
- **Save**—Saves a new contact to the device Contacts database. If the `id` of the contact being saved already exists, the method updates the existing contact.
- **Find**—Searches the device Contacts database and returns an array of Contact objects comprising specified fields.

**Table 5.1  A Brief Description of the Contact's Properties**

| Properties | Description |
|---|---|
| id | Represents a unique identifier of a contact. |
| displayName | Represents the name of the contact displayed to the users. |
| name | Represents an object containing all components of the contact's name. |
| nickname | Represents a casual name of the contact. |
| phoneNumbers | Represents an array of all the contact's phone numbers. |
| e-mails | Represents an array of all the contact's e-mail addresses. |
| addresses | Represents an array of all the contact's addresses. |
| ims | Represents an array of all the contact's IM addresses. |
| organizations | Represents an array of all the contact's organizations. |
| birthday | Represents the birth date of the contact. |
| note | Represents a note about the contact. |
| photos | Represents an array of the contact's photos. |
| categories | Represents an array of all the contact's user-defined categories. |
| urls | Represents an array of Web pages associated with the contact. |

Being frequently used, let us talk about the find method in detail. The format of using the find method is given below:

```
navigator.contacts.find(contactFields, contactSuccess, contactError,
contactFindOptions);
```

where:

- contactFields—Specifies the fields whose values we wish to see in the resulting Contact objects. If * is supplied in this parameter, all fields will be returned. If a zero-length parameter is supplied, then only the id field will be returned. Remember, the specified fields are returned as properties of the Contact objects.
- contactSuccess—A success callback function that is invoked with the contacts that are returned from the Contacts database.
- contactError—An optional error callback function that is invoked if any error occurs.
- contactFindOptions—An optional parameter that specifies the options to filter the contacts. Basically, this parameter contains properties used to filter the results of a contacts.find operation. Below are the two properties that this parameter comprises:
  - filter—Represents the search string used to find contacts.
  - multiple—Boolean value that determines if the find operation should return multiple contacts. Its default value is false.

# Creating Contacts Manually

Let us begin with creating contacts in the Contacts database. Launch the Android emulator and select the People icon on the home page. If there are no existing contacts, the following three buttons will be displayed: `Create a new contact`, `Sign in to an account`, and `Import contacts` (see Figure 5.1a). Click the `Create a new contact` button for creating a new contact. A form will be displayed prompting us to enter information of the new contact (see Figure 5.1b). The form shows four fields, `Name`, `Phone (mobile)`, `Email (home)`, and `Address (home)`, by default. Also, links are provided to enter information related to the `Organization` name, `Phone (work)`, `Email (work)`, and so on. After entering information for the new contact, click the `Done` button to save it. The newly created contact will be displayed in the Contacts List page under its respective character index. For example, if the newly created contact's name begins with the character B, it will appear under the character index B (see Figure 5.1c).

Upon selecting a contact from the Contacts List page, its information will be displayed (see Figure 5.2a). After adding two contacts, the Contacts List page may appear as shown in Figure 5.2b.

You might be wondering if there is any difference in the procedure of creating contacts on a physical device compared to doing so with the Android emulator. Though it might differ from device to device, the main procedure is the same in almost all Android devices. Below is the procedure for creating contacts on physical devices:

- Select the `Settings->Contacts` option from the home page of the device.
- If there are no existing contacts, a `No contacts` message is displayed (see Figure 5.3a).
- Select the `Add Contact` icon on the top right corner of the screen.
- A blank form will be displayed prompting us to enter information of the new contact, as shown in Figure 5.3b. After entering the contact information, click the `Done` button to save it in the Contacts database of the device.
- The newly created contact appears in the Contacts List page under the respective character index (see Figure 5.3c).

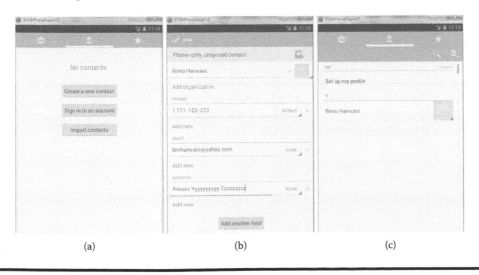

(a)               (b)               (c)

**Figure 5.1** **(a) Three buttons are displayed when no contacts exist. (b) A form prompting us to enter new contact information. (c) The newly created contact is displayed under the respective index character.**

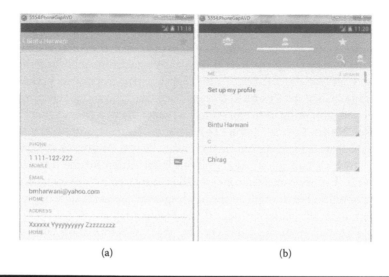

(a)                                                                    (b)

**Figure 5.2    (a) Information on the selected contact is displayed. (b) Contacts are displayed under the respective index character.**

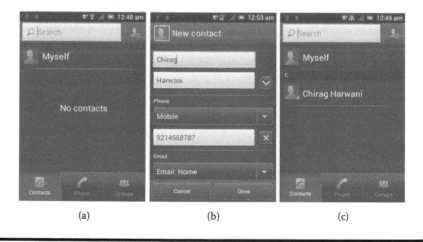

(a)                                   (b)                                   (c)

**Figure 5.3    (a) The** `No contacts` **message is displayed when no contacts exist. (b) A blank form is displayed for entering the information of the new contact. (c) The newly created contact appears under the respective character index.**

Let us learn how contacts are accessed from the Contacts database of the device programmatically.

# Reading Contacts

Let us create an application that fetches all the contacts that exist in the Contacts database and display their names on the screen. So, create an Android project called `PGContactsReadApp`. In the `index.html` file, write the code as shown in Listing 5.1.

**Listing 5.1  Code Written in the `index.html` File**

```
<!DOCTYPE HTML>
<html>
    <head>
    <title>PhoneGap Application</title>
    <script type = "text/javascript" charset = "utf-8" src = "cordova-2.3.0.js">
    </script>
    <script type = "text/javascript">
        function onBodyLoad(){
            document.addEventListener("deviceready", PhonegapLoaded, false);
        }
        function PhonegapLoaded(){
            var options = new ContactFindOptions();
            options.filter = "";
            options.multiple = true;
            filter = ["displayName"];
            navigator.contacts.find(filter, onSuccess, onError, options);
        }
        function onSuccess(contacts) {
            var contnames = "";
            var element = document.getElementById('contactsinfo');
            for(var i = 0;i<contacts.length;i++){
                contnames+ = 'Name: ' + contacts[i].displayName + '<br/>';
            }
            element.innerHTML = contnames;
        }
        function onError(error) {
            alert('Sorry! Some error has occurred');
        }
    </script>
    </head>
    <body onload = "onBodyLoad()">
        Contacts Information
        <div id = "contactsinfo"></div>
    </body>
</html>
```

In the code above, we see that the `ContactFindOptions` object is used to indicate that we want to access multiple rows from the Contacts database. Recall that the `ContactFindOptions` object contains the following three key fields:

- `filter`: The string used to filter the returned results, that is, to limit the number of contacts returned.
- `multiple`: The Boolean value is set to the value `true` to return multiple Contact objects. The default value is `true`.
- `updatedSince`: A JavaScript date object is used to return the Contact objects on the basis of their last updating date. At the time of this writing, this key field is not supported by major mobile platforms.

The `filter` parameter is set to `displayName` to inform us that we want to access only the name of the contact and nothing else. Through the `find()` method, the names of the contacts from the Contacts database are accessed. The `find()` method contains two callback methods, `onSuccess` and `onError`. As the method name suggests, the `onSuccess` method is called when the desired contacts are successfully searched in the Contacts database of the device. Similarly, the `onError` callback method is called when some error occurs while finding the contact(s). The onSuccess callback method returns an array of Contact objects that meet the specified filter and options. The name of the contacts, that is, displayName property, is accessed from the array of Contact objects and displayed through the <div> element of the ID contactsinfo.

To invoke the index.html file that we created in the assets/www directory, the code as shown in Listing 5.2 is written in the Java activity file PGContactsReadAppActivity.java.

**Listing 5.2 Code Written in the Java Activity File: `PGContactsReadAppActivity.java`**

```
package com.phonegap.pgcontactsreadapp;
import android.os.Bundle;
import org.apache.cordova.DroidGap;
public class PGContactsReadAppActivity extends DroidGap {
    @Override
    public void onCreate(Bundle savedInstanceState) {
        super.onCreate(savedInstanceState);
        super.loadUrl("file:///android_asset/www/index.html");
    }
}
```

To access contacts from the Contacts database of the device, we need to add READ _ CONTACTS, WRITE _ CONTACTS, and GET _ ACCOUNTS permissions to the project. After adding the required permissions, the AndroidManifest.xml file will appear as shown in Listing 5.3. Only the statements in bold are added; the rest is the default code.

**Listing 5.3 Code in the `AndroidManifest.xml` File**

```
<?xml version = "1.0" encoding = "utf-8"?>
<manifest xmlns:android = "http://schemas.android.com/apk/res/android"
    package = "com.phonegap.pgcontactsreadapp"
    android:versionCode = "1"
    android:versionName = "1.0" >
    <uses-sdk
        android:minSdkVersion = "11"
        android:targetSdkVersion = "17"/>
    <uses-permission android:name = "android.permission.ACCESS_NETWORK_STATE"/>
    <uses-permission android:name = "android.permission.READ_CONTACTS"/>
    <uses-permission android:name = "android.permission.WRITE_CONTACTS"/>
    <uses-permission android:name = "android.permission.GET_ACCOUNTS"/>
    <application
        android:allowBackup = "true"
        android:icon = "@drawable/ic_launcher"
        android:label = "@string/app_name"
        android:theme = "@style/AppTheme" >
        <activity
        android:name = "com.phonegap.pgcontactsreadapp.PGContactsReadAppActivity"
            android:label = "@string/app_name" >
            <intent-filter>
                <action android:name = "android.intent.action.MAIN"/>
                <category android:name = "android.intent.category.LAUNCHER"/>
            </intent-filter>
        </activity>
    </application>
</manifest>
```

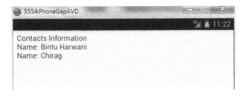

**Figure 5.4    Names of the contacts from the Contacts database are accessed and displayed.**

Our application is ready to run. Upon running the application, the existing contacts in the Contacts database are accessed and their names are displayed on the screen through the `<div>` element, as shown in Figure 5.4.

Now that we have learned the procedure for accessing contacts, let us now focus on how new contacts are added to the Contacts database.

## Adding Contacts

In this application, we will learn to add new contacts to the Contacts database of the device. The application will display a form prompting the user to enter information like name, address, e-mail address, and phone number of the contact. After entering the information for the new contact, when the user selects the `Submit` button, a new contact will be created in the Contacts database with the supplied information.

Let us create a new Android project called `PGContactsAddApp`. To add a new contact, write the code shown in Listing 5.4 in the `index.html` file.

**Listing 5.4    Code Written in the `index.html` File**

```
<!DOCTYPE HTML>
<html>
    <head>
    <title>PhoneGap Application</title>
    <script type = "text/javascript" charset = "utf-8" src = "cordova-2.3.0.js">
    </script>
    <script type = "text/javascript">
    function onBodyLoad() {
        document.addEventListener("deviceready", PhonegapLoaded, false);
    }
    function PhonegapLoaded(){
    document.getElementById("submitButton").addEventListener("click", addContact);
    }
    function addContact(){
        var FullName = document.getElementById("name").value;
        var Address = document.getElementById("add").value;
        var emailID = document.getElementById("email").value;
        var phoneNo = document.getElementById("phone").value;
        var newContact = navigator.contacts.create();
#1
        newContact.displayName = FullName;
#2
        var phoneNums = [1];
#3
        phoneNums[0] = new ContactField('work', phoneNo, true);
```

```
#4
     newContact.phoneNumbers = phoneNums;
#5
     var emailAddresses = [1];
     emailAddresses[0] = new ContactField('home', emailID, true);
     newContact.emails = emailAddresses;
#6
     var addresses = [];
     addresses[0] = new ContactAddress();
     addresses[0].type = 'home';
     addresses[0].streetAddress = Address;
     newContact.addresses = addresses;
     newContact.save(onSuccess, onError);
#7
   }
   function onSuccess(contact) {
     alert("New contact successfully created");

     document.getElementById("addresponse").innerHTML = "Contact successfully
     added";
   }
   function onError(contactError) {
     alert("Error in creating a new contact " + contactError.code);
   }
 </script>
 </head>
 <body onload = "onBodyLoad()">
 <h2> Enter information of the new contact </h2> <br/>
   <form>
      <table>
      <tr><td>Name </td><td> <input type = "text" id = "name"></td></tr>
      <tr><td>Address </td><td> <input type = "text" id = "add"></td></tr>
      <tr><td>Email Address </td><td> <input type = "text" id = "email"></td>
      </tr>
      <tr><td>Phone Number </td><td> <input type = "text" id = "phone"></td>
      </tr>
      </table>
      <input type = "button" id = "submitButton" value = "Submit">
      <div id = "addresponse"></div>
   </form>
 </body>
</html>
```

In the code above, we see that four input text fields are defined with the IDs name, add, email, and phone, respectively. The input fields will prompt users to enter the name, address, e-mail address, and phone number of the new contact. After entering information of the new contact, when the Submit button is clicked, the respective JavaScript function will be invoked to save the entered information in the Contacts database of the device. A few statements used in Listing 5.4 need explanation.

Statement 1 creates a Contact object by name, newContact. Statement 2 assigns the name entered by the user to the displayName property of the newContact object. Multiple information like phone numbers, addresses, e-mail addresses, and so on, are initially kept in arrays, and thereafter the information in arrays is stored in the Contact object with the help of the ContactField object. The ContactField object is a general purpose wrapper that enables us to create a data field and then add it to a contact. A ContactField object has the following three properties:

■ type—A string that defines the field type, that is, whether the field (e-mail, phone number, address, etc.) is related to home, work, mobile, and so on.

■ value—Defines value of the field.

■ pref—A Boolean value is set to true to inform us that the field is a preferred field of the contact. It is used to indicate the preferred phone number, e-mail address, address, and so on, of a contact.

Statement 3 creates an array of one element size, phoneNums. In this array, the work phone number of the contact is kept after wrapping it in the ContactField object (statement 4). Also, the work phone number is declared as the preferred phone number of the contact. By increasing the size of the PhoneNums array, we can store the home phone number of the contact too. The phone number(s) wrapped in the ContactField object is then assigned to the phoneNumbers property of the newContact object (statement 5).

Similarly, statement 5 assigns the home e-mail address of the contact (wrapped inside the ContactField object) to the emails property of the newContact object.

After defining the name, phone number, e-mail address, and address of the contact, the contact is saved in the Contacts database through statement 7.

To load the index.html file, write the code as shown in Listing 5.5 in the Java activity file, PGContactsAddAppActivity.java.

**Listing 5.5  Code Written in the Java Activity File: PGContactsAddAppActivity.java**

```
package com.phonegap.pgcontactsaddapp;
import android.os.Bundle;
import org.apache.cordova.DroidGap;
public class PGContactsAddAppActivity extends DroidGap {
    @Override
    public void onCreate(Bundle savedInstanceState) {
        super.onCreate(savedInstanceState);
        super.loadUrl("file:///android_asset/www/index.html");
    }
}
```

To access, read, and write contacts in the Contacts database of the device, we need to add the following permissions in the AndroidManifest.xml file:

```
<uses-permission android:name = "android.permission.ACCESS_NETWORK_STATE"/>
<uses-permission android:name = "android.permission.READ_CONTACTS"/>
<uses-permission android:name = "android.permission.WRITE_CONTACTS"/>
<uses-permission android:name = "android.permission.GET_ACCOUNTS"/>
```

Our application is complete and ready to run. Upon running the application, a form prompting us to enter information of the new contact will be displayed (see Figure 5.5a). Information like name, address, e-mail address, and phone number of the contact has to be entered in the form, followed by clicking the Submit button. If no error occurs while saving the information of the new contact in the Contacts database, the message Contact successfully added will be displayed, as shown in Figure 5.5b. The newly added contact appears under the respective index character, as shown in Figure 5.5c. Upon clicking on a contact from the Contacts List page, its information will be displayed (see Figure 5.5d).

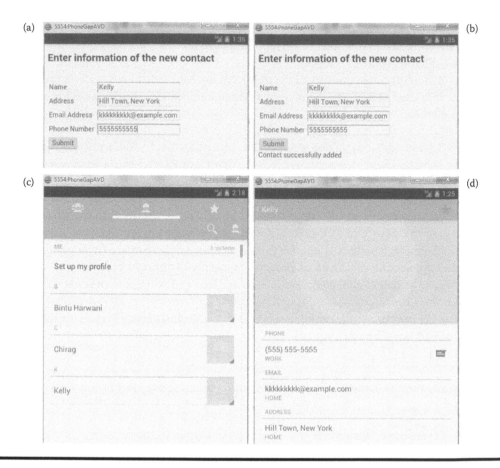

**Figure 5.5** **(a) A form prompting us to enter the information for a new contact. (b) The message** `Contact successfully added` **is displayed when a new contact is successfully added to the Contacts database. (c) The newly added contact appears in the Contacts List page. (d) Information for the selected contact displayed.**

The only limitation that you might observe in the application above is that the detailed information of the contact is missing. That is, though the name, address, e-mail address, and phone number of the contacts are stored, the details are not there. The application does not allow specifying the first and last name of the contact separately. The application does not allow entering the organization name of the contact. Also, we cannot enter the street address, city, state, and country information of the contact. The application does not provide the ability to enter the phone numbers of work and home separately. Separate e-mail addresses for home and work cannot be entered. So, let us enhance this application to enable users to enter detailed information of the contact.

## Adding Detailed Information of the Contacts

We will be making use of the `ContactName`, `ContactAddress`, and `ContactOrganization` objects for keeping detailed information related to the name, address, and organization of a contact. Let us take a quick look at the properties of these objects. Table 5.2 shows the properties of the `ContactName` object that can be used to define a contact's name.

**Table 5.2   A Brief Description of the** `ContactName` **Object Properties**

| Properties | Description |
|---|---|
| `formatted` | Represents the contact's complete name. |
| `familyName` | Represents the contact's surname. |
| `givenName` | Represents the contact's first name. |
| `middleName` | Represents the contact's middle name. |
| `honorificPrefix` | Represents the contact's prefix, for example, Mr., Ms., Dr., etc. |
| `honorificSuffix` | Represents the contact's suffix. |

From Table 5.2, we can see that the `ContactName` object provides properties to enter the complete name of a contact, along with the prefix and suffix.

The `ContactAddress` object provides properties to enter the home and work addresses of the contact. The address can be specified in detail, including street address, city, state, country, and postal code. The object also helps to indicate whether or not the specified address is the preferred address for the contact. Table 5.3 shows the properties of the `ContactAddress` object that can be used to define the contact's address.

The `ContactOrganization` object provides properties to enter the organization information of the contact. We can enter the organization name, title of the contact, department to which he or she belongs, and so on. Table 5.4 shows the properties of the `ContactOrganization` object that can be used to define the contact's organization.

To add detailed information for the contact, the `index.html` file is modified to appear as shown in Listing 5.6.

**Table 5.3   A Brief Description of the** `ContactAddress` **Object Properties**

| Properties | Description |
|---|---|
| `pref` | Boolean value `true` is assigned to this property if the `ContactAddress` object defines the contact's preferred address. |
| `type` | Represents the type of address, i.e., whether it is a home or work address. |
| `formatted` | Represents the full formatted address. |
| `streetAddress` | Represents the full street address. |
| `locality` | Represents the city or locality of the contact. |
| `region` | Represents the state or region of the contact. |
| `postalCode` | Represents the zip code or postal code of the contact. |
| `country` | Represents the country name of the contact. |

**Table 5.4  A Brief Description of the `ContactOrganization` Object Properties**

| Properties | Description |
|---|---|
| pref | Boolean value `true` is assigned to this property if the `ContactOrganization` object defines the contact's preferred organization. |
| type | Represents the type of organization. |
| name | Represents the name of the organization. |
| department | Represents the department of the contact. |
| title | Represents the contact's title at the organization, e.g., whether the contact is the director, manager, developer, etc., in the organization. |

**Listing 5.6  Code Written in the `index.html` File**

```html
<!DOCTYPE HTML>
<html>
    <head>
    <title>PhoneGap Application</title>
    <script type = "text/javascript" charset = "utf-8" src = "cordova-2.3.0.js">
    </script>
    <script type = "text/javascript">
    function onBodyLoad() {
       document.addEventListener("deviceready", PhonegapLoaded, false);
       }
       function PhonegapLoaded(){

       document.getElementById("submitButton").addEventListener("click", addContact);
       }
    function addContact(){
      var firstName = document.getElementById("first_name").value;
      var lastName = document.getElementById("last_name").value;
      var organization = document.getElementById("organization").value;
      var streetAddress = document.getElementById("street_add").value;
      var city = document.getElementById("city").value;
      var state = document.getElementById("state").value;
      var country = document.getElementById("country").value;
      var postalCode = document.getElementById("post_code").value;
      var emailHome = document.getElementById("email_home").value;
      var emailWork = document.getElementById("email_work").value;
      var phoneWork = document.getElementById("phone_work").value;
      var phoneMobile = document.getElementById("phone_mobile").value;
      var newContact = navigator.contacts.create();
      var nameObject = new ContactName();
      nameObject.givenName = firstName;
      nameObject.familyName = lastName;
      nameObject.formatted = firstName + " " + lastName;
      newContact.name = nameObject;
      newContact.displayName = firstName + " " + lastName;
      var organizations = [];
      organizations[0] = new ContactOrganization();
      organizations[0].type = 'work';
      organizations[0].name = organization;
      newContact.organizations = organizations;
      var addresses = [];
      addresses[0] = new ContactAddress();
```

```
        addresses[0].type = 'home';
        addresses[0].streetAddress = streetAddress;
        addresses[0].locality = city;
        addresses[0].region = state;
        addresses[0].country = country;
        addresses[0].postalCode = postalCode;
        newContact.addresses = addresses;
        var emailAddresses = [2];
        emailAddresses[0] = new ContactField('home', emailHome, true);
        emailAddresses[1] = new ContactField('work', emailWork, true);
        newContact.emails = emailAddresses;
        var phoneNums = [2];
        phoneNums[0] = new ContactField('work', phoneWork, true);
        phoneNums[1] = new ContactField('mobile', phoneMobile, true);
        newContact.phoneNumbers = phoneNums;
        newContact.save(onSuccess, onError);
        }
    function onSuccess(contact) {
        alert("New contact successfully created");
        document.getElementById("addresponse").innerHTML = "Contact successfully
        added";
    }
    function onError(contactError) {
        alert("Error in creating a new contact " + contactError.code);
    }
    </script>
    </head>
    <body onload = "onBodyLoad()">
    <h2> Enter information of the new contact </h2> <br/>
        <form>
            <table>
        <tr><td>First Name </td><td> <input type = "text" id = "first_name"></td>
        </tr>
            <tr><td>Last Name </td><td> <input type = "text" id = "last_name"></td>
            </tr>
            <tr><td>Organization </td><td> <input type = "text" id =
            "organization"></td></tr>
            <tr><td>Street Address </td><td> <input type = "text" id = "street_
            add"></td></tr>
            <tr><td>City </td><td> <input type = "text" id = "city"></td></tr>
            <tr><td>State </td><td> <input type = "text" id = "state"></td></tr>
            <tr><td>Country </td><td> <input type = "text" id = "country"></td></tr>
            <tr><td>Postal Code </td><td> <input type = "text" id = "post_code">
            </td></tr>
            <tr><td>Email Address (Home) </td><td> <input type = "text" id = "email_
            home"></td></tr>
            <tr><td>Email Address (Work) </td><td> <input type = "text" id = "email_
            work"></td></tr>
            <tr><td>Phone Number (Work) </td><td> <input type = "text" id = "phone_
            work"></td></tr>
            <tr><td>Phone Number (Mobile) </td><td> <input type = "text" id = "phone_
            mobile"></td></tr>
        </table>
        <input type = "button" id = "submitButton" value = "Submit">
        <div id = "addresponse"></div>
        </form>
    </body>
</html>
```

We can see that a form is created comprising several input text fields. Through the form, the user can enter detailed information for the contact, like first name, last name, organization name, street address, city, state, country, postal code, home e-mail address, work e-mail address, home phone number, and mobile phone number. After entering the information, when the user clicks the Submit button, a Java Script function, addContact, is invoked after ensuring that PhoneGap is loaded properly. In the addContact method, the information entered by the user in different input text fields is accessed and stored in variables. A ContactName object by the name nameObject is created to store the first and last names of the object. Similarly, an organizations array is created and a ContactOrganization object is inserted in it to store the organization name of "work" type. Similarly, an addresses array is created and a ContactAddress object is inserted in it. The home address of the contact, comprising street address, city, state, country, and postal code, is stored in the ContactAddress object. For keeping home and work e-mail addresses of the contact, an array emailAddresses is created, and both types of e-mail addresses are stored in the array after wrapping them in the ContactField objects. Similarly, work and mobile types of phone numbers are stored in the phoneNums array after wrapping in the ContactField objects. Finally, the detailed contact information is saved by calling the save() method.

Upon running the application, a form prompting us to enter detailed information of the new contact will be displayed (see Figure 5.6a). Detailed information here includes first name, last name, organization name, street address, city, state, country, postal code, home e-mail address, work e-mail address, work phone number, and mobile phone number. After entering the detailed information, when the Submit button is pressed, the contact will be added to the Contacts database of the device—provided no error occurs. The added contact will appear in the Contacts List page under the respective index character, as shown in Figure 5.6b. Upon clicking a contact from the Contacts List page, its information will be displayed (see Figure 5.6c).

Now that we understand the procedure of listing and adding contacts, we turn to learning to modify the contact information and the procedure to delete it.

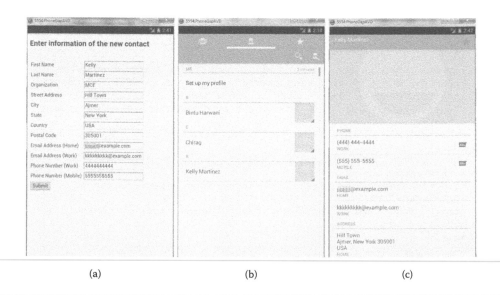

(a)  (b)  (c)

**Figure 5.6  (a) A form prompting us to enter detailed information for a new contact. (b) A newly added contact appears in the Contacts List page. (c) The information for the selected contact is displayed.**

# Deleting and Updating Contacts

In this application, we will learn to delete and update contact information. The application will display the list of existing contacts in the Contacts database of the device, allowing the user to select the one to delete or update. Before physically deleting the selected contact, the user will be prompted for confirmation. Similarly, while updating the contact information, existing information will be displayed allowing the user to modify the desired information.

Let us create a new Android project called PGContactsUpdateApp. To update and delete contact information, write the code as shown in Listing 5.7 in the index.html file.

**Listing 5.7  Code Written in the index.html File**

```
<!DOCTYPE HTML>
<html>
    <head>
    <title>PhoneGap Application</title>
    <script type = "text/javascript" charset = "utf-8" src = "cordova-2.3.0.js">
    </script>
    <script type = "text/javascript">
        function onBodyLoad(){
            document.addEventListener("deviceready", PhonegapLoaded, false);
        }
        function PhonegapLoaded(){
            var options = new ContactFindOptions();
            options.filter = "";
            options.multiple = true;
            filter = ["displayName"];
            document.getElementById("response").innerHTML = "" ;
            navigator.contacts.find(filter, onListContactsSuccess,
            onListContactsError, options);
        }
        function onListContactsSuccess(contacts) {
            var contnames = "";
            var divelement = document.getElementById('contactslist');
            if(contacts.length >0) {
                contnames = "List of Contacts </br></br>";
                for(var i = 0;i<contacts.length;i++){
                contnames+ = '<input type = "radio" name = "contactname" value =
                "'+contacts[i].displayName+'">'+ contacts[i].displayName + '<br/>';
                }
                contnames+ = '<input type = "button" id = "updateButton" value =
                "Update Contact">   ';
                contnames+ = '<input type = "button" id = "deleteButton" value =
                "Delete Contact">';
            }
            else
                contnames = "No contacts exists";
                divelement.innerHTML = contnames;
                document.getElementById("deleteButton").addEventListener("click",
                function() {findSelectedContact("delete");}, false);
                document.getElementById("updateButton").addEventListener("click",
                function() {findSelectedContact("update");}, false);
        }
        function onListContactsError(error) {
            alert('Sorry! Some error has occurred while accessing contacts');
        }
        function findSelectedContact(task) {
```

```
      var contacttofind = "";
      var contactslist = document.getElementById("contactslist").
      getElementsByTagName("INPUT");
      for (var i = 0;i<contactslist.length;i++) {
          if (contactslist[i].type.toUpperCase() = ='RADIO') {
              if(contactslist[i].checked)
                  contacttofind = contactslist[i].value;
          }
      }
      if(contacttofind.trim().length >0) {
          var options = new ContactFindOptions();
          options.filter = contacttofind;
          var fields = ["displayName", "name", "organizations", "addresses",
          "emails", "phoneNumbers"];
          if (task = = 'delete')
              navigator.contacts.find(fields, deleteContact, findError, options);
          else
              navigator.contacts.find(fields, showContactInfo, findError,
              options);
      }
      else
          document.getElementById("response").innerHTML = "No contact selected" ;
}
function deleteContact(contacts) {
      var ask = confirm("Are you sure");
      if(ask){
          contacts[0].remove(removeContactSuccess,removeContactError);
      }
}
function showContactInfo(contacts) {
      var organizationName = emailWork = emailHome = phoneWork = phoneMobile =
      "";
      var firstName = lastName = streetAddress = city = state = country =
      postalCode = "";
      if(contacts[0].name.givenName)
          firstName = contacts[0].name.givenName;
      if(contacts[0].name.familyName)
          lastName = contacts[0].name.familyName;
      if(contacts[0].addresses){
          for (var j = 0; j<contacts[0].addresses.length; j++) {
              if(contacts[0].addresses[j].streetAddress ! = undefined)
                  streetAddress = contacts[0].addresses[j].streetAddress;
              if(contacts[0].addresses[j].locality ! = undefined)
                  city = contacts[0].addresses[j].locality;
              if(contacts[0].addresses[j].region ! = undefined)
                  state = contacts[0].addresses[j].region;
              if(contacts[0].addresses[j].country ! = undefined)
                  country = contacts[0].addresses[j].country;
              if(contacts[0].addresses[j].postalCode ! = undefined)
                  postalCode = contacts[0].addresses[j].postalCode;
          }
      }
      if(contacts[0].organizations){
          for (var j = 0; j<contacts[0].organizations.length; j++) {
              organizationName = contacts[0].organizations[j].name;
          }
      }
      if(contacts[0].emails){
          for (var j = 0; j<contacts[0].emails.length; j++) {
```

```
            if(contacts[0].emails[j].type = ="home" && contacts[0].emails[j].
            value ! = undefined)
                emailHome = contacts[0].emails[j].value;
            if(contacts[0].emails[j].type = ="work" && contacts[0].emails[j].
            value ! = undefined)
                emailWork = contacts[0].emails[j].value;
        }
    }
    if(contacts[0].phoneNumbers){
        for (var j = 0; j<contacts[0].phoneNumbers.length; j++) {
            if(contacts[0].phoneNumbers[j].type = ="work" && contacts[0].
            phoneNumbers[j].value ! = undefined)
                phoneWork = contacts[0].phoneNumbers[j].value;
            if(contacts[0].phoneNumbers[j].type = ="mobile" && contacts[0].
            phoneNumbers[j].value ! = undefined)
                phoneMobile = contacts[0].phoneNumbers[j].value;
        }
    }
    var continfo = "";
    continfo+ = 'Modify the contact information followed by Update button
    <br/> <br/>';
    continfo+ = '<table>';
    continfo+ = '<tr><td>First Name </td><td> <input type = "text" id =
    "first_name" value = "'+firstName+'"></td></tr>';
    continfo+ = '<tr><td>Last Name </td><td> <input type = "text" id = "last_
    name" value = "'+lastName + '"></td></tr>';
    continfo+ = '<tr><td>Organization </td><td> <input type = "text" id =
    "organization" value = "'+organizationName + '"></td></tr>';
    continfo+ = '<tr><td>Street Address </td><td> <input type = "text" id =
    "street_add" size = "30" value = "'+streetAddress + '"></td></tr>';
    continfo+ = '<tr><td>City </td><td> <input type = "text" id = "city"
    value = "'+ city + '"></td></tr>';
    continfo+ = '<tr><td>State </td><td> <input type = "text" id = "state"
    value = "'+ state + '"></td></tr>';
    continfo+ = '<tr><td>Country </td><td> <input type = "text" id =
    "country" value = "'+ country + '"></td></tr>';
    continfo+ = '<tr><td>Postal Code </td><td> <input type = "text" id =
    "post_code" value = "'+postalCode + '"></td></tr>';
    continfo+ = '<tr><td>Email Address (Home) </td><td> <input type = "text"
    id = "email_home" value = "'+ emailHome + '"></td></tr>';
    continfo+ = '<tr><td>Email Address (Work) </td><td> <input type = "text"
    id = "email_work" value = "'+ emailWork + '"></td></tr>';
    continfo+ = '<tr><td>Phone Number (Work) </td><td> <input type = "text"
    id = "phone_work" value = "'+ phoneWork + '"></td></tr>';
    continfo+ = '<tr><td>Phone Number (Mobile) </td><td> <input type = "text"
    id = "phone_mobile" value = "'+ phoneMobile + '"></td></tr>';
    continfo+ = '</table>';
    continfo+ = '<input type = "button" id = "updateContactButton" value =
    "Update">   ';
    continfo+ = '<input type = "button" id = "cancelButton" value =
    "Cancel">';
    var divelement = document.getElementById('contactslist');
    divelement.innerHTML = continfo;
    document.getElementById("updateContactButton").addEventListener("click",
function() {updateContactInfo(contacts[0]);}, false);
    document.getElementById("cancelButton").addEventListener("click",
    PhonegapLoaded);
}
function findError(contactError) {
    alert("Contact Not found");
}
```

```
        function removeContactSuccess(contacts) {
            alert("Contact successfully deleted ");
            PhonegapLoaded();
        }
        function removeContactError(err) {
            alert("Contact could not be deleted. Error = " + err.code);
        }
        function updateContactInfo(contact) {
            var firstName = document.getElementById("first_name").value;
            var lastName = document.getElementById("last_name").value;
            var organization = document.getElementById("organization").value;
            var streetAddress = document.getElementById("street_add").value;
            var city = document.getElementById("city").value;
            var state = document.getElementById("state").value;
            var country = document.getElementById("country").value;
            var postalCode = document.getElementById("post_code").value;
            var emailHome = document.getElementById("email_home").value;
            var emailWork = document.getElementById("email_work").value;
            var phoneWork = document.getElementById("phone_work").value;
            var phoneMobile = document.getElementById("phone_mobile").value;
            var nameObject = new ContactName();
            nameObject.givenName = firstName;
            nameObject.familyName = lastName;
            nameObject.formatted = firstName + " " + lastName;
            contact.name = nameObject;
            contact.displayName = firstName + " " + lastName;
            var organizations = [];
            organizations[0] = new ContactOrganization();
            organizations[0].type = 'work';
            organizations[0].name = organization;
            contact.organizations = organizations;
            var addresses = [];
            addresses[0] = new ContactAddress();
            addresses[0].type = 'home';
            addresses[0].streetAddress = streetAddress;
            addresses[0].locality = city;
            addresses[0].region = state;
            addresses[0].country = country;
            addresses[0].postalCode = postalCode;
            contact.addresses = addresses;
            var emailAddresses = [2];
            emailAddresses[0] = new ContactField('home', emailHome, true);
            emailAddresses[1] = new ContactField('work', emailWork, true);
            contact.emails = emailAddresses;
            var phoneNums = [2];
            phoneNums[0] = new ContactField('work', phoneWork, true);
            phoneNums[1] = new ContactField('mobile', phoneMobile, true);
            contact.phoneNumbers = phoneNums;
            contact.save(onUpdateSuccess, onUpdateError);
        }
    function onUpdateSuccess(contact) {
        alert("Contact successfully updated");
        PhonegapLoaded();
    }
    function onUpdateError(contactError) {
        alert("Error in creating updating contact " + contactError.code);
    }
    </script>
    </head>
    <body onload = "onBodyLoad()">
        <div id = "contactslist"></div>
```

```
        <div id = "response"></div>
    </body>
</html>
```

In the code above, we see that two <div> elements are defined with IDs contactslist and response. The contactslist <div> element is used to display a list of contacts that exists in the Contacts database of the device. After ensuring that PhoneGap is loaded, the find() method is executed to access the contact names from the Contacts database, which in turn are displayed on the screen through the response <div> element. The contact names are displayed in the form of radio buttons to allow users to select a contact that they want to update or delete. Below the list of contacts, two buttons with IDs updateButton and deleteButton are defined. The IDs of the buttons indicate their purpose. After selecting a contact, if the delete-Button is clicked, the findSelectedContact() method is called with the string delete. The findSelectedContact() method detects the selected contact name by checking which radio button is checked. The selected contact name is searched in the Contacts database by calling the find() method, and a confirmation dialog is displayed to the user to avoid any accidental deleting of contacts. If the user confirms deleting of the contact, the remove() method is called to physically delete the selected contact from the Contacts database of the device.

If, after selecting a contact from the contacts list, the user clicks the Update button, the findSelectedContact() method is called with the string update. In the findSelect-edContact() method, the selected contact is searched in the Contacts database of the device, followed by calling the showContactInfo() method. In the showContactInfo() method, the information of the selected contact is accessed from the Contacts database and displayed on the screen. That is, the name, organization, address, phone numbers, and e-mail addresses of the contact are displayed on the screen through input text fields. The user can modify any of the displayed information, followed by clicking the Update button that is displayed at the bottom. The modified contact information is accessed from the input text fields, and the save() method is called to save the modified information of the contact.

To load the index.html file, write the code as shown in Listing 5.8 in the Java activity file PGContactsUpdateAppActivity.java.

**Listing 5.8   Code Written in the Java Activity File: PGContactsUpdateAppActivity.java**

```
package com.phonegap.pgcontactsupdateapp;
import android.os.Bundle;
import org.apache.cordova.DroidGap;
public class PGContactsUpdateAppActivity extends DroidGap {
    @Override
    public void onCreate(Bundle savedInstanceState) {
        super.onCreate(savedInstanceState);
        super.loadUrl("file:///android_asset/www/index.html");
    }
}
```

To access, read, and write the contacts in the Contacts database of the device, add the following permissions in the AndroidManifest.xml file:

```
<uses-permission android:name = "android.permission.ACCESS_NETWORK_STATE"/>
<uses-permission android:name = "android.permission.READ_CONTACTS"/>
<uses-permission android:name = "android.permission.WRITE_CONTACTS"/>
<uses-permission android:name = "android.permission.GET_ACCOUNTS"/>
```

Now our application is ready to run. Upon running the application, existing contacts in the Contacts database of the device are accessed and displayed. Below the listed contacts, two buttons, Update Contact and Delete Contact, will also appear (see Figure 5.7a). We just need to select the contact that we need to modify, followed by clicking the respective button from the bottom to perform the desired operation. If we select either of the buttons without selecting any contact, a message will appear informing No contact selected (see Figure 5.7b).

After selecting a contact when the Delete Contact button is clicked, the user will be prompted for confirmation before physically deleting the contact (see Figure 5.8a). If the user clicks the OK button to confirm deleting of the contact, a message, Contact successfully deleted, appears if no error occurs while deleting the contact from the Contacts database of the device (see Figure 5.8b). The remaining contacts appear in the Contacts List page (see Figure 5.8c). We can see that the deleted contact's name is missing in the contacts list.

To update contact information, we just need to select a contact from the displayed contacts list, followed by clicking the Update Contact button. The existing information of the selected contact will appear as shown in Figure 5.9a. We can edit any of the displayed information, followed by clicking the Update button to apply the changes. In case we change our mind and do not want to apply the modifications, we can select the Cancel button to cancel the update operation. Figure 5.9b shows the form after modifying the contact information. To save the modifications, we select the Update button. If no error occurs while saving the modified information

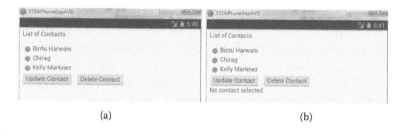

(a)                                    (b)

**Figure 5.7** **(a) The list of contacts is accessed from the Contacts database. (b) The message** No contact selected **is displayed when the** Update Contact **or** Delete Contact **button is selected without selecting any contact.**

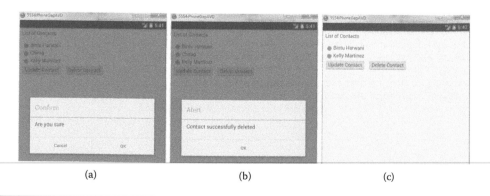

(a)                          (b)                          (c)

**Figure 5.8** **(a) The user is prompted for confirmation before deleting the contact. (b) A message informing us that the selected contact has been successfully deleted from the Contacts database. (c) A list of the remaining contacts is displayed.**

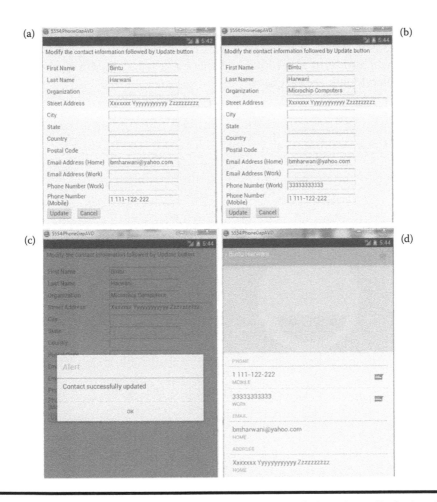

**Figure 5.9** **(a) Existing information on the contact is displayed. (b) A form displaying the information updated by the user. (c) A message informing successful updating of the contact information. (d) The screen showing the updated information of the contact.**

in the Contacts database, the message `Contact successfully updated` appears on the screen, as shown in Figure 5.9c. To confirm if the modifications are successfully applied to the Contacts database, select the contact from the Contacts List page. The updated information of the contact appears (see Figure 5.9d), which confirms that the modifications were successfully applied to the Contacts database.

## Summary

In this chapter, we learned about the role of PhoneGap Contacts API in saving, accessing, and maintaining the contacts information in the Contacts database. We learned about different contact properties that are used for storing information of the contacts. We also learned about methods that are used to find, remove, and save contacts in the Contacts database. Using a step-by-step procedure, we learned to add contacts, access contacts, delete contacts, and update contacts in the Contacts database of the device.

In Chapter 6, we will learn about jQuery Mobile. We will learn about techniques for navigating among different sections of the page. Also, we will learn about pages, dialogs, toolbars, and buttons. We will also learn about jQueryMobile event handling. Finally, we will see how PhoneGap and jQueryMobile are integrated.

# Chapter 6

## jQuery Mobile

In this chapter, we cover:

- Introducing jQuery Mobile
- Declaring a jQuery Mobile page
- Themes
- Handling page navigation
- Using lists
- Creating count bubbles
- Creating inset lists
- Adding list dividers
- Creating collapsible lists
- Creating numbered lists
- Displaying thumbnails and icons in the list
- Applying a search filter
- Creating Split Button lists
- Creating dialogs
- Creating forms in jQuery Mobile
- Displaying input fields, textarea, checkboxes, radio buttons, and drop-down lists
- Displaying date and time pickers
- Using on/off switches and sliders
- Grouping controls

## Introducing jQuery Mobile

jQuery Mobile is an open-source JavaScript user interface (UI) framework built upon the popular jQuery library, created by John Resig. It is one of the top frameworks used for developing applications for mobile devices. A few of the jQuery Mobile features are given below:

- It is built on the very popular and robust jQuery and jQuery UI framework.
- Well-written documentation is available for the jQuery Mobile framework.

- It provides a common UI platform to develop mobile applications across different mobile platforms.
- It makes the applications compatible with different browsers. Remember, there are a lot of differences among browsers. Some browsers are Web kit based and some are not.
- jQueryMobile uses declarative UI building; that is, to build a UI, we do not need to write any JavaScript code, but use the standard Hypertext Markup Language (HTML) tags and apply certain jQueryMobile-specific attributes to enhance them. The UI controls are styled and presented as touch screen controls. That is, jQuery Mobile uses the HTML tags, applies predefined styles, and adapts them to the current browser.
- The UI controls are manipulated as per the mobile device; that is, the UI controls are automatically resized per the available screen space, that is, when the device is oriented from landscape to portrait and vice versa.
- The UI controls are given a professional appearance; that is, there is no need to apply styles to enhance the appearance of UI controls. jQuery Mobile makes the UI controls quite readable and easier to select on a mobile device. jQueryMobile offers five built-in ready-to-use themes: Theme a, Theme b, Theme c, Theme d, and Theme e.
- All forms in jQuery Mobile are submitted through Ajax. That means the data are sent asynchronously to the server, hence increasing the application's response. Also, instead of full-page reload, partial page reloading is done.

To use jQuery Mobile in mobile applications, download it from `http://jquerymobile.com/download/`. The latest version of jQuery Mobile available for download at the time of this writing is 1.2.0. Download the `jquery.mobile-1.2.0.zip` file and unzip it in any folder. Upon unzipping the file, we will find two folders, `demos` and `images`, along with two pairs of jQueryMobile JavaScript and a Cascading Style Sheets (CSS) file. We will be using the .min JavaScript and CSS file in developing the application, as they are minified JavaScript and CSS files.

## Declaring a jQuery Mobile Page

jQuery Mobile uses `data-attributes` to apply styles and extend characteristics of HTML elements. A page in jQuery Mobile is defined by using the `data-role` attribute in the `div` element inside the `body` tag, as shown below:

```
<body>
<div data-role = "page" id = "page_id"></div>
…..
</body>
```

We can see that the value `page` is assigned to the `data-role` attribute for defining a page. A jQuery Mobile page is usually composed of three basic elements: a `header`, `content`, and `footer`. To define page elements, that is, the header, content, and footer of a page, the values `header`, `content`, and `footer` are assigned to the `data-role` attribute, respectively.

A sample format of a page in jQueryMobile is given below:

```
<body>
<div data-role = "page">
<div data-role = "header"></div>
```

```
<div data-role = "content"></div>
<div data-role = "footer"></div>
</div>
</body>
```

**Note:** The data-role is an HTML5 data attribute used to define a page and page structure elements, that is, the page header, content area, and footer.

Let us create an application that defines and displays a page. Launch Eclipse and create a new Android project called JQMIntroApp. After configuring the project for PhoneGap (refer to Chapter 2 for more details), copy the unzipped folder of jQueryMobile into the assets/www folder of our project. In this application, we will simply display a page that comprises a header, content, and footer. The header will display the text, jQuery Mobile Application, in heading 1 style. The content will display the text, Body of the Page, and the footer of the page will display the text, Page Footer. To display the described page, write the code as shown in Listing 6.1 in the index.html file.

**Listing 6.1 Code Written in the index.html File**

```
<!DOCTYPE HTML>
<html>
   <head>
   <title>PhoneGap Application</title>
   <script type = "text/javascript" charset = "utf-8" src = "cordova-2.3.0.js">
   </script>
   <link href = "jquery.mobile-1.2.0/jquery.mobile-1.2.0.min.css" rel =
   "stylesheet" type = "text/css"/>
   <script src = "jquery-1.8.3.min.js" type = "text/javascript"></script>
   <script src = "jquery.mobile-1.2.0/jquery.mobile-1.2.0.min.js" type = "text/
   javascript"></script>
   <script type = "text/javascript">
      function onBodyLoad(){
         document.addEventListener("deviceready", PhonegapLoaded, false);
      }
      function PhonegapLoaded(){
         alert("PhoneGap loaded");
      }
   </script>
   </head>
   <body onload = "onBodyLoad()">
      <div data-role = "page" id = "home">
         <div data-role = "header">
            <h1>jQuery Mobile Application</h1>
         </div>
         <div data-role = "content">
            <p>Body of the Page </p>
         </div>
         <div data-role = "footer">
            <h4> Page Footer </h4>
         </div>
      </div>
   </body>
</html>
```

In the code above, we can see that HTML DOCTYPE declaration is used. It is so because of the simple fact that jQuery Mobile relies on HTML5. jQuery Mobile requires jQuery, so not only mobile framework files, that is, jquery.mobile-1.2.0.min.js and jquery.mobile-1.2.0.min.css, but also the regular jQuery framework, that is, the jquery-1.8.3.min.js file, is included in the HTML file above. We can also optionally use the Viewport metatag given below to initialize page dimensions and zoom level:

```
<meta name = "viewport" content = "width = device-width, initial-scale = 1">
```

We see that the page is defined with the ID home. The page has a header displaying the text, jQuery Mobile Application, in heading 1 font size. The body, that is, content of the page, contains a paragraph element showing the text Body of the Page. The footer of the page shows the text Page footer.

To load the index.html file, code as shown in Listing 6.2 is written in the Java activity file, JQMIntroAppActivity.java.

**Listing 6.2   Code Written in the Java Activity File: JQMIntroAppActivity.java**

```
package com.phonegap.jqmintroapp;
import android.os.Bundle;
import org.apache.cordova.DroidGap;
public class JQMIntroAppActivity extends DroidGap {
   @Override
   public void onCreate(Bundle savedInstanceState) {
      super.onCreate(savedInstanceState);
      super.loadUrl("file:///android_asset/www/index.html");
   }
}
```

Upon running the application, first the onBodyLoad() function will be executed to ensure that PhoneGap is loaded before any of the JavaScript code is loaded. An alert message, PhoneGap loaded, is displayed to confirm that PhoneGap is successfully loaded (see Figure 6.1a). Upon clicking the OK button in the alert dialog, the page will appear as shown in Figure 6.1b. We can see that the header, content, and footer of the page display the text jQuery Mobile Application, Body of the Page, and Page Footer, respectively.

We can see that the page above is displayed in the default theme. If no style is specified in a page, the default theme is used. Let us apply some theme to the page to make it appear dynamic.

As stated earlier, jQuery Mobile includes five predefined style themes.

## Themes

Themes are a collection of styles that are used to apply styles to an application uniformly. Themes can be used to apply foreground color, background color, and fonts to different components of the application uniformly. Themes include multiple color swatches—each consisting of a header bar, content body, and button states.

The default theme includes five swatches named a, b, c, d, and e. Swatch a is the highest level of visual priority (black), b is the secondary level (blue), c is the baseline level (gray), d is

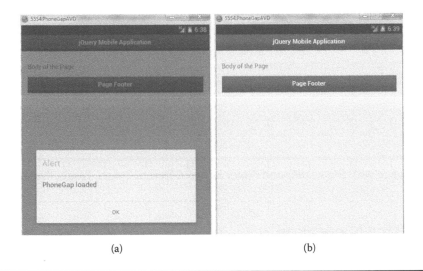

(a)                                    (b)

**Figure 6.1** **(a) The Alert dialog is displayed when PhoneGap is loaded. (b) Page displayed with header, content, and footer.**

an alternate secondary level, and e is an accent swatch. Themes may have additional swatches if required. Also, we can even create our own custom themes using the ThemeRoller tool.

**Note:** If no theme swatch letter is used in a page, the jQuery Mobile framework uses the a swatch for headers and footers and the c swatch for the content of a page.

The data-theme attribute is used to apply the desired theme to a page and its components. To make the header and footer of a page appear in blue and gray colors, respectively, modify the <body> element of the index.html file (refer to Listing 6.1) to appear as shown below. Only the code in bold is modified; the rest is the same as in Listing 6.1.

```
<body onload = "onBodyLoad()">
   <div data-role = "page" id = "home">
      <div data-role = "header" data-theme = "b">
         <h1>jQuery Mobile Application</h1>
      </div>
      <div data-role = "content">
         <p>Body of the Page </p>
      </div>
      <div data-role = "footer" data-theme = "d">
         <h4> Page Footer </h4>
      </div>
   </div>
</body>
```

We can see that the value b is assigned to the data-theme attribute of the page header to make it appear in blue color. Similarly, the value d is assigned to the data-theme attribute of the page footer to make it appear in gray color. Upon running the application, the page will appear with the blue header and gray footer as shown in Figure 6.2.

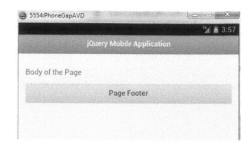

**Figure 6.2 A page with the header and footer in two different colors, respectively.**

## Handling Page Navigation

Unlike traditional Web pages, where each Web page is maintained in a separate HTML file, in mobile programming, multiple pages are defined into a single HTML file. The idea is that once the file is loaded, all the contained pages can be navigated without network requests.

We can define multiple pages in an application by using the `data-role` attribute. By assigning a `page` value to the `data-role` attribute for more than one, we can define multiple pages. For example, the following code defines two pages, Home and Page 2, in an application:

```
<!—Home Page—>
<div data-role = "page" id = "home">
   <div data-role = "header">
      <h1>Home page heading</h1>
   </div>
   <div data-role = "content">
     <p>Body of the Home Page </p>
   </div>
   <div data-role = "footer">
      <p>Footer of the Home Page </p>
   </div>
</div>

<!—Page 2—>
<div data-role = "page" id = "page2" ">
   <div data-role = "header">
      <h1>Page 2 </h1>
   </div>
   <div data-role = "content">
      <p>Body of the Page 2 </p>
   </div>
   <div data-role = "footer">
      <p>Footer of the Page 2 </p>
   </div>
</div>
```

The unique ID is assigned to each page for identifying them and also for implementing navigation among them. For example, if the ID of a page is `page2`, then a hyperlink `href` = `"#page2"` can be used to navigate to `page2`.

The following link, when added in the header or footer of the home page, will enable navigating to page 2:

```
<a href = "#page2">Page 2</a>
```

The link is automatically rendered as a button. We can also exclusively specify a button by associating `data-role = "button"` with the link shown below:

```
<a data-role = "button" href = "#page2" >Page 2</a>
```

The button in the code above will appear on the left side of the header or footer. To make the button appear on the right side, we add `class = "ui-btn-right"` to the link, as shown below:

```
<a data-role = "button" href = "#page2" class = "ui-btn-right">Page 2</a>
```

We can always add an icon to the link. jQuery Mobile includes a number of icons that we can use in our application. For example, the following hyperlink uses the `info` icon for navigating to page 2.

```
<a href = "#page2" data-icon = "info">Page 2</a>
```

In order to add a `Back` button in the header of a page to navigate us one page back in the history, the following code is used:

```
<a href = "#home" data-icon = "arrow-l" data-rel = "back">Back</a>
```

The code above will navigate back to the Home page of the application. The `data-rel = "back"` attribute in the statement above will make the `Back` button mimic a browser's `Back` button.

Let us try the concept of page navigation practically. We will create an application that comprises three pages, `Home`, `Page 2`, and `Page 3`. The Home page will have a link button in its header that, when clicked, will navigate us to `Page 2`. In `Page 2`, there will be a `Back` button in its header that, as expected, when clicked, will navigate us back to the Home page. In the footer of `Page 2`, there will be a link button that, when clicked, will navigate us to `Page 3`. In `Page 3`, there will be two link buttons in the header. The link button on the left, when clicked, will navigate us back to `Page 2`, and the button on the right side, when clicked, will navigate us to the Home page of the application. To create three pages and implement navigation among them, add an html page called `multiplepage.html` to the `assets/www` folder of our Android project, `JQMIntroApp`. In the `multiplepage.html` write the code as shown in Listing 6.3.

**Listing 6.3  Code Written in the `multiplepage.html` File**

```
<!DOCTYPE HTML>
<html>
   <head>
   <title>PhoneGap Application</title>
   <script type = "text/javascript" charset = "utf-8" src = "cordova-2.3.0.js">
   </script>
   <link href = "jquery.mobile-1.2.0/jquery.mobile-1.2.0.min.css" rel =
   "stylesheet" type = "text/css"/>
   <script src = "jquery-1.8.3.min.js" type = "text/javascript"></script>
   <script src = "jquery.mobile-1.2.0/jquery.mobile-1.2.0.min.js" type = "text/
   javascript"></script>
```

```
    <script type = "text/javascript">
      function onBodyLoad(){
          document.addEventListener("deviceready", PhonegapLoaded, false);
      }
      function PhonegapLoaded(){
          alert("PhoneGap loaded");
      }
    </script>
    </head>
    <body onload = "onBodyLoad()">
    <!—Home Page—>
      <div data-role = "page" id = "home">
        <div data-role = "header">
          <h1>jQuery Mobile Application</h1>
          <a data-role = "button" href = "#page2" >Page 2</a>
        </div>
        <div data-role = "content">
          <p>Body of the Home Page </p>
        </div>
      </div>
<!—Page 2—>
      <div data-role = "page" id = "page2" data-add-back-btn = "true">
        <div data-role = "header">
          <h1>Page 2 </h1>
        </div>
        <div data-role = "content">
          <p>Body of the Second Page </p>
        </div>
        <div data-role = "footer">
          <a href = "#page3" data-icon = "info">Page 3</a>
        </div>
      </div>
<!—Page 3—>
      <div data-role = "page" id = "page3">
        <div data-role = "header">
          <h1>Page 3 </h1>
          <a data-role = "button" href = "#page2" data-icon = "arrow-l"
          >Back</a>
          <a data-role = "button" href = "#home" data-icon = "home">Home</a>
        </div>
        <div data-role = "content">
          <p>Body of the Third Page </p>
        </div>
      </div>
    </body>
</html>
```

Open the Java activity file, JQMIntroAppActivity.java and modify the loadUrl() method to load the multiplepage.html file instead of the index.html file, as shown below:

```
super.loadUrl("file:///android_asset/www/multiplepage.html");
```

Our multiple-page application is ready to run. Upon running the application, a page, Home page, will appear on start-up, as shown in Figure 6.3a. The header of the Home page shows the text jQuery Mobile Application. On the left side of the header, a button with the caption Page 2 will appear. Upon clicking the Page 2 button from the Home page, we will be navigated to Page 2. The Page 2 page has a Back button in its header, which is meant for navigating back to the Home page (see Figure 6.3b). The content of Page 2 displays the text,

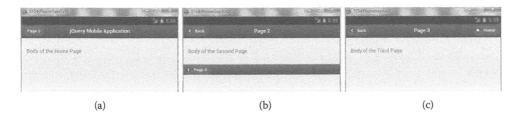

**Figure 6.3**  (a) Home page. (b) Page 2. (c) Page 3.

`Body of the Second Page`. The footer of `Page 2` contains a button with the caption `Page 3`, which, if clicked, will navigate us to `Page 3`. `Page 3` has two buttons, `Back` and `Home`, in its header, as shown in Figure 6.3c. The `Back` button will navigate us to `Page 2`, and the `Home` button, if clicked, will navigate us to the Home page. The content of `Page 3` displays the text, `Body of the Third Page`.

By default, the footer of a page does not have any padding around the buttons. To apply padding around the buttons, `class = "ui-bar"` is added to the footer. By default, the location of the footer depends on the page content; that is, the page footer appears immediately after where the page content ends. It also means that if the page content is less, the page footer will appear somewhere around the middle of the screen instead of at the bottom of the screen. To make the footer of the page appear at a fixed location between page navigations, that is, at the bottom of the screen, irrelevant of the page content size, the `data-position = "fixed"` attribute is used in the footer code. The following statement will apply padding around the buttons in the footer and will also make it appear at a fixed location between page navigations:

```
<div data-role = "footer" class = "ui-bar" data-position = "fixed" >
   <a href = "#page3" data-icon = "info">Page 3</a>
</div>
```

To display an icon-only button and no text, the `data-iconpos` attribute is used in the hyperlink, as shown below:

```
<a href = "#page3" data-icon = "info" data-iconpos = "notext">Page 3</a>
```

Let us apply the following changes in the `multiplepage` application above:

- Make the footer of `Page 2` appear at a fixed location between page navigations, irrelevant of the size of the page content.
- Apply padding around the buttons in the footer of `Page 2`.
- Add a footer in `Page 3` comprising two buttons, `Page 2` and Home. The `Page 2` button will be used for navigating back to `Page 2`, and the `Home` button for navigating to the Home page.

To apply the modifications above, modify the code of `Page 2` and `Page 3` in the `multiplepage.html` file (refer to Listing 6.3) to appear as shown below. Only the code in bold is modified; the rest is the same as in Listing 6.3.

```
<!--Page 2-->
<div data-role = "page" id = "page2" data-add-back-btn = "true">
   <div data-role = "header">
      <h1>Page 2 </h1>
   </div>
   <div data-role = "content">
      <p>Body of the Second Page </p>
   </div>
   <div data-role = "footer" class = "ui-bar" data-position = "fixed" >
      <a href = "#page3" data-icon = "info">Page 3</a>
   </div>
</div>

<!--Page 3-->
<div data-role = "page" id = "page3">
   <div data-role = "header">
      <h1>Page 3 </h1>
      <a data-role = "button" href = "#page2" data-icon = "arrow-l"
      >Back</a>
      <a data-role = "button" href = "#home" data-iconpos = "notext"
      data-icon = "home">Home</a>
   </div>
   <div data-role = "content">
      <p>Body of the Third Page </p>
   </div>
   <div data-role = "footer" class = "ui-bar" data-theme = "b" data-
   position = "fixed" >
      <a href = "#home" data-role = "button">Home</a>
      <a href = "#page2" data-role = "button">Page 2</a>
   </div>
</div>
```

Upon running the application, Page 2 will appear as shown in Figure 6.4a. We can see that the Page 2 footer appears at the bottom, and the button Page 3 contained in it is padded. Upon clicking the Page 3 button, Page 3 will open. Page 3 has a footer containing two buttons, Home and Page 2 (see Figure 6.4b).

jQuery Mobile allows us to group together multiple controls. To do so, we need to wrap the controls in a div tag using the data-role of "controlgroup". In addition, the grouped controls can be aligned horizontally as well as vertically by associating the data-type attribute to the group. For example, the statements below group two buttons, Home and Page 2, and also align them horizontally:

```
<div data-role = "controlgroup" data-type = "horizontal">
   <a href = "#home" data-role = "button">Home</a>
   <a href = "#page2" data-role = "button">Page 2</a>
</div>
```

The value horizontal, when assigned to the data-type attribute, aligns the buttons in the group horizontally. Similarly, for aligning the buttons in a group vertically, the vertical value is assigned to the data-type attribute in the div tag. Let us group the buttons in the footer of Page 3 and align them horizontally. To do so, modify the Page 3 footer to appear as shown below:

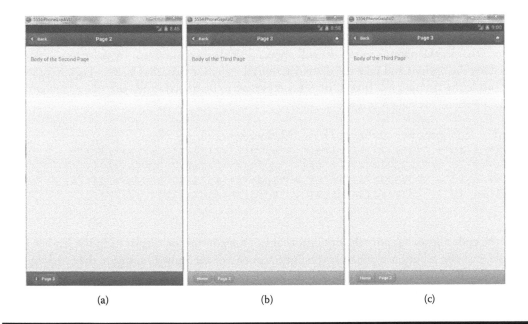

(a)  (b)  (c)

**Figure 6.4  (a) Page 2 with a location-fixed footer and padded button. (b) Page 3 with two buttons in its footer in a blue theme. (c) The buttons in the Page 3 footer arranged as a** `controlgroup`**.**

```
<div data-role = "footer" class = "ui-bar" data-theme = "b" data-position
= "fixed" >
   <div data-role = "controlgroup" data-type = "horizontal">
      <a href = "#home" data-role = "button">Home</a>
      <a href = "#page2" data-role = "button">Page 2</a>
   </div>
</div>
```

The two buttons, Home and Page 2, in the footer of Page 3 will be grouped horizontally and appear as shown in Figure 6.4c.

Now that we understand the creation of pages and navigation among them, let us turn to the procedure for displaying a list of options in an application.

## Using Lists

Lists are used to show options or choices to the users to select from. Lists are displayed by using the standard <ul> tags. The options in the list are defined through the child <li> elements. In order to enhance a list and optimize it for mobile devices, the data-role = "listview" attribute is associated with the <ul> element as shown below:

```
<ul id = "phoneList" data-role = "listview">
   <li>1111111111</li>
   <li>2222222222</li>
   <li>3333333333</li>
   <li>4444444444</li>
</ul>
```

The example above creates a scrollable list with ID `phoneList` showing few phone numbers. Though phone numbers will be displayed in the list above, the user will not be able to click on them. That is, the options in the list will appear as if they are disabled. In order to enable the user to click the options and take the desired action, the anchor tags, that is, `<a>` tags, have to be nested inside the list options. That is, the `<a>` tags have to be nested inside the `<li>` elements of the `<ul>` element, as shown below:

```
<ul id = "phoneList" data-role = "listview">
   <li><a id = "1111111111" href = "#page2">1111111111</a></li>
   <li><a id = "2222222222" href = "#page2">2222222222</a></li>
   <li><a id = "3333333333" href = "#page2">3333333333</a></li>
   <li><a id = "4444444444" href = "#page2">4444444444</a></li>
</ul>
```

By the code above, not only the options, that is, phone numbers, displayed in the list become clickable, but also a button is added at the rightmost end of each row to indicate that clicking on the option will navigate to a page that will do some processing or task on the selected option.

Let us create an application that explains how a list is created and how different features can be applied to it. In the application, we will learn to do the following:

- Initiate a task when an item or option from the list is clicked
- Create count bubbles
- Create inset lists
- Add list dividers
- Create collapsible lists
- Create numbered lists

To do all the said tasks, launch Eclipse and open our Android project called `JQMIntroApp`. Add an HTML page called `listdemo.html` to the `assets/www` folder of our application. In the `listdemo.html`, write the code as shown in Listing 6.4.

**Listing 6.4  Code Written in the `listdemo.html` File**

```
<!DOCTYPE HTML>
<html>
   <head>
   <title>PhoneGap Application</title>
   <script type = "text/javascript" charset = "utf-8" src = "cordova-2.3.0.js">
   </script>
   <link href = "jquery.mobile-1.2.0/jquery.mobile-1.2.0.min.css" rel =
   "stylesheet" type = "text/css"/>
   <script src = "jquery-1.8.3.min.js" type = "text/javascript"></script>
   <script src = "jquery.mobile-1.2.0/jquery.mobile-1.2.0.min.js" type = "text/
   javascript"></script>
   <script type = "text/javascript">
      function onBodyLoad(){
         document.addEventListener("deviceready", PhonegapLoaded, false);
      }
      function PhonegapLoaded(){
         $('#phoneList').children().each(function(){
            var anchor = $(this).find('a');
```

```
            if(anchor){
                anchor.click(function(){
                document.getElementById("selecteditem").innerHTML = "You have selected
                "+anchor.attr('id');
                });
            }
        });
    }
    </script>
    </head>
    <body onload = "onBodyLoad()">
        <div data-role = "page" id = "home">
            <div data-role = "header" data-theme = "b">
                <h1>List Application</h1>
            </div>
            <div data-role = "content">
                <h2> Choose a phone number </h2>
                <ul id = "phoneList" data-role = "listview">
                    <li><a id = "1111111111" href = "#page2">1111111111</a></li>
                    <li><a id = "2222222222" href = "#page2">2222222222</a></li>
                    <li><a id = "3333333333" href = "#page2">3333333333</a></li>
                    <li><a id = "4444444444" href = "#page2">4444444444</a></li>
                    <li><a id = "5555555555" href = "#page2">5555555555</a></li>
                    <li><a id = "6666666666" href = "#page2">6666666666</a></li>
                    <li><a id = "7777777777" href = "#page2">7777777777</a></li>
                    <li><a id = "8888888888" href = "#page2">8888888888</a></li>
                    <li><a id = "9999999999" href = "#page2">9999999999</a></li>
                    <li><a id = "1111122222" href = "#page2">1111122222</a></li>
                </ul>
            </div>
        </div>
<!—Page 2—>
        <div data-role = "page" id = "page2" data-add-back-btn = "true">
            <div data-role = "header" data-theme = "b">
                <h1>Page 2 </h1>
            </div>
            <div data-role = "content">
                <div id = "selecteditem"></div>
            </div>
        </div>
    </body>
</html>
```

In the code above, we see that a home page with the header List Application is created. The content of the page comprises text, Choose a phone number, and a scrollable list. To make the list items selectable, a hyperlink is nested inside each list item. The hyperlink navigates us to Page 2 when any list item from the list is clicked. Page 2 will inform which of the list items is clicked. We see that a Page 2 with header Page 2 is created along with a Back button. The content of Page 2 contains a <div> element with ID selecteditem that will be used to display the list item that is selected from the list.

In the Java activity file, JQMIntroAppActivity.java, modify the loadUrl() to load the listdemo.html file:

```
super.loadUrl("file:///android_asset/www/listdemo.html");
```

Upon running the application, we see that all the list items, that is, phone numbers, are displayed in a scrollable list. The list will be displayed edge to edge by default. We will soon learn to round the corners of the list. Because hyperlinks are nested inside the list items, the phone numbers will appear as touch-friendly buttons with a right-aligned arrow icon (see Figure 6.5a). The list items, that is, phone numbers, will appear in gray color, as lists are styled with the c swatch, that is, in gray color by default. Upon clicking any list item, we will be navigated to Page 2, which will display the selected list item (see Figure 6.5b).

The navigation from the home page to Page 2 when any list item is clicked can be made smoother by associating the data-transition attribute with the hyperlink element. The code given below implements slideup and slidedown transitions in the list items, 1111111111 and 2222222222, for navigating from the home page to Page 2:

```
<ul id = "phoneList" data-role = "listview">
   <li><a id = "1111111111" href = "#page2" data-transition =
   "slideup">1111111111 </a></li>
   <li><a id = "2222222222" href = "#page2" data-transition =
   "slidedown">2222222222 </a></li>
 . . . . . . . . . . . . . . . .
 . . . . . . . . . . . . . . .
</ul>
```

To find the list of transition values that can be applied to data-transition, visit: http://jquerymobile.com/demos/1.2.0/docs/pages/page-transitions.html.

## *Creating Count Bubbles*

jQuery Mobile enables us to add count bubbles, also known as list badges, to the list. Count bubbles are some number, character, or symbol wrapped in a bubble displayed at the end of each list item. We usually see count bubbles while reading e-mails that indicate the number of new

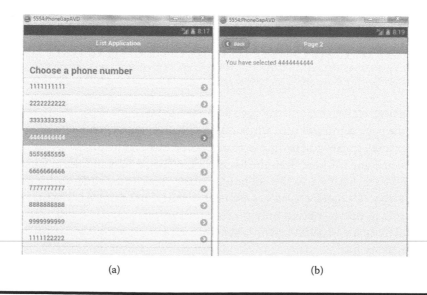

(a)             (b)

**Figure 6.5** **(a) Phone numbers shown in a scrollable list. (b) A selected phone number is displayed on Page 2.**

e-mails that have arrived. To display count bubbles, we need to nest that span class = "ui-li-count" attribute inside the list item, as shown below:

```
<ul id = "phoneList" data-role = "listview">
   <li><a id = "1111111111" href = "#page2"> 1111111111 <span class =
   "ui-li-count"> H </span></a></li>
   <li><a id = "2222222222" href = "#page2"> 2222222222 <span class =
   "ui-li-count"> O </span></a></li>
   .......
   ......
</ul>
```

The code above displays two phone numbers, 1111111111 and 2222222222. To the right of the first phone number, a character H that is enclosed in a bubble will be displayed. The character H indicates that it is a home phone number. Similarly, to the right of the second phone number, 2222222222, a character O wrapped in a bubble will be displayed to inform us that it is an office phone number.

To display the count bubbles in the list that we created in the listdemo.html file (refer to Listing 6.4), modify the <ul> element in the listdemo.html file to appear as shown in Listing 6.5. Only the code in bold is modified; the rest is the same as we saw in Listing 6.4.

**Listing 6.5  Code Written in the <ul> Element in listdemo.html File**

```
<ul id = "phoneList" data-role = "listview">
   <li><a id = "1111111111" href = "#page2"> 1111111111 <span class = "ui-li-
   count"> H </span></a></li>
   <li><a id = "2222222222" href = "#page2"> 2222222222 <span class = "ui-li-
   count"> H </span></a></li>
   <li><a id = "3333333333" href = "#page2"> 3333333333 <span class = "ui-li-
   count"> O </span></a></li>
   <li><a id = "4444444444" href = "#page2"> 4444444444 <span class = "ui-li-
   count"> O </span></a></li>
   <li><a id = "5555555555" href = "#page2"> 5555555555 <span class = "ui-li-
   count"> O </span></a></li>
   <li><a id = "6666666666" href = "#page2">6666666666 <span class = "ui-li-
   count"> H </span></a></li>
   <li><a id = "7777777777" href = "#page2">7777777777 <span class = "ui-li-
   count"> O </span></a></li>
   <li><a id = "8888888888" href = "#page2"> 8888888888 <span class = "ui-li-
   count"> H </span></a></li>
   <li><a id = "9999999999" href = "#page2"> 9999999999 <span class = "ui-li-
   count"> H </span></a></li>
   <li><a id = "1111122222" href = "#page2"> 1111122222 <span class = "ui-li-
   count"> O </span></a></li>
</ul>
```

After adding the count bubbles or list badges to the <ul> element as shown above, when we run the application, we see that count bubbles appear on the right of each phone number (see Figure 6.6a). The characters, H and O, enclosed in the bubble indicate whether the phone number is a home or office number.

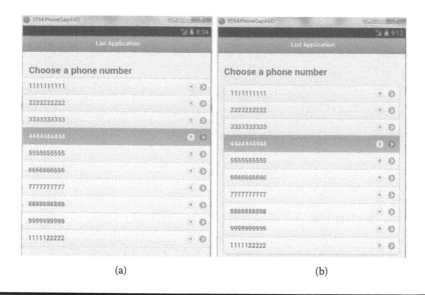

(a)                                        (b)

**Figure 6.6** **(a) Phone numbers are displayed in a scrollable list along with the home and office count bubbles on the right. (b) Inset list showing the phone numbers.**

## Creating Inset Lists

By default, a list is displayed edge to edge, taking up the full width of the device. For a rounded corner list, an inset list is used. An inset list is wrapped inside a block with rounded corners. It does not take up the full width of the device. To create an inset list, the `data-inset = "true"` attribute is added to the `<ul>` element as shown below:

```
<ul id = "phoneList" data-role = "listview" data-inset = "true">
```

To convert a usual list into an inset list, let us add the `data-inset = "true"` attribute to the `<ul>` element shown in Listing 6.5. Upon running the application, the list will appear as an inset list—with rounded corners and with margins from the screen edges (see Figure 6.6b).

## Adding List Dividers

List dividers are used for breaking up a long list into small categories. To represent and differentiate each category, a separate heading is required for each category. A list divider is used to provide heading(s) for the list items shown in a list. To create a list divider, the `data-role = "list-divider"` attribute is added to any list item. To define a list divider or a heading with text, `Choose a phone number`, to our list, modify the `<ul>` element of our `listdemo.html` file to appear as shown in Listing 6.6. Only the code in bold is new; the rest is the same as we saw in Listing 6.5.

**Listing 6.6** **Code Written in the `<ul>` Element in `listdemo.html` File**

```
<ul id = "phoneList" data-role = "listview" data-inset = "true" data-theme = "e" >
   <li data-role = "divider">Choose a phone number</li>
```

```
<li><a id = "1111111111" href = "#page2"> 1111111111 <span class = "ui-li-
count"> H </span></a></li>
<li><a id = "2222222222" href = "#page2"> 2222222222 <span class = "ui-li-
count"> H </span></a></li>
<li><a id = "3333333333" href = "#page2"> 3333333333 <span class = "ui-li-
count"> O </span></a></li>
<li><a id = "4444444444" href = "#page2"> 4444444444 <span class = "ui-li-
count"> O </span></a></li>
<li><a id = "5555555555" href = "#page2"> 5555555555 <span class = "ui-li-
count"> O </span></a></li>
<li><a id = "6666666666" href = "#page2"> 6666666666 <span class = "ui-li-
count"> H </span></a></li>
<li><a id = "7777777777" href = "#page2"> 7777777777 <span class = "ui-li-
count"> O </span></a></li>
<li><a id = "8888888888" href = "#page2"> 8888888888 <span class = "ui-li-
count"> H </span></a></li>
<li><a id = "9999999999" href = "#page2"> 9999999999 <span class = "ui-li-
count"> H </span></a></li>
<li><a id = "1111122222" href = "#page2"> 1111122222 <span class = "ui-li-
count"> O </span></a></li>
</ul>
```

We can see that the above is an inset list to which swatch e of the default theme is applied. The applied swatch will make the list appear in yellow color. Because of the list divider, a heading, Choose a phone number, will be displayed above the list items (see Figure 6.7a).

We can add any number of list dividers. To define two list dividers with text, Friends phone numbers and Client phone numbers, the <ul> element shown in Listing 6.6 can be modified to appear as shown below. The statements in bold define the two headings.

```
<ul id = "phoneList" data-role = "listview" data-inset = "true" data-
theme = "e" >
   <li data-role = "divider">Friends phone numbers</li>
   <li><a id = "1111111111" href = "#page2"> 1111111111 <span class =
   "ui-li-count"> H </span></a></li>
   <li><a id = "2222222222" href = "#page2"> 2222222222 <span class =
   "ui-li-count"> H </span></a></li>
   <li><a id = "3333333333" href = "#page2"> 3333333333 <span class =
   "ui-li-count"> O </span></a></li>
   <li><a id = "4444444444" href = "#page2"> 4444444444 <span class =
   "ui-li-count"> O </span></a></li>
   <li><a id = "5555555555" href = "#page2"> 5555555555 <span class =
   "ui-li-count"> O </span></a></li>
   <li data-role = "divider">Client phone numbers</li>
   <li><a id = "6666666666" href = "#page2"> 6666666666 <span class =
   "ui-li-count"> H </span></a></li>
   <li><a id = "7777777777" href = "#page2"> 7777777777 <span class =
   "ui-li-count"> O </span></a></li>
   <li><a id = "8888888888" href = "#page2"> 8888888888 <span class =
   "ui-li-count"> H </span></a></li>
   <li><a id = "9999999999" href = "#page2"> 9999999999 <span class =
   "ui-li-count"> H </span></a></li>
   <li><a id = "1111122222" href = "#page2"> 1111122222 <span class =
   "ui-li-count"> O </span></a></li>
</ul>
```

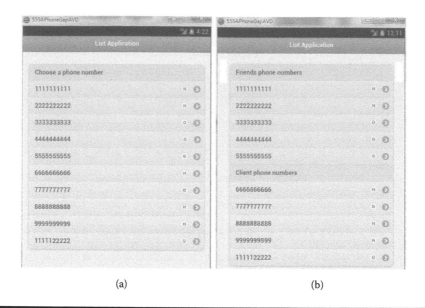

(a)                                                (b)

**Figure 6.7    (a) Phone numbers displayed in an inset list along with a heading. (b) An inset list is displayed with two headings.**

Upon running the application, we see that two headings are displayed that divide the phone numbers shown in the list into two categories, Friends phone numbers and Client phone numbers, respectively (see Figure 6.7b).

## *Creating Collapsible Lists*

For displaying a list of options in a small space, collapsible lists are preferred. When in a collapsed form, all the list items in a collapsible list are hidden and a plus (+) sign is displayed to the left of the list heading. The plus sign indicates that the list is in a collapsed form. Upon clicking the plus sign, the list will be expanded, showing all the hidden list items. In expanded form, the plus sign is replaced by a minus (–) sign. To create a collapsible list, the <ul> element is nested inside a <div> element and the data-role = "collapsible" attribute is associated with that <div> element as shown in the below code:

```
<div data-role = "collapsible">
   <h3>Click to expand the list</h3>
   <ul id = "phoneList" data-role = "listview" >
      <li data-role = "divider">Choose a phone number</li>
      <li><a id = "1111111111" href = "#page2"> 1111111111</a></li>
      <li><a id = "2222222222" href = "#page2"> 2222222222 </a></li>
.................
.................
   </ul>
</div>
```

The code above will display a list that is initially in collapsed form with the heading Click to expand the list. The heading will have a plus sign on its left. Upon clicking the plus sign, the list will be expanded, showing all the hidden list items. The plus sign in the heading will be replaced by a minus sign to indicate that the list is in expanded form. The list will also display a list divider with the text Choose a phone number.

To convert the list that we created in the listdemo.html file in the JQMIntroApp application into a collapsible list, modify the <body> element of that file (refer to Listing 6.4) to appear as shown in Listing 6.7. The statements in bold are responsible for converting a normal list into a collapsible list.

**Listing 6.7   Code Written in the <body> Element of the listdemo.html File**

```
<body onload = "onBodyLoad()">
    <div data-role = "page" id = "home">
        <div data-role = "header" data-theme = "b">
            <h1>List Application</h1>
        </div>
        <div data-role = "content">
            <div data-role = "collapsible" data-theme = "b">
                <h3>Click to expand the list</h3>
                <ul id = "phoneList" data-role = "listview" data-inset = "true" data-
                theme = "e" >
                    <li data-role = "divider">Choose a phone number</li>
                    <li><a id = "1111111111" href = "#page2"> 1111111111 <span class =
                    "ui-li-count"> H </span></a></li>
                    <li><a id = "2222222222" href = "#page2"> 2222222222 <span class =
                    "ui-li-count"> H </span></a></li>
                    <li><a id = "3333333333" href = "#page2"> 3333333333 <span class =
                    "ui-li-count"> O </span></a></li>
                    <li><a id = "4444444444" href = "#page2"> 4444444444 <span class =
                    "ui-li-count"> O </span></a></li>
                    <li><a id = "5555555555" href = "#page2"> 5555555555 <span class =
                    "ui-li-count"> O </span></a></li>
                    <li><a id = "6666666666" href = "#page2"> 6666666666 <span class =
                    "ui-li-count"> H </span></a></li>
                    <li><a id = "7777777777" href = "#page2"> 7777777777 <span class =
                    "ui-li-count"> O </span></a></li>
                    <li><a id = "8888888888" href = "#page2"> 8888888888 <span class =
                    "ui-li-count"> H </span></a></li>
                    <li><a id = "9999999999" href = "#page2"> 9999999999 <span class =
                    "ui-li-count"> H </span></a></li>
                    <li><a id = "1111122222" href = "#page2"> 1111122222 <span class =
                    "ui-li-count"> O </span></a></li>
                </ul>
            </div>
        </div>
    </div>
<!—Page 2—>
    <div data-role = "page" id = "page2" data-add-back-btn = "true">
        <div data-role = "header" data-theme = "b">
            <h1>Page 2 </h1>
        </div>
        <div data-role = "content">
            <div id = "selecteditem"></div>
        </div>
    </div>
</body>
```

Upon running the application, a collapsible list with the heading `Click to expand the list` will be displayed (see Figure 6.8a). Upon clicking the plus sign in the heading, the list will be expanded, revealing all the hidden list items, as shown in Figure 6.8b.

## Creating Numbered Lists

A numbered list is created by using an ordered list `<ol>` element. That is, on replacing the `<ul>` element by `<ol>` in Listing 6.7, we will get a numbered list as shown in Figure 6.8c.

In the output, we can see that the framework adds the numerical index to the left of each list item.

## Displaying Thumbnails and Icons in the List

We can display thumbnails to the left of the list items in a list by nesting an image, that is, `<img>` element, inside the list item, as shown below:

```
<ul id = "phoneList" data-role = "listview" >
  <li data-role = "divider">Choose a phone number</li>
  <li><a id = "1111111111" href = "#page2"> <img src = "images/cell.
  png"/> 1111111111 </a></li>
</ul>
```

The code above will display a thumbnail image to the left of the list item `1111111111` in the list. The framework will scale the image to 80 square pixels. Similarly, we can associate images with other list items too.

Let us create an application that displays thumbnails and icons in the list. So, launch Eclipse and open our Android project called `JQMIntroApp`. Add an HTML file called `listdemo2.html` to the `assets/www` folder. In this application, we will be displaying three different images in the list items, so add a folder called `images` to the `/assets/www` folder of our

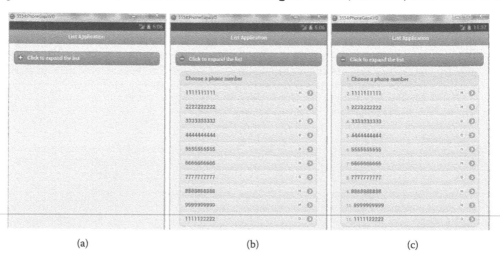

(a)  (b)  (c)

**Figure 6.8** (a) A collapsible list with the heading `Click to expand the list`. (b) A collapsible list in expanded form. (c) A numbered list showing the phone numbers.

application. Paste three image files called cell1.png, cell2.png, and cell3.png to the /assets/www/images folder. To display thumbnails in the list, write the code as shown in Listing 6.8 in the listdemo2.html file.

**Listing 6.8   Code Written in the listdemo2.html File**

```
<!DOCTYPE HTML>
<html>
    <head>
    <title>PhoneGap Application</title>
    <script type = "text/javascript" charset = "utf-8" src = "cordova-2.3.0.js">
    </script>
    <link href = "jquery.mobile-1.2.0/jquery.mobile-1.2.0.min.css" rel =
    "stylesheet" type = "text/css"/>
    <script src = "jquery-1.8.3.min.js" type = "text/javascript"></script>
    <script src = "jquery.mobile-1.2.0/jquery.mobile-1.2.0.min.js" type = "text/
    javascript"></script>
    <script type = "text/javascript">
        function onBodyLoad(){
            document.addEventListener("deviceready", PhonegapLoaded, false);
        }
        function PhonegapLoaded(){
            $('#phoneList').children().each(function(){
                var anchor = $(this).find('a');
                if(anchor){
                    anchor.click(function(){
        document.getElementById("selecteditem").innerHTML = "You have selected
        "+anchor.attr('id');
                    });
                }
            });
        }
    </script>
    </head>
    <body onload = "onBodyLoad()">
        <div data-role = "page" id = "home">
            <div data-role = "header" data-theme = "b">
                <h1>List Application</h1>
            </div>
            <div data-role = "content">
                <ul id = "phoneList" data-role = "listview" data-inset = "true" data-
                theme = "e" >
                    <li data-role = "divider">Choose a phone number</li>
                    <li><a id = "1111111111" href = "#page2"> <img src = "images/cell1.
                    png"/> 1111111111 <span class = "ui-li-count"> H </span></a></li>
                    <li><a id = "2222222222" href = "#page2"> <img src = "images/cell2.
                    png"/> 2222222222 <span class = "ui-li-count"> H </span></a></li>
                    <li><a id = "3333333333" href = "#page2"> <img src = "images/cell3.
                    png"/> 3333333333 <span class = "ui-li-count"> O </span></a></li>
                    <li><a id = "4444444444" href = "#page2"> <img src = "images/cell1.
                    png"/> 4444444444 <span class = "ui-li-count"> O </span></a></li>
                    <li><a id = "5555555555" href = "#page2"> <img src = "images/cell2.
                    png"/> 5555555555 <span class = "ui-li-count"> O </span></a></li>
                    <li><a id = "6666666666" href = "#page2"> <img src = "images/cell3.
                    png"/> 6666666666 <span class = "ui-li-count"> H </span></a></li>
                    <li><a id = "7777777777" href = "#page2"> <img src = "images/cell1.
                    png"/> 7777777777 <span class = "ui-li-count"> O </span></a></li>
                    <li><a id = "8888888888" href = "#page2"> <img src = "images/cell2.
                    png"/> 8888888888 <span class = "ui-li-count"> H </span></a></li>
```

```
            <li><a id = "9999999999" href = "#page2"> <img src = "images/cell3.
            png"/> 9999999999 <span class = "ui-li-count"> H </span></a></li>
            <li><a id = "1111122222" href = "#page2"> <img src = "images/cell1.
            png"/> 1111122222 <span class = "ui-li-count"> O </span></a></li>
          </ul>
        </div>
      </div>
<!—Page 2—>
      <div data-role = "page" id = "page2" data-add-back-btn = "true">
        <div data-role = "header" data-theme = "b">
          <h1>Page 2 </h1>
        </div>
        <div data-role = "content">
          <div id = "selecteditem"></div>
        </div>
      </div>
   </body>
</html>
```

In Listing 6.8, we can see the image elements, <img> (shown in bold), are nested in the list items, <li>. The <img> elements are set to display three images, cell1.png, cell2.png, and cell3.png, as thumbnails in the list items. Hyperlinks in the list items will navigate us to Page 2 when any list item is clicked. Page 2 will display the name of the list item that is clicked.

To load the above listdemo2.html file, open the Java activity file, JQMIntroAppActivity. java, and modify the loadUrl() method as shown below:

```
super.loadUrl("file:///android_asset/www/listdemo2.html");
```

Our application is ready to run. Upon running the application, we see that to the left of each phone number, that is, list item, a thumbnail is displayed as shown in Figure 6.9a.

We can also display smaller icons instead of thumbnails in the list. To display 16 × 16 pixel icons in list items, we need to add the class of ui-li-icon to the image element, as shown in bold below:

```
<ul id = "phoneList" data-role = "listview" data-inset = "true" data-
theme = "e" >
   <li data-role = "divider">Choose a phone number</li>
   <li><a id = "1111111111" href = "#page2"> <img src = "images/cell1.
   png" class = "ui-li-icon"/> 1111111111 <span class = "ui-li-count"> H
   </span></a></li>
   <li><a id = "2222222222" href = "#page2"> <img src = "images/cell2.
   png" class = "ui-li-icon"/> 2222222222 <span class = "ui-li-count"> H
   </span></a></li>
. . . . . . . . . . . . .
. . . . . . . . . .
</ul>
```

Upon adding the class of ui-li-icon to the image element nested in items of the list that we defined in the listdemo2.html file, the images will appear as icons, as shown in Figure 6.9b.

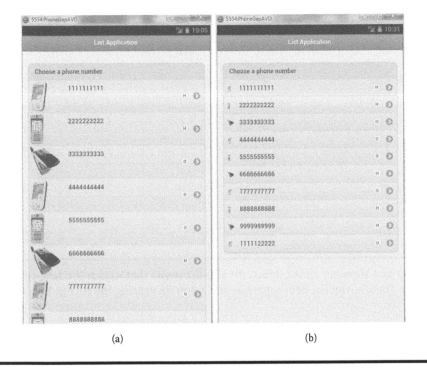

(a)                                      (b)

**Figure 6.9**    (a) List showing thumbnails. (b) List showing icons.

## Applying a Search Filter

A search filter is a very convenient tool for searching for items in a long list. To add a search filter to a list, we need to add the `data-filter = "true"` attribute to the `<ul>` element of the list, as shown in bold below:

```
<ul id = "phoneList" data-role = "listview" data-inset = "true" data-
theme = "e" data-filter = "true" >
   <li data-role = "divider">Choose a phone number</li>
   <li><a id = "1111111111" href = "#page2"> <img src = "images/cell1.
   png" class = "ui-li-icon"/> 1111111111 <span class = "ui-li-count"> H
   </span></a></li>
   <li><a id = "2222222222" href = "#page2"> <img src = "images/cell2.
   png" class = "ui-li-icon"/> 2222222222 <span class = "ui-li-count"> H
   </span></a></li>
   . . . . . . . . . . .
   . . . . . . . . . . .
</ul>
```

jQuery Mobile will automatically add a search field on top of the list that filters as we type. The search field contains a hint text, `Filter items`, as shown in Figure 6.10a. Because no text is yet entered in the search field, all the list items are displayed in the list. As we type text in the search field, the list items start getting filtered. Only the list items that match the text in the search field are displayed (see Figure 6.10b). As we type more text in the search field, the desired list item(s) separates out, as shown in Figure 6.10c.

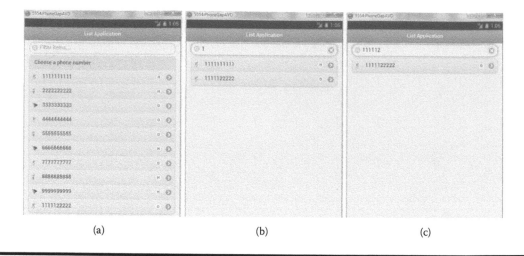

|(a)|(b)|(c)|

**Figure 6.10 (a) List showing all list items. (b) The list items that match the text entered in the search field. (c) The desired list item separates out upon increasing the text in the search field.**

## Creating Split Button Lists

For performing multiple actions per list item, the Split Button list is used. In the Split Button list, in addition to the main list item, there may be an icon or text at the end of each row. The main action is performed when the list item is clicked, and a secondary action is performed when the icon or text at the end of the row is clicked. Hence, two actions can be performed through each list item in the Split Button list.

To create a split button, a secondary link is nested inside the list item, and the jQuery framework will add a vertical line dividing the main list item and secondary link. The code given below defines a Split Button list:

```
<ul id = "phoneList" data-role = "listview" data-inset = "true" >
  <li data-role = "divider">Choose a phone number</li>
  <li><a id = "1111111111" href = "#page2"> 1111111111 </a><a href =
  "#page3">Details</a></li>
  .....................
  .....................
</ul>
```

In the code above, we see that a main list item, 11111111111, is defined along with a secondary link, Details. The main list item and secondary link will do their respective tasks. The main list item, 1111111111, when clicked, will navigate us to Page 2, whereas the secondary link, Details, when clicked, will navigate us to Page 3.

In addition to text, we can also define an icon for the secondary link. Upon defining an icon, the text of the secondary link will be replaced by the icon. To specify an icon, the data-split-icon attribute is added to the <ul> element, as shown in bold in the code given below:

```
<ul data-role = "listview" data-inset = "true" data-split-icon = "star">
```

The code above will represent a star icon as the secondary link and will perform a separate action than the main list item. To display the Split Button list, let us modify the `listdemo2.html` file in the `JQMIntroApp` application to appear as shown in Listing 6.9. The statements in bold are responsible for creating and executing the Split Button list.

**Listing 6.9   Code Written in the `listdemo2.html` File**

```html
<!DOCTYPE HTML>
<html>
    <head>
    <title>PhoneGap Application</title>
    <script type = "text/javascript" charset = "utf-8" src = "cordova-2.3.0.js">
    </script>
    <link href = "jquery.mobile-1.2.0/jquery.mobile-1.2.0.min.css" rel =
    "stylesheet" type = "text/css"/>
    <script src = "jquery-1.8.3.min.js" type = "text/javascript"></script>
    <script src = "jquery.mobile-1.2.0/jquery.mobile-1.2.0.min.js" type = "text/
    javascript"></script>
    <script type = "text/javascript">
        function onBodyLoad(){
            document.addEventListener("deviceready", PhonegapLoaded, false);
            }
            function PhonegapLoaded() {
            $('#phoneList').children().each(function(){
              var anchor = $(this).find('a');
              if(anchor){
                 anchor.click(function(){
            document.getElementById("selecteditem").innerHTML = "You have selected "
            +anchor.attr('id');
                 });
              }
            });
        }
    </script>
    </head>
    <body onload = "onBodyLoad()">
        <div data-role = "page" id = "home">
            <div data-role = "header" data-theme = "b">
                <h1>List Application</h1>
            </div>
            <div data-role = "content">
                <ul id = "phoneList" data-role = "listview" data-inset = "true" data-
                split-icon = "star" data-theme = "e" data-filter = "true" >
                    <li data-role = "divider">Choose a phone number</li>
                    <li><a id = "1111111111" href = "#page2"> <img src = "images/cell1.
                    png" class = "ui-li-icon"/> 1111111111 <span class = "ui-li-count">
                    H </span></a><a href = "#page3">Details</a></li>
                    <li><a id = "2222222222" href = "#page2"> <img src = "images/cell2.
                    png" class = "ui-li-icon"/> 2222222222 <span class = "ui-li-count">
                    H </span></a><a href = "#page3">Details</a></li>
                    <li><a id = "3333333333" href = "#page2"> <img src = "images/cell3.
                    png" class = "ui-li-icon"/> 3333333333 <span class = "ui-li-count">
                    O </span></a><a href = "#page3">Details</a></li>
                    <li><a id = "4444444444" href = "#page2"> <img src = "images/cell1.
                    png" class = "ui-li-icon"/> 4444444444 <span class = "ui-li-count">
                    O </span></a><a href = "#page3">Details</a></li>
```

```
        <li><a id = "5555555555" href = "#page2"> <img src = "images/cell2.
        png" class = "ui-li-icon"/> 5555555555 <span class = "ui-li-count">
        O </span></a><a href = "#page3">Details</a></li>
        <li><a id = "6666666666" href = "#page2"> <img src = "images/cell3.
        png" class = "ui-li-icon"/> 6666666666 <span class = "ui-li-count">
        H </span></a><a href = "#page3">Details</a></li>
        <li><a id = "7777777777" href = "#page2"> <img src = "images/cell1.
        png" class = "ui-li-icon"/> 7777777777 <span class = "ui-li-count">
        O </span></a><a href = "#page3">Details</a></li>
        <li><a id = "8888888888" href = "#page2"> <img src = "images/cell2.
        png" class = "ui-li-icon"/> 8888888888 <span class = "ui-li-count">
        H </span></a><a href = "#page3">Details</a></li>
        <li><a id = "9999999999" href = "#page2"> <img src = "images/cell3.
        png" class = "ui-li-icon"/> 9999999999 <span class = "ui-li-count">
        H </span></a><a href = "#page3">Details</a></li>
        <li><a id = "1111122222" href = "#page2"> <img src = "images/cell1.
        png" class = "ui-li-icon"/> 1111122222 <span class = "ui-li-count">
        O </span></a><a href = "#page3">Details</a></li>
      </ul>
    </div>
  </div>
<!—Page 2—>
    <div data-role = "page" id = "page2" data-add-back-btn = "true">
      <div data-role = "header" data-theme = "b">
        <h1>Page 2 </h1>
      </div>
      <div data-role = "content">
        <div id = "selecteditem"></div>
      </div>
    </div>
<!—Page 3—>
    <div data-role = "page" id = "page3" data-add-back-btn = "true">
      <div data-role = "header" data-theme = "b">
        <h1>Page 3 </h1>
      </div>
      <div data-role = "content">
        <p> Welcome to Page 3 </p>
      </div>
    </div>
  </body>
</html>
```

We can see that the secondary link is represented by a star icon. Also, the secondary link, that is, the star, when clicked, will navigate us to Page 3 of the application. The main list item, when clicked, will navigate to Page 2 to display the clicked list item.

Upon running the application, we get a Split Button list where the main list items show the phone numbers and the secondary links are represented by star icons (see Figure 6.11a). The main list item, when clicked, will navigate us to Page 2, which displays the list item that is clicked (see Figure 6.11b). All secondary link icons are set to navigate to Page 3; hence, upon clicking any of the secondary icons (see Figure 6.11c), we will be navigated to Page 3, as shown in Figure 6.11d.

## Creating Dialogs

Dialogs, as we know, play a major role in displaying important messages, getting data from the user, and seeking confirmation before taking certain action. To open a dialog, we need to add the

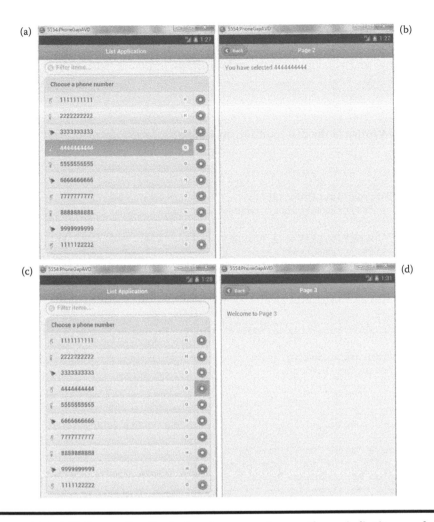

**Figure 6.11** (a) A Split Button list displaying phone numbers as the main list item and star icons as the secondary link. (b) `Page 2` displaying the clicked list item. (c) The secondary link icon being clicked. (d) `Page 3` opens upon clicking the secondary link icon.

`data-rel = "dialog"` attribute to the anchor, that is, `<a>` element. The statement below shows a link that, when clicked, will open a dialog:

```
<a href = "#dialog" data-rel = "dialog">Open dialog</a>
```

We can also optionally add the `data-transition` attribute to the hyperlink for applying an animation effect. For example, the following link, when clicked, will open a dialog with an animation effect:

```
<a href = "#dialog1" data-rel = "dialog" data-transition = "pop">Open
Dialog </a>
```

Let us create an application that displays dialogs. The application will display a button in the header of the home page that, when clicked, will open a dialog. So, launch Eclipse and open our

Android project called JQMIntroApp. Add an HTML file called dialogdemo.html to the assets/www folder. As stated earlier, the application comprises a home page and a dialog. To define the home page and a dialog, write the code as shown in Listing 6.10 in the dialogdemo. html file.

**Listing 6.10   Code Written in the dialogdemo.html File**

```html
<!DOCTYPE HTML>
<html>
   <head>
   <title>PhoneGap Application</title>
   <script type = "text/javascript" charset = "utf-8" src = "cordova-2.3.0.js">
   </script>
   <link href = "jquery.mobile-1.2.0/jquery.mobile-1.2.0.min.css" rel =
   "stylesheet" type = "text/css"/>
   <script src = "jquery-1.8.3.min.js" type = "text/javascript"></script>
   <script src = "jquery.mobile-1.2.0/jquery.mobile-1.2.0.min.js" type = "text/
   javascript"></script>
   <script type = "text/javascript">
      function onBodyLoad(){
         document.addEventListener("deviceready", PhonegapLoaded, false);
      }
      function PhonegapLoaded(){
         alert("PhoneGap loaded");
      }
   </script>
   </head>
   <body onload = "onBodyLoad()">
<!—Home Page—>
   <div data-role = "page" id = "home">
      <div data-role = "header" data-theme = "b">
         <h1>Dialog Application</h1>
         <a href = "#dialog" data-rel = "dialog">Open dialog</a>
      </div>
      <div data-role = "content">
         <p>Body of the Home Page </p>
      </div>
   </div>
<!—Dialog Box—>
   <div data-role = "dialog" id = "dialog" >
      <div data-role = "header" data-theme = "b">
         <h1>Dialog Box </h1>
      </div>
      <div data-role = "content">
         <p>Body of the Dialog </p>
      </div>
   </div>
</body>
</html>
```

In the code above, we can see that a home page and a dialog are defined. The home page shows the text, Dialog Application, in its header. The header also contains a button with the caption Open dialog, which will be used for opening the dialog. The content of the home page displays the text, Body of the Home Page. The dialog page displays the text, Dialog Box, in its header. The content of the dialog displays the text, Body of the Dialog.

(a)                                                    (b)

**Figure 6.12   (a) Home page showing a header with the button** `Open dialog`**. (b) The dialog opens up displaying the text,** `Body of the Dialog`**.**

To load the `dialogdemo.html` file, open the Java activity file, `JQMIntroAppActivity.java`, and modify the `loadUrl()` method as shown below:

```
super.loadUrl("file:///android_asset/www/dialogdemo.html");
```

Upon running the application, we see that the home page shows a heading, `Dialog Application`, along with the button `Open dialog` (see Figure 6.12a). Upon clicking the `Open dialog` button, the dialog box opens up as shown in Figure 6.12b. The dialog box shows the text, `Body of the Dialog`, and a cross icon at the top left corner for closing the dialog.

The dialog above is very simple and can be used for displaying alert messages. But, it cannot be used for getting feedback from the user. Let us modify our application to create a dialog that asks the user for confirmation. The dialog will ask the user whether he or she wants to delete the file. Two buttons, `Yes` and `Cancel`, will also be displayed. Respective action will take place when the user clicks the `Yes` or `Cancel` button. For converting our simple dialog to a dialog that prompts for confirmation, modify the `dialogdemo.html` file to appear as shown in Listing 6.11. Only the code in bold is new; the rest is the same as we saw in Listing 6.10.

**Listing 6.11   Code Written in the** `dialogdemo.html` **File**

```
<!DOCTYPE HTML>
<html>
  <head>
  <title>PhoneGap Application</title>
  <script type = "text/javascript" charset = "utf-8" src = "cordova-2.3.0.js">
  </script>
  <link href = "jquery.mobile-1.2.0/jquery.mobile-1.2.0.min.css" rel =
  "stylesheet" type = "text/css"/>
  <script src = "jquery-1.8.3.min.js" type = "text/javascript"></script>
  <script src = "jquery.mobile-1.2.0/jquery.mobile-1.2.0.min.js" type = "text/
  javascript"></script>
  <script type = "text/javascript">
    function onBodyLoad(){
      document.addEventListener("deviceready", PhonegapLoaded, false);
    }
    function PhonegapLoaded(){
      document.getElementById("yes").addEventListener("click", yesMessage);
      document.getElementById("cancel").addEventListener("click", cancelMessage);
  }
    function yesMessage(){
```

```
        document.getElementById("response").innerHTML = "Yes! Go ahead and delete
        the file";
    }
    function cancelMessage(){
        document.getElementById("response").innerHTML = "Cancel the command";
    }
    </script>
    </head>
    <body onload = "onBodyLoad()">
        <!--Home Page-->
        <div data-role = "page" id = "home">
            <div data-role = "header" data-theme = "b">
                <h1>Dialog Application</h1>
                <a href = "#dialog" data-rel = "dialog">Open dialog</a>
            </div>
            <div data-role = "content">
                <p>Body of the Home Page </p>
                <div id = "response"></div>
            </div>
        </div>
<!--Dialog Box-->
        <div data-role = "page" id = "dialog" >
            <div data-role = "header" data-theme = "b">
                <h1>Dialog Box </h1>
            </div>
            <div data-role = "content">
                <p>Want to delete this file. Are you sure ? </p>
                <a href = "#home" data-role = "button" data-rel = "back" id = "yes"
                >Yes</a>
                <a href = "#home" data-role = "button" data-rel = "back" id =
                "cancel">Cancel</a>
            </div>
        </div>
    </body>
</html>
```

We can see that two buttons with the captions Yes and Cancel are added to the dialog. Both the buttons are set to navigate to the home page. The click event listeners are linked with the Yes and Cancel buttons so that the desired action can be initiated when the click event occurs on either of the buttons. Functions called yesMessage() and cancelMessage() will be called respectively when the Yes and Cancel buttons are clicked in the dialog. The yesMessage() function displays a message, Yes! Go ahead and delete the file, in the home page to confirm that the Yes button in the dialog is clicked. Similarly, the cancelMessage() function displays a message, Cancel the command, to inform us that the Cancel button in the dialog is clicked. The messages in the home page are displayed through the <div> element with the ID response.

Upon running the application, we get a home page on start-up. The home page displays a button, Open dialog, in its header (see Figure 6.13a). Upon clicking the Open dialog button, the dialog opens up. The dialog displays a message, Want to delete this file. Are you sure? Two buttons, Yes and Cancel, are also displayed in the dialog (see Figure 6.13b). Upon clicking the Yes button in the dialog, we will be navigated to the home page that displays a message, Yes! Go ahead and delete the file (see Figure 6.13c). When the Cancel button in the dialog is clicked, the home page will be displayed showing the message Cancel the command (see Figure 6.13d).

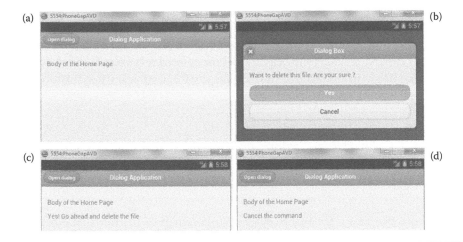

**Figure 6.13** (a) `Home` page showing a header with the button `Open dialog`. (b) The dialog opens up asking for confirmation. (c) `Home` page indicating that the `Yes` button is clicked from the dialog. (d) `Home` page informing that the `Cancel` button is clicked in the dialog.

## Creating Forms in jQuery Mobile

Where dialogs are usually used for getting limited data from the user, forms are used for getting large amounts of information from the user. The information entered in the forms can be submitted to the server too. A form can make the data entry task quite convenient for the user by using different types of controls. In addition to displaying a one line input field, a form can display a multiline text area, drop-down lists, date and time pickers, checkboxes, radio buttons, and much more.

Every form field in jQuery Mobile is wrapped within the following tag:

```
<div data-role = "fieldcontain">
</div>
```

### Input Field

The input field is used for entering single-line data. The statements given below display an input text field for entering an e-mail address:

```
<div data-role = "fieldcontain">
    <label for = "email">Email: </label>
    <input type = "text" name = "email" id = "email" value = ""/>
</div>
```

We can see that the input text field has a label associated with it. That is, the label is grouped with the associated input field. The tag `<div>` with the `data-role = "fieldcontain"` attribute helps in aligning the label and the form field. jQuery Mobile automatically resizes the form fields per the available screen size.

## *TextArea*

While working with the textarea, if we do not define the rows and columns limit, the textarea will automatically expand in width and height when the entered text exceeds the available size. To limit the width and height of the textarea and to make scroll bars appear when the text exceeds the available size, the following statements are used:

```
<div data-role = "fieldcontain">
   <label for = "custommsg">Custom Message</label>
   <textarea cols = "40" rows = "3" name = "custommsg" id = "custommsg">
   </textarea>
</div>
```

The code above provides a textarea to enter custom remarks. The initial size of the textarea will be 3 rows and 40 columns. If the entered text exceeds the defined size, the scroll bars will appear automatically.

## *Checkboxes and Radio Buttons*

Both checkboxes and radio buttons are used for displaying different options. The difference between radio buttons and checkboxes is that radio buttons enable single selection, whereas checkboxes enable multiple selections. That is, only a single option can be selected from a set of radio buttons, whereas more than one option can be selected from a set of checkboxes. For displaying options through radio buttons and checkboxes, the `fieldset` tag is required:

```
<fieldset data-role = "controlgroup">
```

This `fieldset` tag is used to group together different controls, including radio buttons or checkboxes. For example, the following code will create four radio buttons by the name `periodtosend`. The radio buttons will provide the following four options to select from: `Daily`, `Monthly`, `Yearly`, and `Specified date & time`.

```
<div data-role = "fieldcontain">
   <fieldset data-role = "controlgroup">
      <legend>Send</legend>
      <input type = "radio" name = "periodtosend" id = "daily" value =
      "Daily">
      <label for = "daily">Daily</label>
      <input type = "radio" name = "periodtosend" id = "monthly" value =
      "Monthly">
      <label for = "monthly">Monthly</label>
      <input type = "radio" name = "periodtosend" id = "yearly" value =
      "Yearly">
      <label for = "yearly">Yearly</label>
      <input type = "radio" name = "periodtosend" id = "specific" value =
      "Specified date & time" checked = "checked">
      <label for = "specific">Specific</label>
   </fieldset>
</div>
```

Each of the four radio buttons has its own individual value and label. In addition to having separate labels, the radio buttons in the code above have a common label, Send. The common label is assigned in radio buttons and checkboxes through the legend tag. By default, the radio buttons and checkboxes are organized vertically, that is, one below the other. To make the checkboxes or radio button appear horizontally, the horizontal value is assigned to the data-type attribute in the fieldset tag. The following statement will make the checkboxes or radio buttons appear horizontally:

```
<fieldset data-role = "controlgroup" data-type = "horizontal">
```

## Drop-Down Lists

To show the drop-down list, the <select> tag is used. The following code shows a drop-down list containing a couple of templates enabling the user to select one of them.

```
<div data-role = "fieldcontain">
   <label for = "template">Select Template</label>
   <select name = "template" id = "template">
      <option value = "Many Happy Returns of the Day">Many Happy Returns
      of the Day</option>
      <option value = "All the Best for Exams">All the Best for Exams
      </option>
      <option value = "Wish you a very Happy Birthday">Wish you a very
      Happy Birthday</option>
      <option value = "Have a nice and safe journey">Have a nice and safe
      journey</option>
      <option value = "Tommorrow will be Holiday">Tommorrow will be
      Holiday</option>
   </select>
</div>
```

We can see that the templates, for example, Many Happy Returns of the Day, All the Best for Exams, and so on, are displayed in the form of a drop-down list. Also, a label, Select Template, is displayed for the drop-down list.

## Displaying Date and Time Pickers

In order to extend jQuery Mobile features or provide some new functionality, we can always add plug-ins. For example, jQuery Mobile does not include a date picker. To include a date picker in our applications, we use an extension to jQuery Mobile, the jQuery Mobile Datebox. The jQuery Mobile Datebox is a multimode date and time picker for jQueryMobile. Download jQuery Mobile Datebox from the following link, http://dev.jtsage.com/jQM-DateBox/.

To invoke a date picker in an application, we need to associate the data-role = "datebox" attribute to an input field. For example, the statement given below defines an input box with an icon on the right. Upon clicking the icon, a date picker will be invoked enabling the user to choose the desired date. The chosen date will then be assigned to the associated input field.

```
<div data-role = "fieldcontain">
   <label for = "date">Select Date:</label>
```

```
<input name = "date" id = "date" type = "date" data-role = "datebox"
data-options = '{"mode": "calbox", "overrideDateFormat":"%m/%d/%Y"}'/>
</div>
```

Let us create an application that displays a form containing all the controls that we discussed above. The application will display an SMS Sending Form that asks the user to choose a contact to whom the SMS has to be sent. The form will also display a list of templates enabling the user to choose one of them. The template drop-down list displays some very commonly used SMSs, like Many Happy Returns of the Day, All the Best for Exams, Wish you a very Happy Birthday, and so on. In addition to selecting a built-in template, the user can also write a custom message. The form also displays a date picker and time picker to specify the date and time for sending the SMS. The form displays certain radio buttons that help the user to determine if the SMS has to be sent to the chosen contact daily, monthly, yearly, or only on the specified date and time. The data entered along with different options selected in the form will be displayed at the bottom of the form upon clicking the Submit button.

Launch Eclipse and open our Android project called JQMIntroApp. Add an HTML file called formdemo.html to the assets/www folder. To define a form comprising input text field, textarea, drop-down lists, date picker, time picker, and radio buttons, write the code as shown in Listing 6.12 in the formdemo.html file.

**Listing 6.12  Code Written in the `formdemo.html` File**

```
<!DOCTYPE HTML>
<html>
    <head>
    <title>PhoneGap Application</title>
    <script type = "text/javascript" charset = "utf-8" src = "cordova-2.3.0.js">
    </script>
    <link href = "jquery.mobile-1.2.0/jquery.mobile-1.2.0.min.css" rel =
    "stylesheet" type = "text/css"/>
    <script src = "jquery-1.8.3.min.js" type = "text/javascript"></script>
    <script src = "jquery.mobile-1.2.0/jquery.mobile-1.2.0.min.js" type = "text/
    javascript"></script>
    <script src = "jqm-datebox-1.1.0.core.js" type = "text/javascript"></script>
    <script src = "jqm-datebox-1.1.0.mode.calbox.js" type = "text/javascript">
    </script>
    <script src = "jqm-datebox-1.1.0.mode.datebox.js" type = "text/javascript">
    </script>
    <link href = "jqm-datebox-1.1.0.css" rel = "stylesheet" type = "text/css"/>
    <script type = "text/javascript">
        function onBodyLoad(){
            document.addEventListener("deviceready", PhonegapLoaded, false);
        }
        function PhonegapLoaded(){
            document.getElementById("submit").addEventListener("click", dispData);
        }
        function dispData(){
            var datainfo = '';
            datainfo = 'Information entered is '+
            document.getElementById("contactname").value +', '+
            document.getElementById("email").value +', '+
            document.getElementById("template").value +', '+
            document.getElementById("custommsg").value +', '+
            document.getElementById("date").value +', '+
```

```
            document.getElementById("time").value;
            datainfo+ = ', '+ $('input[name = periodtosend]:checked').val();
            document.getElementById("response").innerHTML = datainfo;
    }
</script>
</head>
<body onload = "onBodyLoad()">
    <div data-role = "page" id = "home">
    <div data-role = "header" data-theme = "b">
        <h1>SMS Sending Form</h1>
    </div>
    <div data-role = "content">
        <form>
            <div data-role = "fieldcontain">
                <label for = "contact">Contact: </label>
                <select name = "contactname" id = "contactname">
                <option value = "Bintu Harwani">Bintu Harwani</option>
                <option value = "Chirag">Chirag</option>
                <option value = "Kelly Martinez">Kelly Martinez</option>
                <option value = "Laura">Laura</option>
                <option value = "David">David</option>
                </select>
            </div>
            <div data-role = "fieldcontain">
                <label for = "email">Email: </label>
                <input type = "text" name = "email" id = "email" value = ""/>
            </div>
            <div data-role = "fieldcontain">
                <label for = "template">Select Template</label>
                <select name = "template" id = "template">
                    <option value = "Many Happy Returns of the Day">Many Happy Returns
                    of the Day</option>
                    <option value = "All the Best for Exams">All the Best for Exams
                    </option>
                    <option value = "Wish you a very Happy Birthday">Wish you a very
                    Happy Birthday</option>
                    <option value = "Have a nice and safe journey">Have a nice and safe
                    journey</option>
                    <option value = "Tommorrow will be Holiday">Tommorrow will be
                    Holiday</option>
                </select>
            </div>
            <div data-role = "fieldcontain">
                <label for = "custommsg">Custom Message</label>
                <textarea cols = "40" rows = "8" name = "custommsg" id = "custommsg">
                </textarea>
            </div>
            <div data-role = "fieldcontain">
                <label for = "date">Select Date:</label>
                <input name = "date" id = "date" type = "date" data-role = "datebox"
                data-options = '{"mode": "calbox", "overrideDateFormat":"%m/%d/%Y"}'/>
                </div>
                <div data-role = "fieldcontain">
                    <label for = "time">Select Time:</label>
                    <input name = "time" id = "time" type = "date" data-role =
                    "datebox" data-options = '{"mode": "timebox"}'/>
                </div>
                <div data-role = "fieldcontain">
                    <fieldset data-role = "controlgroup">
                        <legend>Send</legend>
```

```
                <input type = "radio" name = "periodtosend" id = "daily" value =
                "Daily">
                <label for = "daily">Daily</label>
                <input type = "radio" name = "periodtosend" id = "monthly" value
                = "Monthly">
                <label for = "monthly">Monthly</label>
                <input type = "radio" name = "periodtosend" id = "yearly" value
                = "Yearly">
                <label for = "yearly">Yearly</label>
                <input type = "radio" name = "periodtosend" id = "specific"
                value = "Specified date & time" checked = "checked">
                <label for = "specific">Specific</label>
            </fieldset>
        </div>
        <div data-role = "fieldcontain">
        <input type = "button" id = "submit" name = "submit" value = "Submit"/>
            </div>
        </form>
        <div id = "response"></div>
        </div>
      </div>
    </div>
  </body>
</html>
```

To load the `formdemo.html` file, open the Java activity file, `JQMIntroAppActivity.java`, and modify the `loadUrl()` method as shown below:

```
super.loadUrl("file:///android_asset/www/formdemo.html");
```

Upon running the application, we see that a blank form appears on start-up (see Figure 6.14a). Select the contact to whom the SMS has to be sent from the drop-down list, enter the e-mail address of the receiver, select a template from the drop-down list, and enter the custom message, if required. We assume that the SMS will be automatically sent on the scheduled date and time. To specify the date of sending the SMS, we make use of the date picker. The date picker will be invoked upon selecting an icon that appears on the right side in the `Select Date` input field (see Figure 6.14b). To specify the time of sending the SMS, we will use the time picker. The time picker opens up (see Figure 6.14c) upon clicking the icon in the `Select Time:` input box. Select the radio box that determines whether we want to send the SMS repetitively. For example, we can choose a radio button to send the SMS to the chosen contact name daily, monthly, yearly, or only on the specified date and time. Upon clicking the `Submit` button, all the information entered in the form will be displayed at the bottom of the form, as shown in Figure 6.14d.

## *On/Off Switches*

To display the on/off switch or two options from where the user can select either of them, jQuery Mobile wraps HTML `<select>` to make it appear as an on/off switch. For example, the following code displays two options, `Male` and `Female`, as an on/off switch. The user can choose either of the options to specify gender:

```
<div data-role = "fieldcontain">
   <label for = "gender">Gender:</label>
```

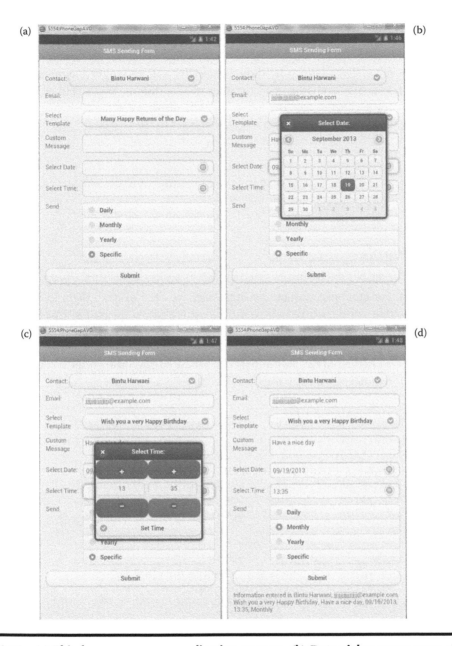

**Figure 6.14    (a) This form appears on application start-up. (b) Date picker opens upon clicking the icon in the** Select Date: **input box. (c) Time picker opens upon clicking the icon in the** Select Time: **input box. (d) Data entered in the form is displayed below the form.**

```
<select name = "gender" id = "gender" data-role = "slider">
    <option value = "Male">Male</option>
    <option value = "Female">Female</option>
</select>
</div>
```

## Sliders

To make the user enter a value from within the given range of values, jQuery Mobile wraps an input field with a slider. The value set by sliding the slider will be assigned automatically to the input field. That is, the user can either directly enter a value into the input field or use the slider to specify a value in the given range. The following code displays a slider for the age of a person between the range of 0 and 100. The default age value is set to 10.

```
<div data-role = "fieldcontain">
   <label for = "age">Age:</label>
   <input type = "range" name = "age" id = "age" value = "10" min = "0"
   max = "100" data-highlight = "true"/>
</div>
```

## Grouping Controls

jQuery Mobile also allows us to vertically or horizontally group together different controls, including `select` tags. For grouping multiple `select` tags, we need to wrap them in a `fieldset` using the `data-role` of the `controlgroup`. We can also use the `data-type` attribute in the `fieldset` tag to align the group horizontally or vertically. The `horizontal` value, when assigned to the `data-type` attribute, will align the grouped controls horizontally. Similarly, the `vertical` value is assigned to the `data-type` attribute to align the group vertically. The following code aligns a group of `select` tags horizontally:

```
<div data-role = "fieldcontain">
   <fieldset data-role = "controlgroup" data-type = "horizontal">
      <legend>Preference</legend>
      <label for = "type">Room Type</label>
      <select name = "type" id = "type">
         <option value = "Ordinary">Ordinary Room</option>
         <option value = "Luxury Room">Luxury Room</option>
         <option value = "Suite">Suite</option>
      </select>
      <label for = "food">Food</label>
      <select name = "food" id = "food">
         <option value = "Breakfast">Breakfast</option>
         <option value = "Lunch">Lunch</option>
         <option value = "Dinner">Dinner</option>
      </select>
      <label for = "meal">Meal</label>
      <select name = "meal" id = "meal">
         <option value = "Vegetarian">Vegetarian</option>
         <option value = "Non Vegetarian">Non Vegetarian</option>
      </select>
   </fieldset>
</div>
```

We can see three `select` tags with the names, `type`, `food`, and `meal`, which are aligned horizontally, where the `type` select tag displays options for room types. The `food` select tag displays three food options, `Breakfast`, `Lunch`, and `Dinner`. The `meal` select tag shows two meal options, `Vegetarian` and `Non Vegetarian`.

Let us create an application that helps us learn how to use checkboxes, sliders, and on/off switches, combine select fields in a group, and so on, in a form. The application will display a `Hotel Room Reservation` form that asks a user to enter his or her name, specify his or her gender and age, and choose the desired room type, type of meal, that is, vegetarian or nonvegetarian, and so on. The information supplied in the form will be displayed at the bottom of the form upon clicking the `Submit` button.

Launch Eclipse and open our Android project called `JQMIntroApp`. Add an HTML file called `formdemo2.html` to the `assets/www` folder. To define a form comprising the search field, slider, on/off switch, checkboxes, and select fields, write the code as shown in Listing 6.13 in the `formdemo2.html` file.

**Listing 6.13   Code Written in the `formdemo2.html` File**

```html
<!DOCTYPE HTML>
<html>
   <head>
   <title>PhoneGap Application</title>
   <script type = "text/javascript" charset = "utf-8" src = "cordova-2.3.0.js">
   </script>
   <link href = "jquery.mobile-1.2.0/jquery.mobile-1.2.0.min.css" rel =
   "stylesheet" type = "text/css"/>
   <script src = "jquery-1.8.3.min.js" type = "text/javascript"></script>
   <script src = "jquery.mobile-1.2.0/jquery.mobile-1.2.0.min.js" type = "text/
   javascript"></script>
   <script type = "text/javascript">
       function onBodyLoad(){
           document.addEventListener("deviceready", PhonegapLoaded, false);
       }
       function PhonegapLoaded(){
           document.getElementById("submit").addEventListener("click", dispData);
       }
       function dispData(){
           var datainfo = '';
           datainfo = 'Information entered is '+ document.getElementById("search").
           value +', '+ document.getElementById("name").value +', '+ document.
           getElementById("gender").value +', '+ document.getElementById("age").value;
           if(document.getElementById('photography').checked) {
               datainfo+ = ', '+ document.getElementById("photography").value;
           }
           if(document.getElementById('writing').checked) {
               datainfo+ = ', '+ document.getElementById("writing").value;
           }
           if(document.getElementById('swimming').checked) {
               datainfo+ = ', '+ document.getElementById("swimming").value;
           }
               datainfo+ = ', '+ document.getElementById("type").value;
               datainfo+ = ', '+ document.getElementById("food").value;
               datainfo+ = ', '+ document.getElementById("meal").value;
               document.getElementById("response").innerHTML = datainfo;
       }
   </script>
   </head>
   <body onload = "onBodyLoad()">
       <div data-role = "page" id = "home">
           <div data-role = "header" data-theme = "b">
             <h1>Hotel Room Reservation</h1>
           </div>
```

```
<div data-role = "content">
<form>
   <div data-role = "fieldcontain">
      <label for = "search">Search:</label>
      <input type = "search" name = "search" id = "search" value = ""/>
   </div>
   <div data-role = "fieldcontain">
      <label for = "name">Name:</label>
      <input type = "text" name = "name" id = "name" value = ""/>
   </div>
   <div data-role = "fieldcontain">
      <label for = "gender">Gender:</label>
      <select name = "gender" id = "gender" data-role = "slider">
         <option value = "Male">Male</option>
         <option value = "Female">Female</option>
      </select>
   </div>
   <div data-role = "fieldcontain">
      <label for = "age">Age:</label>
      <input type = "range" name = "age" id = "age" value = "10" min = "0"
      max = "100" data-highlight = "true"/>
   </div>
   <div data-role = "fieldcontain">
      <fieldset data-role = "controlgroup">
         <legend>Hobbies:</legend>
         <input type = "checkbox" name = "photography" id = "photography"
         value = "Photography">
         <label for = "photography">Photography</label>
         <input type = "checkbox" name = "writing" id = "writing" value =
         "Writing">
         <label for = "writing">Writing</label>
         <input type = "checkbox" name = "swimming" id = "swimming" value =
         "Swimming">
         <label for = "swimming">Swimming</label>
      </fieldset>
   </div>
   <div data-role = "fieldcontain">
      <fieldset data-role = "controlgroup" data-type = "horizontal">
         <legend>Preference</legend>
         <label for = "type">Room Type</label>
         <select name = "type" id = "type">
            <option value = "Ordinary">Ordinary Room</option>
            <option value = "Luxury Room">Luxury Room</option>
            <option value = "Suite">Suite</option>
         </select>
         <label for = "food">Food</label>
         <select name = "food" id = "food">
            <option value = "Breakfast">Breakfast</option>
            <option value = "Lunch">Lunch</option>
            <option value = "Dinner">Dinner</option>
         </select>
         <label for = "meal">Meal</label>
         <select name = "meal" id = "meal">
            <option value = "Vegetarian">Vegetarian</option>
            <option value = "Non Vegetarian">Non Vegetarian</option>
         </select>
      </fieldset>
   </div>
   <div data-role = "fieldcontain">
      <input type = "button" id = "submit" name = "submit" value = "Submit"/>
   </div>
```

```
      </form>
      <div id = "response"></div>
      </div>
   </body>
</html>
```

To load the `formdemo2.html` file, open the Java activity file, `JQMIntroAppActivity.java`, and modify the `loadUrl()` method as is shown below:

```
super.loadUrl("file:///android_asset/www/formdemo2.html");
```

Upon running the application, we see that a blank form appears on start-up (see Figure 6.15a). Enter the name of the guest, select the gender from the on/off switch, specify the age by using

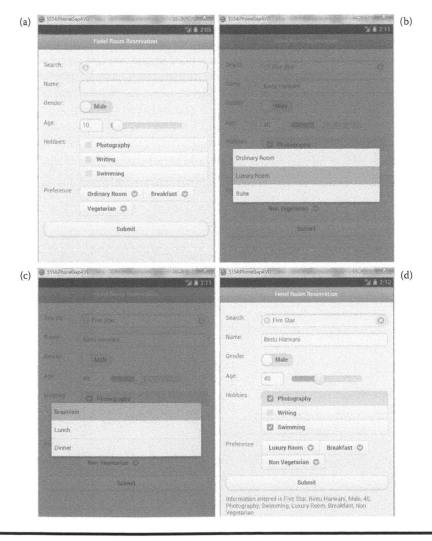

**Figure 6.15** **(a)** This form appears on application start-up. **(b)** Different available room types are displayed by the first select field. **(c)** The second select field defines the options to select a meal type. **(d)** The data entered in the form is displayed below the form.

the slider, and specify the hobbies by checking the desired checkboxes. Three select tags are combined in a `controlgroup` to define the guest's preferences. For example, the first `select` tag displays options to select the room type desired by the guest (see Figure 6.15b). The second `select` tag displays options, `Breakfast`, `Lunch`, and `Dinner`, to specify the meal type. The third `select` tag displays two options, `Vegetarian` and `Non  Vegetarian`, to define the kind of meal the guest prefers. After filling out the form, when the `Submit` button is clicked, all the information entered in the form will be displayed at the bottom of the form as shown in Figure 6.15d.

## Summary

In this chapter, we learned to use jQuery Mobile in mobile applications. We learned to apply themes and handle page navigations. We also learned how to create lists, create count bubbles, add list dividers, and create collapsible lists and numbered lists. Additionally, we learned to display thumbnails and icons in the lists and apply a search filter to the list. We learned to create Split Button lists and dialogs too. Finally, we learned to create forms in jQuery Mobile to fetch information from the users. We learned to display input fields, textarea, checkboxes, radio buttons, dropdown lists, date picker, time picker, and on/off switch and sliders in the forms.

Chapter 7 focuses on using Storage API. We will learn to create database tables. In addition, we will learn how to execute Structured Query Language (SQL) statements for fetching rows from the database tables, as well as how to delete, update, and insert data in the storage.

# *Chapter 7*

# Storing Data

In this chapter, we cover:

- Using Storage API
- Methods of the Storage API
- Creating a database
- Creating tables and inserting rows
- Listing rows
- Deleting rows
- Editing rows

## Using Storage API

Almost all mobile applications require information to be stored so that it can be accessed and reused in the future. PhoneGap provides the JavaScript library to implement storage capability in mobile devices. More precisely, the Storage API implements a simple database that can be used in mobile applications for maintaining information. We can use Structured Query Language (SQL) statements to add, edit, delete, and update information in the implemented database. The popular Storage API methods that are used in mobile applications for storing data are provided below.

## Methods of the Storage API

### *openDatabase*

The `openDatabase` method creates a new SQLite database and returns a `Database` object. The returned `Database` object is then used to store the data. The format for using the method is given below:

```
openDatabase(name, version, display_name, size);
```

where:

- name—Represents the name of the database.
- version—Represents the version of the database.
- display _ name—Represents the display name of the database.
- size—Represents the size of the database in bytes.

For example, the statement given below opens a database called greetings. The display name of the database is Greetings Database, its version is 1.0, and its size is 1000000 bytes:

```
var db = window.openDatabase("greetings", "1.0", "Greetings Database",
1000000);
```

If the database greetings does not exist, the openDatabase() method creates it and then opens it.

### *transaction*

The transaction method performs a database transaction to manipulate the database. The method contains callback methods that in turn execute SQL statements on the associated database. The transaction method's callback methods are called with an SQLTransaction object. For example, the transaction method given below contains three callback methods, insertRow, errorIns, and successIns:

```
db.transaction(insertRow, errorIns, successIns);
```

If the SQL statements used in the insertRow method are successfully executed, the successIns method will be called; otherwise, the errorIns method will be called.

### *executeSql*

The executeSql method is used to execute SQL statements on the associated database. For example, the executeSql method given below creates a table called Templates consisting of two columns, the id and Template:

```
function insertRow(tx) {
tx.executeSql('CREATE TABLE IF NOT EXISTS Templates (id INTEGER PRIMARY
KEY AUTOINCREMENT, Template TEXT NOT NULL)');
}
```

We can see that the id column is of the integer type. Similarly, the executeSql method given below accesses all the rows of the Templates table:

```
tx.executeSql('SELECT * FROM Templates',[], successQuery, errorQuery);
```

The executeSql method given above contains two callback methods, successQuery and errorQuery. The successQuery callback method will be called with an SQLResultSet object when the supplied SQL statement is executed successfully. For example, the callback method, `successQuery`, given below is called with the `SQLTransaction` and `SQLResultSet` objects:

```
function successQuery(tx,result){
```

The `SQLResultSet` object has the following three properties:

■ `insertId`—Represents the row ID of the row in which the SQL statement is inserted into the database. If the SQL statement is not an insert statement, then the `insertId` property is not set.
■ `rowAffected`—Represents the count of the rows that were changed by the SQL statement. If the statement did not affect any rows, then the value of this property is set to 0.
■ `rows`—Represents an `SQLResultSetRowList` that represents the rows returned by the SQL statement. If no rows are returned, then this object will be empty.

For example, the code given below shows how to display the three properties of the `SQLResultSet` object:

```
function execQuery(tx) {
    tx.executeSql('SELECT * FROM Templates',[], successQuery, errorQuery);
}
function successQuery(tx, results) {
    console.log("Insert ID = " + results.insertId);
    console.log("Rows Affected = " + results.rowAffected);
    console.log("Insert ID = " + results.rows.length);
}
```

## *SQLResultSetList*

We saw that the `rows` property of the `SQLResultSet` object is an `SQLResultSetRowList` that contains the rows returned from an SQL query. The `SQLResultSetList` object has a property called `length`. The `length` property represents the number of rows returned by the SQL query. The `SQLResultSetList` object also has a method called `item()` that returns the row at the specified index. The returned row is in the form of a JavaScript object. The properties of the JavaScript object represent the columns of the database. For example, the statement given below displays the value in the `Template` column of the first row:

```
result.rows.item(0).Template
```

## *SQLError*

`SQLError` is an object that is thrown when an error occurs while manipulating a database. It has the following two properties:

■ **Code**—Represents the error code. The error codes are in the form of constants. A few of them are shown below:
   − `SQLError.UNKNOWN _ ERR`
   − `SQLError.DATABASE _ ERR`

- SQLError.VERSION _ ERR
- SQLError.TOO _ LARGE _ ERR
- SQLError.QUOTA _ ERR
- SQLError.SYNTAX _ ERR
- SQLError.CONSTRAINT _ ERR
- SQLError.TIMEOUT _ ERR

■ **Message**—Represents a description of the error.

Let us use the above-mentioned methods for storing and managing information in mobile applications.

## Creating a Database

Let us understand the concept of the Storage API through a running example. We will create an application that stores templates that are usually used while sending a Short Message Service (SMS). Frequently used templates like Happy Birthday to you, Have a nice day, Many Happy returns of the day, and so on, will be stored in a database so that they can be fetched while sending an SMS. The first step of using the Storage API is to create a database. When the database is successfully created, information is stored in the table(s) that is created inside the database. So, let us go ahead and create a new Android project called PGApplication and configure it to use PhoneGap.

The application will create a database called greetings. A message will be displayed to inform us if the database is successfully created or some error occurred while creating it. The application will consist of a single page with a single <div> element. The <div> element will be used to display the response, that is, whether the database is successfully created or not. To define a page and create a database, the code as shown in Listing 7.1 is written in the index.html file.

**Listing 7.1  Code Written in the index.html File**

```
<!DOCTYPE HTML>
<html>
   <head>
   <title>PhoneGap Application</title>
   <script type = "text/javascript" charset = "utf-8" src = "cordova-2.3.0.js">
   </script>
   <link href = "jquery.mobile-1.2.0/jquery.mobile-1.2.0.min.css" rel =
   "stylesheet" type = "text/css"/>
   <script src = "jquery-1.8.3.min.js" type = "text/javascript"></script>
   <script src = "jquery.mobile-1.2.0/jquery.mobile-1.2.0.min.js" type = "text/
   javascript"></script>
   <script src = "template.js" type = "text/javascript"></script>
   </head>
   <body onload = "onBodyLoad()">
      <div data-role = "page" id = "home">
         <div data-role = "header" data-theme = "b" >
            <h1> PGApplication </h1>
         </div>
         <div data-role = "content">
            <div id = "homepageresult"></div>
         </div>
```

```
        </div>
    </body>
</html>
```

We can see that a home page is defined with a heading PGApplication. The heading will appear in a blue theme. The content of the page contains a <div> element of the ID homepageresult that will be used for displaying the response of creating the database. To keep things clean, we do not merge JavaScript code in the HTML file but store it in a separate file. So, create a file, template.js, and write the JavaScript code as shown in Listing 7.2 in it.

**Listing 7.2  Code Written in the template.js File**

```
function onBodyLoad(){
    document.addEventListener("deviceready", PhonegapLoaded, false);
}
function PhonegapLoaded(){
    var homepageresult = document.getElementById('homepageresult');
    try {
        var db = window.openDatabase("greetings", "1.0", "Greetings Database",
        1000000);
        homepageresult.innerHTML = "Database created and opened successfully ";
        } catch (e) {
        homepageresult.innerHTML = "Error occurred while creating the database";
    }
}
```

In the JavaScript code above we see that after ensuring that PhoneGap is loaded, a database called greetings is created that is 1 MB. The version and display name of the database are set to 1.0 and Greetings Database, respectively. If the method for creating the database, openDatabase(), executes successfully, a message, Database created and opened successfully, is displayed through the <div> element of the ID homepageresult that we defined in the home page. The same <div> element can also be used to display an error message. If some error occurs while creating the database, a message, Error occurred while creating the database, is displayed on the home page.

To load the index.html file, code as shown in Listing 7.3 is written in the Java activity file, PGApplicationActivity.java.

**Listing 7.3  Code Written in the Java Activity File: PGApplicationActivity.java**

```
package com.phonegap.pgapplication;
import android.os.Bundle;
import org.apache.cordova.DroidGap;
public class PGApplicationActivity extends DroidGap {
    @Override
    public void onCreate(Bundle savedInstanceState) {
        super.onCreate(savedInstanceState);
        super.loadUrl("file:///android_asset/www/index.html");
    }
}
```

Our application is ready to run. Upon running the application, if the database is created successfully, we get a message, Database created and opened successfully, as shown in Figure 7.1.

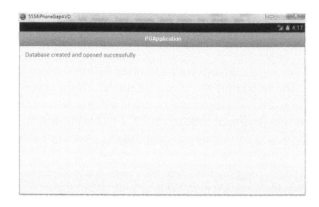

**Figure 7.1  The message `Database created and opened successfully` appears upon the successful creation of the database.**

The next task after the creation of a database is the creation of tables. In this application, we want to keep and manage information on templates. By templates we mean a string of texts that are commonly used while sending an SMS. For example, `All the Best for Exams`, `Happy Birthday to you`, `See you tomorrow`, and so on, are a couple of commonly used templates. To store templates, we need to create a `Templates` table.

Using the Storage API, we want to perform the following essential tasks:

- Add new row(s), that is, templates to the `Templates` table
- Access templates from the `Templates` table
- Edit or modify templates in the `Templates` table
- Delete template(s) from the `Templates` table

We will be creating a separate page dedicated to each of the mentioned tasks. We will be creating pages for adding templates, listing templates, editing templates, and deleting templates. All the pages will be accessed through link buttons. That is, we need a page that will display different link buttons to invoke the pages above. Let us call that page a `Templates` page.

It means, that in addition to a `home` page, we need to create a `Templates` page that will act as a menu for all the other pages. The footer of the `Templates` page will contain four buttons, `Add Template`, `List Templates`, `Delete Template`, and `Edit Template`. These four buttons, when clicked, will open the respective page to perform the desired task on the `Templates` table.

## Creating Tables and Inserting Rows

To the `index.html` file that we created earlier (refer to Listing 7.1), we need to add code to define the following two pages:

- `Templates` page—Page containing buttons to invoke other pages for performing adding, listing, deleting, and editing templates.

■ Add Template page—Page for adding a new template. In this page, we need to define two fields, an input text field and an Add button. The input text field will be used for entering a template, and the Add button will be used for initiating the task of inserting the template into the Templates table. In addition to the two fields, we also need a <div> element to display the result of inserting a row into the table, that is, whether the task of inserting a row in the Templates table was successful or not.

To define the Templates and Add Template pages, the code shown in Listing 7.4 is written in the index.html file. Only the code in bold is new; the rest is the same as we saw in Listing 7.1.

**Listing 7.4  Code Written in the `index.html` File**

```
<!DOCTYPE HTML>
<html>
    <head>
    <title>PhoneGap Application</title>
    <script type = "text/javascript" charset = "utf-8" src = "cordova-2.3.0.js">
    </script>
    <link href = "jquery.mobile-1.2.0/jquery.mobile-1.2.0.min.css" rel =
    "stylesheet" type = "text/css"/>
    <script src = "jquery-1.8.3.min.js" type = "text/javascript"></script>
    <script src = "jquery.mobile-1.2.0/jquery.mobile-1.2.0.min.js" type = "text/
    javascript"></script>
    <script src = "template.js" type = "text/javascript"></script>
    </head>
    <body onload = "onBodyLoad()">
    <!—Home Page—>
        <div data-role = "page" id = "home">
            <div data-role = "header" data-theme = "b" >
                <h1> PGApplication </h1>
            </div>
            <div data-role = "content">
                <div id = "homepageresult"></div>
            </div>
            <div data-role = "footer" class = "ui-bar" data-theme = "b" data-position
            = "fixed" >
                <a href = "#templates">Templates</a>
            </div>
        </div>
        <!—Templates Page—>
        <div data-role = "page" id = "templates" data-add-back-btn = "true" >
            <div data-role = "header" data-theme = "b">
                <h1> Templates </h1>
            </div>
            <div data-role = "content">
            </div>
            <div data-role = "footer" data-position = "fixed" data-theme = "b" >
                <a data-role = "button" href = "#addtemplates">Add Template</a>
                <a data-role = "button" href = "#listtemplates" onclick =
                "javascript:listTemplate();">List Templates</a>
                <a data-role = "button" href = "#deltemplates" onclick =
                "javascript:deleteTemplates();">Delete Template</a>
                <a data-role = "button" href = "#edittemplates" onclick =
                "javascript:editTemplate();">Edit Template</a>
            </div>
```

```
            </div>
            <!—Add Template Page—>
            <div data-role = "page" id = "addtemplates">
                <div data-role = "header" data-theme = "b">
                    <h1> Add Template </h1>
                    <a data-role = "button" href = "#templates">Back</a>
                    <a data-role = "button" href = "#home">Home</a>
                </div>
                <div data-role = "content">
                    Enter Template <input type = "text" id = "templatedata" onfocus =
                    'javascript:document.getElementById("addtemplateresult").innerHTML =
                    "";'>
                    <input type = "button" id = "addTemplateButton" value = "Add
                    template"/>
                    <div id = "addtemplateresult"></div>
                </div>
            </div>
        </body>
    </html>
```

We can see that the footer is added to the home page that contains a link button with the caption Templates. The link button, when clicked, will navigate us to the Templates page.

The Templates page shows the heading Templates. The page shows a Back button that can be clicked to go back to the home page or the previous page in the browsing history. The Templates page defines a footer containing four buttons, Add Template, List Templates, Delete Template, and Edit Template. These buttons will make us navigate to four different pages to perform the tasks of adding, listing, deleting, and editing templates in the Templates table. We will soon learn to create a Templates table. The main thing to observe here is that the List Templates, Delete Template, and Edit Template buttons, in addition to navigating to their respective pages, also execute the JavaScript functions, listTemplate(), deleteTemplates(), and editTemplate(), respectively. These methods are meant for filling the body or content of the respective pages with the data to be acted upon.

The code above also defines the Add Template page with the heading Add Template. The header of this page contains two buttons, Back and Home, to navigate us to the Templates and home pages, respectively. The content of the page defines an input text field, button, and <div> element. The input text field will provide a text box for entering information for the new template, the button will execute the code to save the new template into the Templates table, and the <div> element of the ID addtemplateresult will be used to display the result of executing the method for inserting row(s) into the Templates table, that is, whether the template is successfully added to the Templates table or not.

Upon running the application, the home page will appear on start-up. The home page confirms that the database greetings is created and opened successfully. The home page also displays a footer containing a Templates button (see Figure 7.2a). The Templates button, when clicked, will navigate us to the Templates page as shown in Figure 7.2b. The Templates page header contains a Back button for backward navigation. The page also contains a footer that shows four buttons, Add Template, List Templates, Delete Template, and Edit Template. The Add Template button, when clicked, will navigate us to the Add Template page as shown in Figure 7.2c. The Add Template page shows an input text field that can be used for entering the template that we want to add to the Templates table.

As this point, we have just defined the Add Template page and have not yet written JavaScript code to perform the task of inserting new row(s) into the Templates table. Let us do so now.

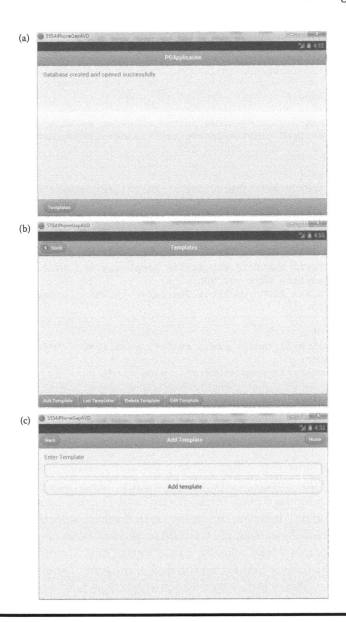

**Figure 7.2** (a) `Home` page showing the `Templates` button in its footer. (b) `Templates` page showing buttons in its header and footer. (c) `Add Template` page displaying a form for adding a new template.

The structure of the `Templates` table will comprise the following two columns:

■ Integer column, `id`—To be used for identifying the template.
■ Text column, `Template`—To be used for storing template content.

To add the template text entered by the user in the `Add Template` page into the `Templates` table, modify the `template.js` file to appear as shown in Listing 7.5. Only the code in bold is new; the rest is the same as we saw in Listing 7.2.

**Listing 7.5   Code Written in the `template.js` File**

```
function onBodyLoad(){
    document.addEventListener("deviceready", PhonegapLoaded, false);
}
function PhonegapLoaded(){
    var homepageresult = document.getElementById('homepageresult');
    homepageresult.innerHTML = "Welcome to our PhoneGap Build Application";
    document.getElementById("addTemplateButton").addEventListener("click",
    addTemplate);
}
function addTemplate(){
    var db = window.openDatabase("greetings", "1.0", "Greetings Database",
    1000000);
    db.transaction(tryAddingRow, errorAdding, rowAdded);
}
function tryAddingRow(tx) {
    var templateData = document.getElementById("templatedata").value;
    tx.executeSql('CREATE TABLE IF NOT EXISTS Templates (id INTEGER PRIMARY KEY
    AUTOINCREMENT, Template TEXT NOT NULL)');
    tx.executeSql('INSERT INTO Templates(Template) VALUES("'+ templateData + '")',
    rowAdded, errorAdding);
}
function rowAdded() {
    document.getElementById("addtemplateresult").innerHTML = "New Template
    successfully added";
    document.getElementById("templatedata").value = "";
}
function errorAdding(err) {
    document.getElementById("addtemplateresult").innerHTML = "Error occurred while
    adding template: " + err.code;
}
```

We can see that the home page is set to display a welcome message. The `click` event listener is associated with the Add Template button in the Add Template page, so that whenever the Add Template button is clicked, the `addTemplate` function is called.

In the `addTemplate()` function, the `greetings` database is opened. Once the `greetings` database is successfully opened, the `tryAddingRow()` function is called that creates a Templates table consisting of two columns, `id` and `Template`. The function also accesses the template text entered by the user in the input text field of the Add Template page and inserts it into the Templates table by calling the `executeSql()` method.

If the new row is successfully inserted into the Templates table, the `rowAdded()` function will be called to display a message, New Template successfully added, via the `<div>` element of ID `addtemplateresult`. If some error occurs while inserting the row, then the message Error occurred while adding template is displayed along with the error code on the screen.

Upon running the application, we get a home page with the Templates button in its footer. Upon clicking the Templates button, the Templates page will be invoked showing four buttons in its footer, Add Template, List Templates, Delete Template, and Edit Template. Upon clicking the Add Template button, the Add Template page opens. Let us add a template, Best of Luck for Exams, followed by clicking the Add template button (see Figure 7.3a). If the template is successfully added to the Templates table, the message New Template successfully added is displayed on the screen, as shown in Figure 7.3b.

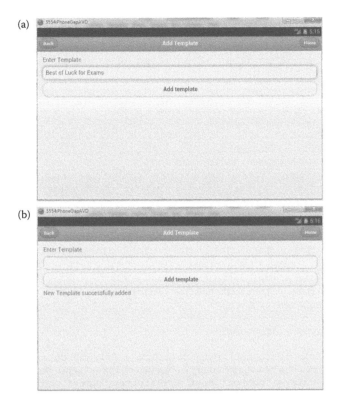

**Figure 7.3** **(a) Adding a new template through the Add Template page. (b) The message New Template successfully added is displayed upon the successful addition of the template.**

After learning the procedure of inserting rows in the Templates table, let us learn the procedure of retrieving the rows from the Templates table and displaying them on the screen.

## Listing Rows

We need to add a new page to the index.html file for displaying the rows that will be accessed from the Templates table. So, let us add a page with the heading List Templates to the index.html file. The code written in the index.html file is shown in Listing 7.6. Only the code in bold is newly added; the rest is the same as we saw in Listing 7.4.

**Listing 7.6 Code Written in the index.html File**

```
<!DOCTYPE HTML>
<html>
   <head>
   <title>PhoneGap Application</title>
   <script type = "text/javascript" charset = "utf-8" src = "cordova-2.3.0.js">
   </script>
   <link href = "jquery.mobile-1.2.0/jquery.mobile-1.2.0.min.css" rel =
   "stylesheet" type = "text/css"/>
   <script src = "jquery-1.8.3.min.js" type = "text/javascript"></script>
```

```
<script src = "jquery.mobile-1.2.0/jquery.mobile-1.2.0.min.js" type = "text/
javascript"></script>
<script src = "template.js" type = "text/javascript"></script>
</head>
<body onload = "onBodyLoad()">
<!—Home Page—>
   <div data-role = "page" id = "home">
      <div data-role = "header" data-theme = "b" >
         <h1> PGApplication </h1>
      </div>
      <div data-role = "content">
         <div id = "homepageresult"></div>
      </div>
      <div data-role = "footer" class = "ui-bar" data-theme = "b" data-position
      = "fixed" >
         <a href = "#templates">Templates</a>
      </div>
   </div>
<!—Templates Page—>
   <div data-role = "page" id = "templates">
      <div data-role = "header" data-theme = "b">
         <a data-role = "button" href = "##home">Home</a>
         <h1> Templates </h1>
      </div>
      <div data-role = "content">
      </div>
      <div data-role = "footer" data-position = "fixed" data-theme = "b" >
         <a data-role = "button" href = "#addtemplates">Add Template</a>
         <a data-role = "button" href = "#listtemplates" onclick = "javascript:
         listTemplate();">List Templates</a>
         <a data-role = "button" href = "#deltemplates" onclick = "javascript:
         deleteTemplates();">Delete Template</a>
         <a data-role = "button" href = "#edittemplates" onclick = "javascript:
         editTemplate();">Edit Template</a>
      </div>
   </div>
<!—Add Templates Page—>
   <div data-role = "page" id = "addtemplates">
      <div data-role = "header" data-theme = "b">
         <h1> Add Template </h1>
         <a data-role = "button" href = "#templates">Back</a>
         <a data-role = "button" href = "#home">Home</a>
      </div>
      <div data-role = "content">
         Enter Template <input type = "text" id = "templatedata" onfocus =
         'javascript:document.getElementById("addtemplateresult").innerHTML = "";'>
         <input type = "button" id = "addTemplateButton" value = "Add
         template"/>
         <div id = "addtemplateresult"></div>
      </div>
   </div>
<!—List Templates Page—>
   <div data-role = "page" id = "listtemplates">
      <div data-role = "header" data-theme = "b">
         <h1> List Templates </h1>
         <a data-role = "button" href = "#templates">Back</a>
         <a data-role = "button" href = "#home">Home</a>
      </div>
      <div data-role = "content">
         <div id = "listtemplateresult"></div>
      </div>
```

```
        </div>
    </body>
</html>
```

For showing the list of templates accessed from the Templates table, a page with the ID listtemplates is defined. The page is assigned to the heading List Templates. The link button, List Templates, in the Templates page, when clicked, will navigate us to the List Templates page. In addition to navigating to the Templates page, the List Templates button will also execute the JavaScript function listTemplate(). The list-Template() function will access the rows from the Templates table and display in the content of the List Templates page.

The List Template page's header also contains two buttons, Back and Home. The Back button is for navigating back to the Templates page, and the Home button is for navigating to the home page of the application. Recall, the Templates page acts as a menu and contains the link buttons for navigating to other pages of the application. The content of the page contains a <div> element of ID listtemplateresult that will be used for displaying the rows accessed from the Templates table. This <div> element can also be used for displaying errors if any occur while accessing rows from the Templates table.

To access information from the templates from the Templates table and display it on the screen, the code shown in Listing 7.7 is written in the template.js file. Only the code in bold is newly added; the rest is the same as we saw in Listing 7.5.

**Listing 7.7   Code Written in the `template.js` File**

```
function onBodyLoad(){
    document.addEventListener("deviceready", PhonegapLoaded, false);
}
function PhonegapLoaded(){
    var homepageresult = document.getElementById('homepageresult');
    homepageresult.innerHTML = "Welcome to our PhoneGap Build Application";
    document.getElementById("addTemplateButton").addEventListener("click",
    addTemplate);
}
function addTemplate(){
    var db = window.openDatabase("greetings", "1.0", "Greetings Database",
    1000000);
    db.transaction(tryAddingRow, errorAdding, rowAdded);
}
function tryAddingRow(tx) {
    var templateData = document.getElementById("templatedata").value;
    tx.executeSql('CREATE TABLE IF NOT EXISTS Templates (id INTEGER PRIMARY KEY
    AUTOINCREMENT, Template TEXT NOT NULL)');
    tx.executeSql('INSERT INTO Templates(Template) VALUES("'+ templateData + '")',
    rowAdded, errorAdding);
}
function rowAdded() {
    document.getElementById("addtemplateresult").innerHTML = "New Template
    successfully added";
    document.getElementById("templatedata").value = "";
}
function errorAdding(err) {
    document.getElementById("addtemplateresult").innerHTML = "Error occurred while
    adding template: " + err.code;
}
```

```
function listTemplate(){
   var db = window.openDatabase("greetings", "1.0", "Greetings Database",
   1000000);
   db.transaction(tryFetchingRows, errorFetchingRows);
}
function tryFetchingRows(tx) {
   tx.executeSql('SELECT * FROM Templates',[], successFetching,
   errorFetchingRows);
}
function successFetching(tx, result){
   var templatesinfo = "";
   var len = result.rows.length;
   var listtemplateresult = document.getElementById("listtemplateresult");
   if (len >0) {
      templatesinfo + = '<ul id = "listoftemplates" data-role = "listview" data-
      inset = "true" data-theme = "b" >';
      for (var i = 0; i<len; i++){
         templatesinfo + = '<li>'+ result.rows.item(i).Template + '</li>';
      }
      templatesinfo + = '</ul>';
      listtemplateresult.innerHTML = templatesinfo;
   }
   else
      listtemplateresult.innerHTML = "There are no templates defined";
      $("#listtemplateresult").trigger("create");
}
function errorFetchingRows(err) {
   document.getElementById("listtemplateresult").innerHTML = "Error occurred while
   fetching templates: " + err.code;
}
```

The listTemplate() function opens the greetings database. When the database is opened successfully, the tryFetchingRows() function is called. In the tryFetching-Rows() function, the SQL SELECT command is executed using the executeSql() method to access all rows from the Templates table. If no error occurs while accessing rows, the suc-cessFetching() function is called that wraps all the accessed rows in the <ul> element. That is, the accessed rows are arranged to appear as a list before being displayed on the List Templates page. The list of templates is displayed on the List  Templates page via the <div> element of ID listtemplateresult. If there are no rows in the Templates table, the message There  are  no  templates  defined is displayed through the listtem-plateresult <div> element. This <div> element will also be used to display an error mes-sage, Error  occurred  while  fetching  templates, along with the error code if any error occurs while accessing rows from the Templates table.

Upon running the application, open the Templates page from the home page. From the Templates page (see Figure 7.4a), click the List  Templates button to navigate to the List Templates page. The List  Templates page (see Figure 7.4b) shows the rows, that is, the templates accessed from the Templates table in list appearance.

## Deleting Rows

To delete rows or templates from the Templates table, we need to define a Delete  Templates page in the index.html file. All the rows in the Templates table are accessed and displayed in the Delete  Templates page as checkboxes. The idea behind showing the templates in a

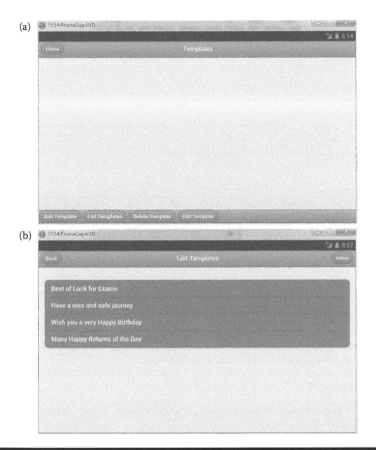

**Figure 7.4** (a) `Templates` page showing buttons in its header and footer. (b) Templates accessed from the `Templates` database and displayed in the `List Templates` page.

checkbox appearance is to enable the user to check the templates that need to be deleted, followed by clicking the `Delete template` button. For defining the `Delete Templates` page, the code shown in Listing 7.8 is written in the `index.html` file. Only the code in bold is newly added; the rest is the same as we saw in Listing 7.6.

**Listing 7.8    Code Written in the `index.html` File**

```
<!DOCTYPE HTML>
<html>
   <head>
   <title>PhoneGap Application</title>
   <script type = "text/javascript" charset = "utf-8" src = "cordova-2.3.0.js">
   </script>
   <link href = "jquery.mobile-1.2.0/jquery.mobile-1.2.0.min.css" rel =
   "stylesheet" type = "text/css"/>
   <script src = "jquery-1.8.3.min.js" type = "text/javascript"></script>
   <script src = "jquery.mobile-1.2.0/jquery.mobile-1.2.0.min.js" type = "text/
   javascript"></script>
   <script src = "template.js" type = "text/javascript"></script>
   </head>
   <body onload = "onBodyLoad()">
```

```
    <!—Home Page—>
        <div data-role = "page" id = "home">
            <div data-role = "header" data-theme = "b" >
                <h1> PGApplication </h1>
            </div>
            <div data-role = "content">
                <div id = "homepageresult"></div>
            </div>
            <div data-role = "footer" class = "ui-bar" data-theme = "b" data-position
            = "fixed" >
                <a href = "#templates">Templates</a>
            </div>
        </div>
<!—Templates Page—>
        <div data-role = "page" id = "templates">
            <div data-role = "header" data-theme = "b">
                <a data-role = "button" href = "#home">Home</a>
                <h1> Templates </h1>
            </div>
            <div data-role = "content">
            </div>
            <div data-role = "footer" data-position = "fixed" data-theme = "b" >
                <a data-role = "button" href = "#addtemplates">Add Template</a>
                <a data-role = "button" href = "#listtemplates" onclick = "javascript:
                listTemplate();">List Templates</a>
                <a data-role = "button" href = "#deltemplates" onclick = "javascript:
                deleteTemplates();">Delete Template</a>
                <a data-role = "button" href = "#edittemplates" onclick = "javascript:
                editTemplate();">Edit Template</a>
            </div>
        </div>
<!—Add Templates Page—>
        <div data-role = "page" id = "addtemplates">
            <div data-role = "header" data-theme = "b">
                <h1> Add Template </h1>
                <a data-role = "button" href = "#templates">Back</a>
                <a data-role = "button" href = "#home">Home</a>
            </div>
            <div data-role = "content">
                Enter Template <input type = "text" id = "templatedata" onfocus =
                'javascript:document.getElementById("addtemplateresult").innerHTML =
                "";'>
                <input type = "button" id = "addTemplateButton" value = "Add
                template"/>
                <div id = "addtemplateresult"></div>
            </div>
        </div>
<!—List Templates Page—>
        <div data-role = "page" id = "listtemplates">
            <div data-role = "header" data-theme = "b">
                <h1> List Templates </h1>
                <a data-role = "button" href = "#templates">Back</a>
                <a data-role = "button" href = "#home">Home</a>
            </div>
            <div data-role = "content">
                <div id = "listtemplateresult"></div>
            </div>
        </div>
<!—Delete Templates Page—>
        <div data-role = "page" id = "deltemplates" >
            <div data-role = "header" data-theme = "b" >
```

```
        <h1> Delete Templates </h1>
        <a data-role = "button" href = "#templates">Back</a>
        <a data-role = "button" href = "#home">Home</a>
      </div>
      <div data-role = "content">
        <div id = "deltemplateresult"></div>
      </div>
      <div data-role = "footer" data-theme = "b" data-position = "fixed" >
        <a data-role = "button" href = "#" onclick = "javascript:delete
        TemplateFromTable();">Delete Template</a>
      </div>
    </div>
  </body>
</html>
```

We can see that the Delete Templates page is accessible through the Delete Template button present in the footer of the Templates page. The Delete  Template button, when clicked, not only opens up the Delete  Template page but also automatically executes the JavaScript function deleteTemplates() to display content in the Delete  Template page to work on. That is, the deleteTemplates() function will access the rows from the Templates table and display them in the form of checkboxes in the Delete  Template page. The Delete  Template page contains two buttons, Back and Home, in its header to enable us to navigate back to the Templates page and the Home page. The content of the page defines a <div> element of ID deltemplateresult that will be used to display the rows to be deleted. The <div> element will also be used to display the error messages if any occur while accessing or deleting rows from the Templates table. The footer of the page defines a Delete Template button that, when clicked, will invoke the JavaScript function deleteTemplate-FromTable() to initiate the procedure of deleting rows from the Templates table.

To implement the task of deleting rows from the Templates table, the code shown in Listing 7.9 is written in the JavaScript template.js file. Only the code in bold is newly added; the rest is the same as we saw in Listing 7.7.

### Listing 7.9   Code Written in the `template.js` File

```
function onBodyLoad(){
   document.addEventListener("deviceready", PhonegapLoaded, false);
}
function PhonegapLoaded(){
   var homepageresult = document.getElementById('homepageresult');
   homepageresult.innerHTML = "Welcome to our PhoneGap Build Application";
   document.getElementById("addTemplateButton").addEventListener("click",
   addTemplate);
}
function addTemplate(){
   var db = window.openDatabase("greetings", "1.0", "Greetings Database",
   1000000);
   db.transaction(tryAddingRow, errorAdding, rowAdded);
}
function tryAddingRow(tx) {
   var templateData = document.getElementById("templatedata").value;
   tx.executeSql('CREATE TABLE IF NOT EXISTS Templates (id INTEGER PRIMARY KEY
   AUTOINCREMENT, Template TEXT NOT NULL)');
   tx.executeSql('INSERT INTO Templates(Template) VALUES("'+ templateData + '")',
   rowAdded, errorAdding);
}
```

```
function rowAdded() {
   document.getElementById("addtemplateresult").innerHTML = "New Template
   successfully added";
   document.getElementById("templatedata").value = "";
}
function errorAdding(err) {
   document.getElementById("addtemplateresult").innerHTML = "Error occurred while
   adding template: " + err.code;
}
function listTemplate(){
   var db = window.openDatabase("greetings", "1.0", "Greetings Database",
   1000000);
   db.transaction(tryFetchingRows, errorFetchingRows);
}
function tryFetchingRows(tx) {
   tx.executeSql('SELECT * FROM Templates',[], successFetching,
   errorFetchingRows);
}
function successFetching(tx, result){
   var templatesinfo = "";
   var len = result.rows.length;
   var listtemplateresult = document.getElementById("listtemplateresult");
   if (len >0) {
      templatesinfo + = '<ul id = "listoftemplates" data-role = "listview" data-
      inset = "true" data-theme = "b" >';
      for (var i = 0; i<len; i++){
         templatesinfo + = '<li>'+ result.rows.item(i).Template + '</li>';
      }
      templatesinfo + = '</ul>';
      listtemplateresult.innerHTML = templatesinfo;
   }
   else
      listtemplateresult.innerHTML = "There are no templates defined";
      $("#listtemplateresult").trigger("create");
}
function errorFetchingRows(err) {
   document.getElementById("listtemplateresult").innerHTML = "Error occurred while
   fetching templates: " + err.code;
}
function deleteTemplates() {
   var db = window.openDatabase("greetings", "1.0", "Greetings Database",
   1000000);
   db.transaction(fetchTemplatesToDelete, errorFetchingTemplateToDelete);
}
function fetchTemplatesToDelete(tx) {
   tx.executeSql('SELECT * FROM Templates',[], showTemplatesToDelete,
   errorFetchingTemplateToDelete);
}
function showTemplatesToDelete(tx, result) {
   var tempinfo = "";
   var len = result.rows.length;
   var deltemplateresult = document.getElementById("deltemplateresult");
   if (len >0){
      tempinfo+ = 'Choose the templates to delete followed by Delete button
<br/><br/>';
      tempinfo+ = '<div data-role = "fieldcontain">';
      tempinfo+ = '<fieldset data-role = "controlgroup">';
      for (var i = 0; i<len; i++){
         tempinfo+ = '<input type = "checkbox" name = "'+result.rows.item(i).id+'"
         id = "'+result.rows.item(i).id+'" value = "'+result.rows.item(i).id+'">';
```

```
            tempinfo+ = '<label for = "'+result.rows.item(i).id+'">'+ result.rows.
            item(i).Template + '</label>';
         }
         tempinfo+ = '</fieldset>';
         tempinfo+ = '</div>';
         deltemplateresult.innerHTML = tempinfo;
      }
      else
         deltemplateresult.innerHTML = "There are no templates defined";
         $("#deltemplateresult").trigger("create");
}
function errorFetchingTemplateToDelete(err) {
      document.getElementById("deltemplateresult").innerHTML = "Error occurred while
      accessing templates: " + err.code;
}
function deleteTemplateFromTable() {
      var db = window.openDatabase("greetings", "1.0", "Greetings Database",
      1000000);
      db.transaction(tryDeletingTemplates, errorDeletingTemplates);
}
function tryDeletingTemplates(tx) {
      var idsToDelete = "";
      var deldiv = document.getElementById("deltemplateresult").
      getElementsByTagName("INPUT");
      for (var i = 0;i<deldiv.length;i++) {
         if (deldiv[i].type.toUpperCase() = ='CHECKBOX') {
            if(deldiv[i].checked)
               idsToDelete + = deldiv[i].value+", ";
         }
      }
      if(idsToDelete.trim().length >0) {
         idsToDelete = idsToDelete.substring(0, idsToDelete.length - 2);
         tx.executeSql('DELETE FROM Templates where id in (' +idsToDelete + ')', [],
         templatesDeleted, errorDeletingTemplates);
      }
      else
         document.getElementById("deltemplateresult").innerHTML = "No template
         selected " ;
      $("#deltemplist").trigger("create");
}
function templatesDeleted() {
document.getElementById("deltemplateresult").innerHTML = "Selected templates
successfully deleted";
      $("#deltemplateresult").trigger("create");
}
function errorDeletingTemplates(err) {
      document.getElementById("deltemplateresult").innerHTML = "Error occurred while
      deleting templates: " + err.code;
}
```

The task of deleting rows from the Templates table consists of the following two subtasks:

■ Fetching rows from the Templates table and displaying them in the content of the Delete Template page in the form of checkboxes. This subtask is performed by the deleteTemplates() function that is automatically called upon clicking the Delete Template button in the Templates page.

■ Execute the SQL DELETE command to delete the rows or checkboxes chosen by the user from the Templates table. This subtask is performed by the deleteTemplateFrom-Table() function that is called when the Delete Template button is clicked from the Delete Templates page.

The deleteTemplates() function opens the greetings database and calls the fetch-TemplatesToDelete() function if the database is opened successfully. In the fetchTem-platesToDelete() function, the SQL SELECT statement is executed to access all the rows from the Templates table. If the rows are successfully accessed, the showTemplatesToDe-lete() function is called to make the rows, that is, templates, accessed from the Templates table appear as checkboxes. The checkboxes are grouped as controlgroup, aligned vertically, and assigned to the <div> element with the ID deltemplateresult of the Delete Templates page for display. If some error occurs while opening the database or accessing rows from the Templates table, the errorFetchingTemplateToDelete() function is called to display the error message Error occurred while accessing templates, along with the error code, on the Delete Templates page via the <div> element of the ID deltemplateresult.

To delete the templates that are displayed as checkboxes in the Delete Templates page, the user just needs to check any number of checkboxes followed by clicking the Delete Template button in the footer of the page. Upon clicking the Delete Template button, the JavaScript function deleteTemplateFromTable() will be invoked.

The deleteTemplateFromTable() function opens the greetings database and calls the tryDeletingTemplates() function if the database is opened successfully. In the tryDeletingTemplates() function, the checkboxes in the Delete Templates page are scanned and the IDs of the selected templates are retrieved from the checked checkboxes. Thereafter, the SQL DELETE command is executed to delete the templates with the retrieved IDs. If the rows from the Templates table are successfully deleted, a message, Selected templates successfully deleted, is displayed on the Delete Templates page via the <div> element of ID deltemplateresult. The same <div> element will also be set to display an error message, Error occurred while deleting templates, along with the error code if anything goes wrong while deleting rows from the Templates table.

Upon running the application, the home page will open by default. Upon clicking the Templates button in the footer of the home page, the Templates page will open. Click the Delete Template button in the footer of the Templates page to open the Delete Templates page. The Delete Templates page accesses all the templates, that is, rows in the Templates table, and displays them in the form of checkboxes, as shown in Figure 7.5a. The Delete Templates page also shows a Delete Template button in its footer. After checking the templates that we want to delete, when we click the Delete Template button in the footer, the selected templates (rows) will be deleted from the Templates table. If the rows are successfully deleted from the Templates table, a message, Selected templates suc-cessfully deleted, is displayed on the screen as shown in Figure 7.5b. Upon opening the Delete Templates page again, only the left-out templates will be displayed on the screen, as shown in Figure 7.5c, which confirms that the selected rows are successfully deleted from the Templates table.

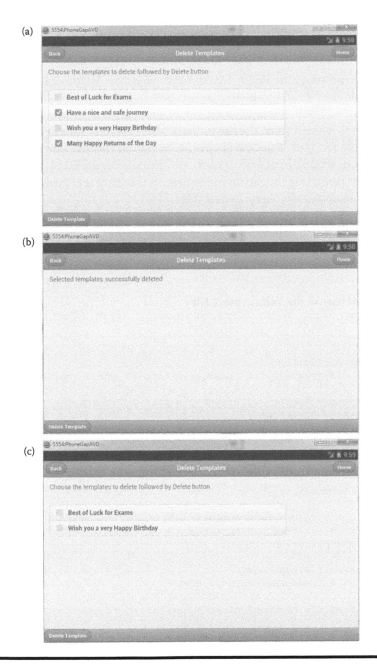

**Figure 7.5** (a) Selecting the templates for deleting. (b) The message displayed upon successful deletion of the templates. (c) The left-out templates are displayed.

## Editing Rows

Sometimes, we may require updating or editing the templates that are stored in the Templates table. To edit rows or templates in the Templates table, we need to define the following two pages:

- The first page displays the templates as a list, allowing the user to select the template to edit.
- The second page displays the selected template from the list in editable form.

Let us call these two pages the Edit Template page and Template Modification Form. All the rows in the Templates table are accessed and displayed in the Edit Template page in list appearance. The user can click on any of the templates shown in the list to edit it. When any template is selected from the list in the Edit Template page, another page, the Template Modification Form, will open, showing the selected template in an input text field. The Template Modification Form will also display an Edit Template button so that the user, after modifying the displayed template in the input text field, can click the Edit Template button to update the Templates table.

To define the two pages, Edit Template page and Template Modification Form, modify the index.html to appear as shown in Listing 7.10. Only the code in bold is newly added; the rest is the same as we saw in Listing 7.8.

**Listing 7.10 Code Written in the `index.html` File**

```
<!DOCTYPE HTML>
<html>
    <head>
    <title>PhoneGap Application</title>
    <script type = "text/javascript" charset = "utf-8" src = "cordova-2.3.0.js">
    </script>
    <link href = "jquery.mobile-1.2.0/jquery.mobile-1.2.0.min.css" rel =
    "stylesheet" type = "text/css"/>
    <script src = "jquery-1.8.3.min.js" type = "text/javascript"></script>
    <script src = "jquery.mobile-1.2.0/jquery.mobile-1.2.0.min.js" type = "text/
    javascript"></script>
    <script src = "template.js" type = "text/javascript"></script>
    </head>
    <body onload = "onBodyLoad()">
    <!-Home Page->
        <div data-role = "page" id = "home">
            <div data-role = "header" data-theme = "b" >
                <h1> PGApplication </h1>
            </div>
            <div data-role = "content">
                <div id = "homepageresult"></div>
            </div>
            <div data-role = "footer" class = "ui-bar" data-theme = "b" data-position
            = "fixed" >
                <a href = "#templates">Templates</a>
            </div>
        </div>
<!-Templates Page->
        <div data-role = "page" id = "templates">
            <div data-role = "header" data-theme = "b">
                <a data-role = "button" href = "#home">Home</a>
                <h1> Templates </h1>
            </div>
            <div data-role = "content">
            </div>
            <div data-role = "footer" data-position = "fixed" data-theme = "b" >
                <a data-role = "button" href = "#addtemplates">Add Template</a>
                <a data-role = "button" href = "#listtemplates" onclick = "java
```

```
                    script:listTemplate();">List Templates</a>
                    <a data-role = "button" href = "#deltemplates" onclick = "javascript:
                    deleteTemplates();">Delete Template</a>
                    <a data-role = "button" href = "#edittemplates" onclick = "javascript:
                    editTemplate();">Edit Template</a>
                </div>
            </div>
<!-Add Templates Page->
        <div data-role = "page" id = "addtemplates">
            <div data-role = "header" data-theme = "b">
                <h1> Add Template </h1>
                <a data-role = "button" href = "#templates">Back</a>
                <a data-role = "button" href = "#home">Home</a>
            </div>
            <div data-role = "content">
                Enter Template <input type = "text" id = "templatedata" onfocus =
                'javascript:document.getElementById("addtemplateresult").innerHTML =
                "";'>
                <input type = "button" id = "addTemplateButton" value = "Add
                template"/>
                <div id = "addtemplateresult"></div>
            </div>
        </div>
<!-List Templates Page->
        <div data-role = "page" id = "listtemplates">
            <div data-role = "header" data-theme = "b">
                <h1> List Templates </h1>
                <a data-role = "button" href = "#templates">Back</a>
                <a data-role = "button" href = "#home">Home</a>
            </div>
            <div data-role = "content">
                <div id = "listtemplateresult"></div>
            </div>
        </div>
<!-Delete Templates Page->
        <div data-role = "page" id = "deltemplates" >
            <div data-role = "header" data-theme = "b" >
                <h1> Delete Templates </h1>
                <a data-role = "button" href = "#templates">Back</a>
                <a data-role = "button" href = "#home">Home</a>
            </div>
            <div data-role = "content">
                <div id = "deltemplateresult"></div>
            </div>
            <div data-role = "footer" data-theme = "b" data-position = "fixed" >
                <a data-role = "button" href = "#" onclick = "javascript:delete
                TemplateFromTable();">Delete Template</a>
            </div>
        </div>
<!-Edit Template Page->
        <div data-role = "page" id = "edittemplates">
            <div data-role = "header" data-theme = "b">
                <h1>Edit Template </h1>
                <a data-role = "button" href = "#templates">Back</a>
                <a data-role = "button" href = "#home">Home</a>
            </div>
            <div data-role = "content">
                <div id = "edittemplateresult"></div>
            </div>
        </div>
<!-Template Modification Form->
```

```
    <div data-role = "page" id = "templatemodificationform">
       <div data-role = "header" data-theme = "b">
         <h1>Template Modification Form </h1>
         <a data-role = "button" href = "#edittemplates" onclick = "javascript:
         editTemplate();">Back</a>
         <a data-role = "button" href = "#home">Home</a>
       </div>
       <div data-role = "content">
          <div id = "modifytemplateresult"></div>
       </div>
    </div>
  </body>
</html>
```

When the `Edit Template` button is clicked from the `Templates` page, we will be navigated to the `Edit Template` page and the JavaScript function `editTemplate()` will be executed, which will do the job of accessing rows from the `Templates` table and displaying them in the form of a list.

We can see that the `Edit Template` page contains two buttons, `Back` and `Home`, to be used for navigating to the `Templates` and `Home` pages, respectively. The `<div>` element with the ID `edittemplateresult` is added to the content of the page that will be used for displaying the template rows in the form of a list. The `<div>` element can also be used for displaying error messages if any occur. When any template is selected from the list displayed in the `Edit Template` page, the `Template Modification Form` will open showing the selected template.

The `Template Modification Form` contains two buttons, `Back` and `Home`, in its header. The `Back` button, when clicked, will navigate us to the `Edit Template` page. The `Home` button, when clicked, will navigate us to the `Home` page of the application. A `<div>` element with the ID `modifytemplateresult` is defined in the content of the page that will be used for displaying the selected template in an editable input text field along with an `Edit Template` button. A user can modify the content of the displayed template in the input text field and subsequently click the `Edit Template` button to save the modifications in the `Templates` table.

Next, we need to write the JavaScript code to perform the following tasks:

■ Access the template rows from the `Templates` table
■ Display the accessed template rows in a list
■ Display the selected template in the editable input text field
■ Update the `Templates` table to save the modifications

To do all the tasks above, modify the JavaScript file `template.js` to appear as shown in Listing 7.11. Only the code in bold is newly added; the rest is the same as we saw in Listing 7.9.

**Listing 7.11  Code Written in the `template.js` File**

```
function onBodyLoad(){
    document.addEventListener("deviceready", PhonegapLoaded, false);
}
function PhonegapLoaded(){
   var homepageresult = document.getElementById('homepageresult');
   homepageresult.innerHTML = "Welcome to our PhoneGap Build Application";
```

```
        document.getElementById("addTemplateButton").addEventListener("click",
        addTemplate);
}
function addTemplate(){
        var db = window.openDatabase("greetings", "1.0", "Greetings Database",
        1000000);
        db.transaction(tryAddingRow, errorAdding, rowAdded);
}
function tryAddingRow(tx) {
        var templateData = document.getElementById("templatedata").value;
        tx.executeSql('CREATE TABLE IF NOT EXISTS Templates (id INTEGER PRIMARY KEY
        AUTOINCREMENT, Template TEXT NOT NULL)');
        tx.executeSql('INSERT INTO Templates(Template) VALUES("'+ templateData + '")',
        rowAdded, errorAdding);
}
function rowAdded() {
        document.getElementById("addtemplateresult").innerHTML = "New Template
        successfully added";
        document.getElementById("templatedata").value = "";
}
function errorAdding(err) {
        document.getElementById("addtemplateresult").innerHTML = "Error occurred while
        adding template: " + err.code;
}
function listTemplate(){
        var db = window.openDatabase("greetings", "1.0", "Greetings Database",
        1000000);
        db.transaction(tryFetchingRows, errorFetchingRows);
}
function tryFetchingRows(tx) {
        tx.executeSql('SELECT * FROM Templates',[], successFetching,
        errorFetchingRows);
}
function successFetching(tx, result){
        var templatesinfo = "";
        var len = result.rows.length;
        var listtemplateresult = document.getElementById("listtemplateresult");
        if (len >0) {
                templatesinfo + = '<ul id = "listoftemplates" data-role = "listview" data-
                inset = "true" data-theme = "b" >';
                for (var i = 0; i<len; i++){
                        templatesinfo + = '<li>'+ result.rows.item(i).Template + '</li>';
                }
                templatesinfo + = '</ul>';
                listtemplateresult.innerHTML = templatesinfo;
        }
        else
                listtemplateresult.innerHTML = "There are no templates defined";
                $("#listtemplateresult").trigger("create");
}
function errorFetchingRows(err) {
        document.getElementById("listtemplateresult").innerHTML = "Error occurred while
        fetching templates: " + err.code;
}
function deleteTemplates() {
        var db = window.openDatabase("greetings", "1.0", "Greetings Database",
        1000000);
        db.transaction(fetchTemplatesToDelete, errorFetchingTemplateToDelete);
}
function fetchTemplatesToDelete(tx) {
```

```
      tx.executeSql('SELECT * FROM Templates',[], showTemplatesToDelete,
      errorFetchingTemplateToDelete);
}
function showTemplatesToDelete(tx, result) {
   var tempinfo = "";
   var len = result.rows.length;
   var deltemplateresult = document.getElementById("deltemplateresult");
   if (len >0){
      tempinfo+ = 'Choose the templates to delete followed by Delete button
<br/><br/>';
      tempinfo+ = '<div data-role = "fieldcontain">';
      tempinfo+ = '<fieldset data-role = "controlgroup">';
      for (var i = 0; i<len; i++){
         tempinfo+ = '<input type = "checkbox" name = "'+result.rows.item(i).id+'"
         id = "'+result.rows.item(i).id+'" value = "'+result.rows.item(i).id+'">';
         tempinfo+ = '<label for = "'+result.rows.item(i).id+'">'+ result.rows.
         item(i).Template + '</label>';
      }
      tempinfo+ = '</fieldset>';
      tempinfo+ = '</div>';
      deltemplateresult.innerHTML = tempinfo;
   }
   else
      deltemplateresult.innerHTML = "There are no templates defined";
      $("#deltemplateresult").trigger("create");
}
function errorFetchingTemplateToDelete(err) {
   document.getElementById("deltemplateresult").innerHTML = "Error occurred while
   accessing templates: " + err.code;
}
function deleteTemplateFromTable() {
   var db = window.openDatabase("greetings", "1.0", "Greetings Database",
   1000000);
   db.transaction(tryDeletingTemplates, errorDeletingTemplates);
}
function tryDeletingTemplates(tx) {
   var idsToDelete = "";
   var deldiv = document.getElementById("deltemplateresult").
   getElementsByTagName("INPUT");
   for (var i = 0;i<deldiv.length;i++) {
      if (deldiv[i].type.toUpperCase() = ='CHECKBOX') {
         if(deldiv[i].checked)
            idsToDelete + = deldiv[i].value+", ";
      }
   }
   if(idsToDelete.trim().length >0) {
      idsToDelete = idsToDelete.substring(0, idsToDelete.length - 2);
      tx.executeSql('DELETE FROM Templates where id in (' +idsToDelete + ')', [],
      templatesDeleted, errorDeletingTemplates);
   }
   else
      document.getElementById("deltemplateresult").innerHTML = "No template
      selected " ;
      $("#deltemplist").trigger("create");
}
function templatesDeleted() {
   document.getElementById("deltemplateresult").innerHTML = "Selected templates
   successfully deleted";
   $("#deltemplateresult").trigger("create");
}
function errorDeletingTemplates(err) {
```

```
    document.getElementById("deltemplateresult").innerHTML = "Error occurred while
    deleting templates: " + err.code;
}
function editTemplate(){
    var db = window.openDatabase("greetings", "1.0", "Greetings Database",
    1000000);
    db.transaction(fetchTemplatesToEdit, errorFetchingTemplatesToEdit);
}
function fetchTemplatesToEdit(tx) {
    tx.executeSql('SELECT * FROM Templates',[], displayingTemplatesToEdit,
    errorFetchingTemplatesToEdit);
}
function displayingTemplatesToEdit(tx, result){
    var templistinfo = "";
    var len = result.rows.length;
    var edittemplateresult = document.getElementById("edittemplateresult");
    if (len >0){
        templistinfo + = '<ul id = "ListofTemplates" data-role = "listview" data-
        inset = "true" data-theme = "b" >';
        templistinfo + = '<li data-role = "divider">Tap the templates to edit</li>';
        for (var i = 0; i<len; i++){
            templistinfo+ = '<li><a id = "'+result.rows.item(i).id+'" href =
            "#templatemodificationform" onclick = "javascript:tryFetchingSelected
            Template(' + result.rows.item(i).id +');">' + result.rows.item(i).
            Template + '</a></li>';
        }
        templistinfo+ = '</ul>';
        edittemplateresult.innerHTML = templistinfo;
    }
    else
        edittemplateresult.innerHTML = "There are no templates defined";
        $("#edittemplateresult").trigger("create");
}
function errorFetchingTemplatesToEdit(err) {
document.getElementById("edittemplateresult").innerHTML = "Error occurred while
accessing templates: " + err.code;
}
function tryFetchingSelectedTemplate(templateID){
    var db = window.openDatabase("greetings", "1.0", "Greetings Database", 1000000);
    db.transaction(function(tx){
        fetchSelectedTemplate(tx, templateID)}, errorFetchingSelectedTemplate);
}
function fetchSelectedTemplate(tx, templateID){
    tx.executeSql('SELECT * FROM Templates where id in ('+ templateID + ')',[],
    showSelectedTemplate, errorFetchingSelectedTemplate);
}
function showSelectedTemplate(tx, result){
    var showtemplate = "";
    var len = result.rows.length;
    var modifytemplateresult = document.getElementById("modifytemplateresult");
    if (len >0){
        showtemplate+ = 'Template <input type = "text" id = "newtemplatedata" value
        = "'+result.rows.item(0).Template +'">';
        showtemplate+ = '<input type = "button" id = "editTemplateButton" value =
        "Edit Template"/>';
        modifytemplateresult.innerHTML = showtemplate;
    }
    else
        modifytemplateresult.innerHTML = "No template defined";
        $("#modifytemplateresult").trigger("create");
```

```
document.getElementById("editTemplateButton").addEventListener("click", function()
{
    editTemplateTable(result.rows.item(0).id;}, false);
}
function errorFetchingSelectedTemplate(err) {
    document.getElementById("edittempresult").innerHTML = "Error occurred while
    accessing template: " + err.code;
}
function editTemplateTable(templateID){
    var db = window.openDatabase("greetings", "1.0", "Greetings Database",
    1000000);
    db.transaction(function(tx){
    tryEditingTemplateTable(tx, templateID)}, errorEditingTemplateTable);
}
function tryEditingTemplateTable(tx, templateID){
    var newtempdata = document.getElementById("newtemplatedata").value;
    tx.executeSql('UPDATE Templates Set Template = "'+newtempdata + '" where id in
    ('+ templateID + ')',[], templateTableEdited, errorEditingTemplateTable);
}
function templateTableEdited(tx, result){
    alert("Template table successfully edited");
}
function errorEditingTemplateTable(err) {
    alert("Error occurred while editing Templates table: " + err.code);
}
```

As stated earlier, when the Edit Template button is clicked from the Templates page, we will be navigated to the Edit Template page and the JavaScript function editTemplate()will be automatically executed to display the content in the Edit Template page.

The editTemplate() function opens the greetings database and calls the fetchTemplatesToEdit() function. In the fetchTemplatesToEdit() function, the SQL SELECT statement is executed to fetch all the rows from the Templates table. If the rows are successfully accessed from the Templates table, the displayingTemplatesToEdit() function is called to make the accessed templates appear as a list. That is, all the templates are wrapped in the <li> element and enclosed in the <ul> element. The templates in list appearance are then assigned to the <div> element of the ID edittemplateresult for display on the Edit Template page. The same <div> element will also be used to display a message, There are no templates defined, if there are no rows in the Templates table or an error message, Error occurred while accessing templates, along with the error code, if some error occurs while accessing the Templates table.

Whenever any template from the list is selected in the Edit Template page, the Template Modification Form should open, showing the selected template in an editable input text field. In order to do so, a hyperlink that navigates to the Template Modification Form and that calls the JavaScript function tryFetchingSelectedTemplate() is nested inside each <li> element. As a result, when any list item, that is, template, is clicked in the list, we will be navigated to the Template Modification Form and the JavaScript function tryFetchingSelectedTemplate() will be executed. The ID of the template will also be passed to the tryFetchingSelectedTemplate() function. The tryFetchingSelectedTemplate() function opens the greetings database and calls the fetchSelectedTemplate() function that retrieves the template with the supplied ID from the Templates table. If the specified template is successfully accessed from the Templates table, the showSelectedTemplate() function is called that displays the selected template in an input text field along with an Edit Template button. The input text field and Edit Template button will be displayed through the `<div>` element of the ID `modifytemplateresult` in the `Template Modification Form`. A click event listener is associated with the `Edit Template` button so that after modifying the template in the input text field, when the user clicks the `Edit Template` button, the `editTemplateTable()` function is called that executes the SQL UPDATE statement to update the `Templates` table; that is, the function updates the `Templates` table, saving the modified template. If the `Templates` table is successfully updated, an alert dialog appears showing the message `Template table successfully edited`. If something goes wrong while updating the `Templates` table, the alert dialog displays the message `Error occurred while editing Templates table` along with the error code.

Upon running the application, the home page, as usual, is opened by default. Upon clicking the `Templates` button in the footer of the home page, the `Templates` page will open. Click the `Edit Template` button in the footer of the `Templates` page to open the `Edit Template` page. The `Edit Template` page will show all the rows, that is, templates, in the `Templates` table as a list (see Figure 7.6a). Each template displayed in the list is clickable. Upon clicking a template from the list, a `Template Modification Form` will open, showing the selected template in an input text field (see Figure 7.6b). After modifying the template, when the user clicks the `Edit Template` button, the modified template will be saved in the `Templates` table. If the `Templates` table is successfully edited, an alert dialog will appear showing the message `Template table successfully edited`, as shown in Figure 7.6c.

## Summary

In this chapter, we explored the role of the Storage API for developing mobile applications. We learned the methods required in creating a database, creating tables, and inserting rows in the database tables. We learned the procedure for accessing rows from the table and listing them on the screen. We also learned the steps required in deleting and editing rows in the tables.

Chapter 8 mainly focuses on using geolocation. We will learn how to use geolocation methods and options. We will also learn how to use accelerometer in mobile applications, as well as about accelerometer methods and how device orientation is observed. Finally, we will learn how to capture video, audio, and images.

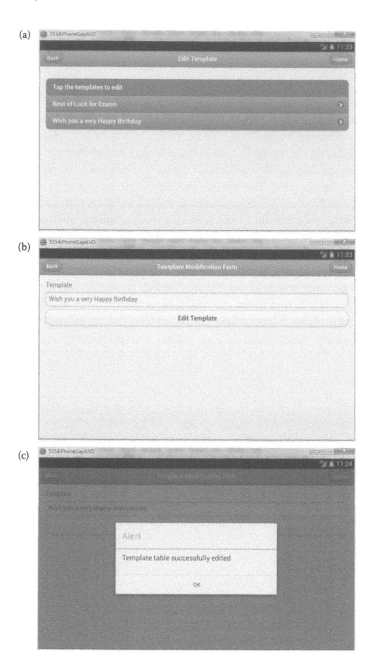

**Figure 7.6** **(a) Existing templates displayed in the Edit Template page. (b) Selected template opened for editing. (c) Alert dialog informing of successful editing of the template.**

## Chapter 8

# Using PhoneGap API

In this chapter, we cover:

- Using Accelerometer API
- Using Camera API
- Using Capture API—Capturing audio and video
- Using Geolocation API—Getting a device's current location and watching a device's location
- Using Google Maps API—Displaying Google Maps
- Combining the Geolocation and Google Maps APIs—Displaying Google Maps centered at the device location, displaying markers on the map, drawing lines on the map, finding the distance between two positions, dragging markers, and computing distances
- Using the Geocoder class
- Using Compass API

## Using Accelerometer API

An accelerometer is a sensor that provides information about the current position of the device, detecting its motion, tilt, and acceleration. This sensor is available on most modern smartphones. Using the accelerometer, we can develop applications that respond to the position or motion of the device. PhoneGap provides the Accelerometer API that enables us to access the accelerometer sensor of the device and use its information in Web applications.

To access the accelerometer sensor in Web applications, we need to first create an `Acceleration` object. The `Acceleration` object is a read-only object that contains accelerometer data, that is, device motion in the X, Y, and Z directions at a specific time. Below are the `Acceleration` object's properties:

- x—Represents the amount of acceleration along the X axis.
- y—Represents the amount of acceleration along the Y axis.
- z—Represents the amount of acceleration along the Z axis.
- `timestamp`—Timestamp for creation, is expressed in milliseconds.

187

## Using Accelerometer Methods

Let us learn about the methods that are required in the creation of the `Acceleration` object. Below is the first one.

### getCurrentAcceleration() Method

An `Acceleration` object can be created by calling `getCurrentAcceleration()`, as shown in the example below:

```
navigator.accelerometer.getCurrentAcceleration(onSuccess, onError);
```

The method above, if executed successfully, will create an `Acceleration` object that can be accessed from the `onSuccess` callback method, as shown below:

```
function onSuccess(acceleration) {
    alert('X Coordinate: ' + acceleration.x + '\n' +
    'Y Coordinate: ' + acceleration.y + '\n' +
    'Acceleration Z: ' + acceleration.z + '\n' +
    'Timestamp: ' + acceleration.timestamp + '\n');
};
```

We can see that the `Acceleration` object's `x`, `y`, `z`, and `timestamp` properties are used for displaying acceleration of the device along the three axes, along with the timestamp. In case some error occurs while creating an `Acceleration` object, the `onError` callback method will be called to display the error message, as shown below:

```
function onError() {
    alert('Error occurred while using Accelerometer');
};
```

The `getCurrentAcceleration()` method is called every time there is a change in the acceleration of the device; hence, it results in high consumption of CPU and battery power. To avoid consumption of CPU, the `watchAcceleration()` method is preferred. Let us now learn more.

### watchAcceleration() Method

The `watchAcceleration()` method watches or gets the acceleration data of the device in the specified time interval. For example, the following statements will watch the device acceleration after every second:

```
var options = {frequency: 1000};
var watchID = navigator.accelerometer.watchAcceleration(onSuccess,
onError, options);
```

We can see that in addition to the two callback methods, `onSuccess` and `onError`, the `watchAcceleration()` method uses an `options` object with a `frequency` parameter. The `frequency` parameter specifies the time interval between watching and measuring of acceleration. The time interval is specified in milliseconds.

## *clearWatch()* Method

To stop watching or getting the acceleration data through the Acceleration object created earlier, the clearWatch() method is used. The reference or ID of the Acceleration object is passed to this method as shown below:

```
navigator.accelerometer.clearWatch(watchID);
```

The statement above stops the measuring of acceleration data through the Acceleration object of the ID watchID.

Let us apply the knowledge gained so far in measuring acceleration of an Android device. So, create an Android project called PGAccelerometerApp and configure it for using PhoneGap. In the assets/www folder, open the index.html file and write the code as shown in Listing 8.1.

**Listing 8.1   Code Written in the index.html File**

```
<!DOCTYPE HTML>
<html>
    <head>
    <title>PhoneGap Application</title>
    <script type = "text/javascript" charset = "utf-8" src = "cordova-2.3.0.js">
    </script>
    <script type = "text/javascript">
    function onBodyLoad() {
        document.addEventListener("deviceready", PhonegapLoaded, false);
    }
    function PhonegapLoaded(){
        var options = {frequency: 500};
        navigator.accelerometer.watchAcceleration(onSuccess, onError, options);
    }
    function onSuccess(acceleration) {
        Xaxis = document.getElementById("Xaxis");
        Yaxis = document.getElementById("Yaxis");
        Zaxis = document.getElementById("Zaxis");
        Xaxis.innerHTML = "X Coordinate: " + acceleration.x;
        Yaxis.innerHTML = "Y Coordinate: " + acceleration.y;
        Zaxis.innerHTML = "Z Coordinate: " + acceleration.z;
    }
    function onError() {
        alert("Error occurred while using Accelerometer");
    }
    </script>
    </head>
    <body onload = "onBodyLoad()">
        <h3>Accelerometer</h3>
        <div id = "Xaxis"></div>
        <div id = "Yaxis"></div>
        <div id = "Zaxis"></div>
        </form>
    </body>
</html>
```

In the code above, we can see that three <div> elements of IDs Xaxis, Yaxis, and Zaxis are defined that will be used to display the acceleration data of the device along the three axes,

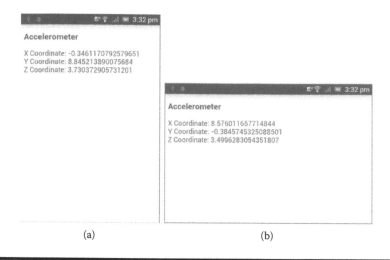

(a)  (b)

**Figure 8.1  (a) The X, Y, and Z coordinate values when the device is in portrait mode. (b) The coordinates along the three axes when the device switches to landscape mode.**

respectively. After PhoneGap is loaded, the options object of the watchAcceleration() method is defined to measure the acceleration data of the device every half second, that is, every 500 milliseconds. The onSuccess callback method will be called if no error occurs in the execution of the watchAcceleration() method. In the onSuccess callback method, the three <div> elements with IDs Xaxis, Yaxis, and Zaxis are accessed and the acceleration data along the three axes are displayed through them. If anything goes wrong while accessing the acceleration data, the onError callback method is called to display the error message through the alert dialog.

Upon running the application when the device is in portrait mode, the acceleration data along the X, Y, and Z axes will be displayed as shown in Figure 8.1a. Upon switching the device to landscape mode, the acceleration data along the three axes will appear as shown in Figure 8.1b.

## Using Camera API

Every smartphone comes with a camera, and it is quite obvious that developers need to access and use it in applications. The PhoneGap Camera API enables Web applications to access the device camera and the images in the local photo storage of the device.

To obtain or access a picture using the device camera, the getPicture() method is called as shown below:

```
navigator.camera.getPicture(onCameraSuccess, onCameraError,
cameraOptions);
```

The onCameraSuccess callback method is called when the image is obtained successfully. The getPicture() method returns either the Uniform Resource Identifier (URI) pointing to the image file on the device's file system or the base64-encoded string representing the content of the image. The onCameraError callback method is called when either the task of obtaining an image is canceled or some error occurs while obtaining the image. The cameraOptions object is used to define parameters that configure the obtained image, its format, and so on. The `cameraOptions` object supports the properties as shown in Table 8.1.

The following shows a sample code to define `cameraOptions` and the calling `getPicture()` method:

**Table 8.1  Properties Supported by the `CameraOptions` Object**

| *Property* | *Description* |
|---|---|
| `Quality` | Represents a value in percentage that determines the quality of the image. 100% quality means the retrieved image will be of the highest quality and is not reduced or compressed. Because the file size of the highest-quality image becomes quite large, it is recommended to set the quality percentage at around 50%. |
| `destinationType` | Determines how the image information is returned. Following are the two possible values for this parameter: <br> • `Camera.DestinationType.FILE_URI`—Provides the file URI or path to the image file in the device's local file system. <br> • `Camera.DestinationType.DATA_URL`—Provides the binary data of the image in base64-encoded string format. <br> It is very easy to work with file URIs compared with the raw binary image data. |
| `sourceType` | Defines the source of the picture to capture or retrieve, that is, whether to retrieve the image through a device camera or from a saved photo album. The possible values of this parameter are `Camera.SourceType.CAMERA`, `Camera.SourceType.PHOTOLIBRARY`, and `Camera.SourceType.SAVEDPHOTOALBUM`. <br> In most of the mobile platforms, both `PHOTOLIBRARY` and `SAVEDPHOTOALBUM` refer to the photo album. |
| `allowEdit` | Boolean value that determines if editing can be applied to the retrieved image before sending it to the application. For example, if this parameter is set to `true`, an editing screen will be launched that can be used to edit the image. This parameter works only on the iPhone. |
| `encodingType` | Determines the kind of picture to return, i.e., whether we want the JPEG or PNG format of the retrieved image. Below are the possible values for this parameter: <br> • `Camera.EncodingType.JPEG`—Used to return an image in JPEG format. It is the most commonly used encoding type. <br> • `Camera.EncodingType.PNG`—Used to return an image in PNG format. This type is not supported on all platforms. |
| `targetWidth` and `targetHeight` | Determines the height and width of the retrieved image in pixels. The image will be scaled to the specified width and height maintaining the aspect ratio. |

*(Continued)*

**Table 8.1  Properties Supported by the `CameraOptions` Object (Continued)**

| Property | Description |
|---|---|
| mediaType | Determines the media type. Below are the possible options:<br>• DEFAULT—Returns the image using the format specified in the destinationType parameter.<br>• ALLMEDIA—Enable selection from all media types.<br>• PICTURE—Returns the photographs only.<br>• VIDEO—Returns the video files only. When the VIDEO option is chosen, only a file URI is returned to the calling application. |

```
var cameraOptions = {
   quality : 50,
   sourceType : Camera.PictureSourceType.CAMERA,
   destinationType : Camera.DestinationType.FILE_URI,
   allowEdit : true,
   encodingType: Camera.EncodingType.JPEG,
   targetWidth: 100,
   targetHeight: 200};
   navigator.camera.getPicture(onSuccess, onFail, cameraOptions);
   function onSuccess(data) {
   capturedImage = document.getElementById("capturedImage");
   capturedImage.src = data;
}
function onFail(err) {
   alert('Command Cancelled or Error occurred while retrieving the image:
   ' + err);
}
```

Let us create an application to see how PhoneGap's Camera API is used for invoking the device's default camera application to access the image(s). So, create an Android project called PGCameraApp and configure it for using PhoneGap. In the assets/www folder, open the index.html file and write the code as shown in Listing 8.2.

**Listing 8.2  Code Written in the `index.html` File**

```
<!DOCTYPE HTML>
<html>
   <head>
   <title>PhoneGap Application</title>
   <script type = "text/javascript" charset = "utf-8" src = "cordova-2.3.0.js">
   </script>
   <script type = "text/javascript">
   function onBodyLoad() {
      document.addEventListener("deviceready", PhonegapLoaded, false);
   }
   function PhonegapLoaded(){
      document.getElementById("captureImage").addEventListener("click",
      captureImage);
   }
   function captureImage(){
```

```
     var cameraOptions = {
        quality : 50,
        sourceType : Camera.PictureSourceType.CAMERA,
        destinationType : Camera.DestinationType.FILE_URI,
        encodingType: Camera.EncodingType.JPEG,
        targetWidth: 100,
        targetHeight: 200};
        navigator.camera.getPicture(displayImage, onError, cameraOptions);
  }
  function displayImage(data){
     capturedImage = document.getElementById("capturedImage");
     capturedImage.style.display = 'block';
     capturedImage.src = data;
  }
  function onError(err) {
     alert('Some error occurred while capturing image: ' + err);
  }
  </script>
  </head>
  <body onload = "onBodyLoad()">
     <button id = "captureImage"onclick = "captureImage();">Capture Image</
     button><br/>
     <img id = "capturedImage" style = "display:none;width:400px;height:300px;"
></img>
  </body>
</html>
```

In the code above, we can see a button with the caption `Capture Image` is defined along with an `<img>` element. The `Capture Image` button, when clicked, will call the JavaScript function `captureImage()` to initiate the task of obtaining an image using the device's camera application. The `<img>` element is assigned the ID `capturedImage` and will be used to display the obtained image.

In the JavaScript function `captureImage()`, the `cameraOptions` object is defined. The properties in `cameraOptions` recommend the quality of the obtained image to 50%, return the file URI of the obtained image, return the image in JPEG format, and scale the obtained image to 100 pixels wide by 200 pixels high, maintaining the aspect ratio. After setting the `cameraOptions` object, the `getPicture()` method is called. The `displayImage` callback method will be called if the image is obtained successfully. In the `displayImage` callback method, the `<img>` element with the ID `capturedImage` is accessed and the URI of the obtained image is assigned to it for display.

The `onError` callback will be called to display an error message if any error occurs while obtaining the image.

Next, we need to write permissions in the `AndroidManifest.xml` file to access the device camera, use it, and store the obtained image in the device storage. Listing 8.3 shows the code in the `AndroidManifest.xml` file. Only the code in bold is new; the rest is the default code.

**Listing 8.3   Code in the `AndroidManifest.xml` File**

```
<?xml version = "1.0" encoding = "utf-8"?>
  <manifest xmlns:android = "http://schemas.android.com/apk/res/android"
  package = "com.phonegap.pgcameraapp"
  android:versionCode = "1"
  android:versionName = "1.0" >
  <uses-sdk
```

```
    android:minSdkVersion = "11"
    android:targetSdkVersion = "17"/>
  <uses-permission
    android:name = "android.permission.ACCESS_NETWORK_STATE"/>
  <uses-feature android:name = "android.hardware.camera"/>
  <uses-permission android:name = "android.permission.CAMERA"/>
  <uses-permission
    android:name = "android.permission.WRITE_EXTERNAL_STORAGE"/>
  <application
    android:allowBackup = "true"
    android:icon = "@drawable/ic_launcher"
    android:label = "@string/app_name"
    android:theme = "@style/AppTheme" >
    <activity android:name = "com.phonegap.pgcameraapp.PGCameraAppActivity"
        android:label = "@string/app_name" >
      <intent-filter>
        <action android:name = "android.intent.action.MAIN"/>
        <category android:name = "android.intent.category.LAUNCHER"/>
      </intent-filter>
    </activity>
  </application>
</manifest>
```

Our application is ready to run. Upon running the application, a button, `Capture Image`, will be displayed as shown in Figure 8.2a. Upon clicking the `Capture Image` button, the standard camera application will open, enabling us to take a picture (see Figure 8.2b). The clicked image will be displayed in the image element of the Hypertext Markup Language (HTML) page as shown in Figure 8.2c.

## Using the Capture API

The PhoneGap Capture API allows an application to capture audio, video, and images using the built-in application on a mobile device. The device's default camera application is used to capture pictures and videos, while the device's default voice recorder application is used for capturing audio clips. The Capture API interacts with the device's default capture application and enables multiple captures with a single API call.

**Note:** The Camera API can capture only images, but supports alternate sources for the image files. The Camera API is supported by PhoneGap for backward compatibility.

The methods to capture audio, image, and video are provided below:

■ To capture one or more audio files, the `captureAudio()` method is used as shown below:

```
navigator.device.capture.captureAudio(CaptureSuccess, CaptureError,
captureOptions);
```

■ To capture one or more image files, the `captureImage()` method is used as shown below:

```
navigator.device.capture.captureImage(onCaptureSuccess, onCaptureEr-
ror, captureOptions);
```

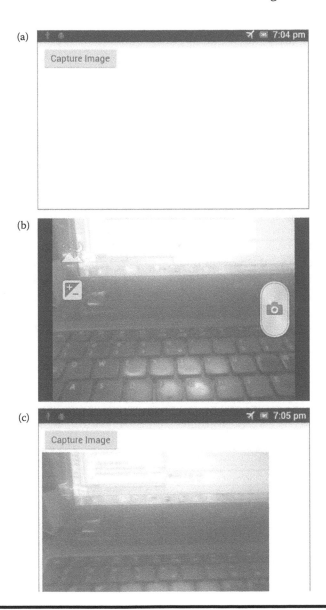

**Figure 8.2** (a) The `Capture Image` **button appears upon application start-up.** (b) **The standard camera application is invoked to click images.** (c) **The clicked image appears in the** `<img>` **element of the HTML page.**

■ To capture one or more video files, the `captureVideo()` method is used as shown below:

```
navigator.device.capture.captureVideo(onCaptureSuccess, onCaptureEr-
ror, captureOptions);
```

Let us understand the concept of capturing audio, video, and image one by one. We will begin with capturing audio.

## *Capturing Audio*

To capture one or more audio files, the `captureAudio()` method is called as shown below:

```
navigator.device.capture.captureAudio(captureAudioSuccess, captureAudio-
Error, captureOptions);
```

The `captureAudioSuccess` callback method will be called after the audio is captured by the capture application on the device. The `captureAudioError` callback method is called when either the capturing task is canceled or some error occurs while capturing. The `capture-Options` object supports the parameters that can be used to configure the capturing task. The list of parameters supported by the `captureOptions` object is given below:

- **Limit**—Determines the number of audio clips to capture. This value must be greater than or equal to 1. The default value is 1.
- **Duration**—Determines the maximum duration of audio clips in seconds.
- **Mode**—Determines the mode of capturing audio, such as audio/wav or audio/amr. Wav and amr are the audio formats.

For example, the statements given below capture two audio clips of 10 seconds duration:

```
var captureOptions = {limit:2, duration:10};
navigator.device.capture.captureAudio(captureAudioSuccess, captureAudio-
Error, captureOptions);
```

If audio is captured successfully, the `captureAudioSuccess` callback will be called; otherwise, the `captureAudioError` callback will be called. An array of media files containing information about the captured audio will be passed to the `captureAudioSuccess` callback method. The media file array passed to the function supports the following properties:

- `name`—Represents the name of the file along with the extension.
- `fullPath`—Represents the full path of the media file.
- `type`—Represents the file's Multipurpose Internet Mail Extensions (MIME) type.
- `lastModifiedDate`—Represents the date and time the media file was last modified.
- `size`—Represents the file's size in bytes.

The `captureAudioSuccess` callback method loops through the media file array and processes each of the media files generated during the capture as shown below:

```
function captureAudioSuccess(mediaFiles) {
   var len, i;
   len = mediaFiles.length;
   if(len > 0) {
      for(i = 0; i < len; i + = 1) {
         alert("File: "+mediaFiles[i].name+ "\n"+
         "is stored at: "+mediaFiles[i].fullPath+"\n"+
         "Size of the file is: "+mediaFiles[i].size);
      }
   } else {
      alert("Error occurred while capturing audio");
   }
}
```

We see that the `captureAudioSuccess` callback loops through the media file array, isolates each media file, and displays its name, path, and size. The `captureAudioError` callback method is called to display an error message when either the capturing task is canceled or some error occurs, as shown below:

```
function captureAudioError(err) {
    alert("Error occurred while recording audio:" +err);
}
```

Let us apply the knowledge gained so far in creating an application that uses the device's default voice recorder to capture audio(s). Create an Android project called `PGMediaApp` and configure it for using PhoneGap. In the `assets/www` folder, open the `index.html` file and write the code as shown in Listing 8.4.

**Listing 8.4   Code Written in the `index.html` File**

```
<!DOCTYPE HTML>
<html>
    <head>
    <title>PhoneGap Application</title>
    <script type = "text/javascript" charset = "utf-8" src = "cordova-2.3.0.js">
    </script>
    <script type = "text/javascript">
    function onBodyLoad() {
        document.addEventListener("deviceready", PhonegapLoaded, false);
    }
    function PhonegapLoaded(){ document.getElementById("recordAudio").
    addEventListener("click", captureAudio);
    }
    function captureAudio() { navigator.device.capture.captureAudio
    (captureAudioSuccess, captureAudioError, {limit: 1});
    }
    function captureAudioSuccess(mediaFiles) {
        var len, i;
        len = mediaFiles.length;
        if(len > 0) {
            for(i = 0; i < len; i + = 1) {
                alert("Audio recorded successfully"+"\n"+
                "File: "+mediaFiles[i].name+ "\n"+
                "is stored at: "+mediaFiles[i].fullPath+"\n"+
                "Size of the file is: "+mediaFiles[i].size);
            }
        }
    }
    function captureAudioError(err) {
        alert("Error occurred while recording audio:" +err);
    }
    </script>
    </head>
    <body onload = "onBodyLoad()">
        <button id = "recordAudio">Capture Audio</button>
    </body>
</html>
```

We can see that a button with the ID `recordAudio` and caption `Capture Audio` is defined in the `<body>` of the HTML file. The `Capture Audio` button, when clicked, invokes the captureAudio() method, which in turn invokes the device's default audio recorder. If the audio is recorded successfully, the captureAudioSuccess callback method is called to display the filename of the recorded audio path where it is stored on the device and the file size. If some error occurs while capturing the audio, the captureAudioError callback is called to display the reason for the error on the screen.

To access the device's default voice recorder, record audio, and save the recorded audio in the device storage, add the following permission statements to the <manifest> element in the AndroidManifest.xml file:

```
<uses-permission android:name = "android.permission.ACCESS_NETWORK_STATE"/>
<uses-permission android:name = "android.permission.WRITE_EXTERNAL_STORAGE"/>
<uses-permission android:name = "android.permission.RECORD_AUDIO"/>
<uses-permission android:name = "android.permission.MODIFY_AUDIO_SETTINGS"/>
```

Upon running the application, a button, Capture Audio, will appear as shown in Figure 8.3a. Upon clicking the Capture Audio button, the standard audio application in the device will open, enabling us to record and play audio (see Figure 8.3b). Upon clicking the record button, the application will begin recording the user's voice as shown in Figure 8.3c. Upon clicking the Stop button, the audio recording will stop. Two options will appear, Discard and Done (see Figure 8.3d). The Discard button will cancel the recorded audio. The Done button, if clicked, will save the recorded audio in the device storage and will appear in the My recordings list of the device. Upon clicking the Done button, an alert dialog will appear, informing us that the audio recorded successfully along with the audio filename, its path, and file size, as shown in Figure 8.3e. The recorded audio will appear in the My recording list of the device (see Figure 8.3f).

## *Capturing Video*

To capture video on a device, the captureVideo() method is used as shown below:

```
navigator.device.capture.captureVideo(captureVideoSuccess,
captureVideoError, captureOptions);
```

The captureVideoSuccess callback is called if the video is captured successfully. An array of media file objects, each describing the captured video clip file, is passed to the callback. The media file array supports the same properties, name, fullPath, type, lastModification-tionDate, and size that we saw in the captureAudio() method.

The captureVideoError callback is called if the capture process is canceled or some error occurs while capturing video. The captureOptions object defines the parameters to configure video capturing. The following are the parameters supported by the captureOptions object:

- **Limit**—Represents the maximum number of video clips that can be captured at a time. The value of this parameter must be greater than or equal to 1. Its default value is 1.
- **Duration**—Represents the maximum duration of the video clip in seconds.
- **Mode**—Represents the mode of video capture, like video/quicktime, video/3gpp, and so on.

**Figure 8.3** (a) `Capture Audio` **appears on application start-up. (b) The standard audio application in the device is invoked. (c) Recording audio. (d) Audio recording stopped. (e) Alert dialog informing us that** `audio recorded successfully`**. (f) The recorded audio appears in the** `My recordings` **list of the device.**

Below are example captures of a video clip that is 30 seconds in duration:

```
var captureOptions = {limit: 1, duration: 30};
navigator.device.capture.captureVideo(captureVideoSuccess,
captureVideoError, captureOptions);
function captureVideoSuccess(mediaFiles) {
    var len, i;
    len = mediaFiles.length;
    if(len > 0) {
        for(i = 0; i < len; i + = 1) {
            alert("Video Clip: "+mediaFiles[i].name+ "\n"+
            "is stored at: "+mediaFiles[i].fullPath+"\n"+
            "Size of the video clip is: "+mediaFiles[i].size);
        }
    }
}
```

```
function captureVideoError(err) {
   alert("Error occurred while recording video:" +err);
}
```

The captureVideoSuccess callback will be called if the captureVideo() method executes successfully; that is, the device's default application successfully records the video(s). The media file array of the recorded video clips is passed to the captureVideoSuccess callback where the filename, path, and size of each video recorded clip are displayed.

The PGMediaApp that we just created earlier captures audio. Let us modify the same application to record video too. That is, in addition to the Capture Audio button, we will add one more button, Capture Video, to the application. When the user clicks the Capture Video button, the device's video recorder application will be invoked to record the video clip(s). So, open the Android project, PGMediaApp. Open the index.html file in the assets/www folder and modify its code to appear as shown in Listing 8.5. Only the code in bold is modified; the rest is the same as we saw in Listing 8.4.

**Listing 8.5   Code Written in the index.html File**

```
<!DOCTYPE HTML>
<html>
   <head>
   <title>PhoneGap Application</title>
   <script type = "text/javascript" charset = "utf-8" src = "cordova-2.3.0.js">
   </script>
   <script type = "text/javascript">
   function onBodyLoad() {
      document.addEventListener("deviceready", PhonegapLoaded, false);
   }
   function PhonegapLoaded(){ document.getElementById("recordAudio").
   addEventListener("click", captureAudio); document.
   getElementById("recordVideo").addEventListener("click", captureVideo);
   }
   function captureAudio() {
      navigator.device.capture.captureAudio(captureAudioSuccess,
      captureAudioError, {limit: 1});
   }
   function captureAudioSuccess(mediaFiles) {
      var len, i;
      len = mediaFiles.length;
      if(len > 0) {
         for(i = 0; i < len; i + = 1) {
            alert("Audio recorded successfully"+"\n"+
            "File: "+mediaFiles[i].name+ "\n"+
            "is stored at: "+mediaFiles[i].fullPath+"\n"+
            "Size of the file is: "+mediaFiles[i].size);
         }
      }
   }
   function captureAudioError(err) {
      alert("Error occurred while recording audio:" +err);
   }
   function captureVideo() { navigator.device.capture.captureVideo
   (captureVideoSuccess, captureVideoError, {limit: 1});
   }
   function captureVideoSuccess(mediaFiles) {
      var len, i;
```

```
        len = mediaFiles.length;
        if(len > 0) {
            for(i = 0; i < len; i + = 1) {
                alert("Video recorded successfully" + "\n" +
                "Video Clip filename: " + mediaFiles[i].name + "\n"+
                "is stored at: " + mediaFiles[i].fullPath + "\n" +
                "Size of the video clip is: " + mediaFiles[i].size);
            }
        }
        else
            alert("Video is not recorded");
    }
    function captureVideoError(err) {
        alert("Error occurred while recording video:" +err);
    }
</script>
</head>
<body onload = "onBodyLoad()">
    <button id = "recordAudio">Capture Audio</button>   
    <button id = "recordVideo">Capture Video</button>
</body>
</html>
```

We can see that a button with the ID `recordVideo` and caption `Capture Video` is added in the `<body>` of the HTML file. The `Capture Video` button, when clicked, invokes the `captureVideo()` method, which in turn invokes the device's camera application to record video. If the video is recorded successfully, the `captureVideoSuccess` callback method is called to display detailed information of the recorded video, for example, the filename of the video, path where it is stored on the device, and file size. If some error occurs while capturing the video, the `captureVideoError` callback is called to display the error that occurred while recording the video.

To access the device's camera to record video, we need to add the following permission statement in the `<manifest>` element in the `AndroidManifest.xml` file:

```
<uses-permission android:name = "android.permission.CAMERA"/>
```

Now our application is ready to run. Upon running the application, we find two buttons, `Capture Audio` and `Capture Video`, as shown in Figure 8.4a. Upon clicking the `Capture Video` button, the standard camera application in the device will open, enabling us to record video (see Figure 8.4b). Upon clicking the record button, video will begin recording, as shown in Figure 8.4c. Upon clicking the stop button, video recording will stop. The recorded video clip will be saved in the storage of the device. An alert dialog informing us of the successful recording of the video along with the filename, its path, and size will appear as shown in Figure 8.4d. The recorded video will appear in the storage of the device (see Figure 8.4e).

## Capturing Images

Earlier, we saw how the Camera API can be used for retrieving images. Let us now look at how the images are captured using the Capture API. To capture an image on a device, the `capture Image()` method is used as shown below:

```
navigator.device.capture.captureImage(captureImageSuccess,
captureImageError, captureOptions);
```

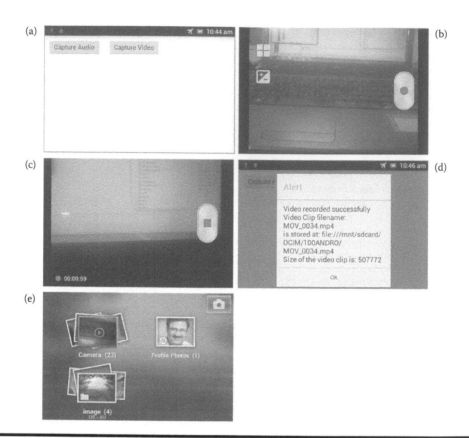

**Figure 8.4** **(a)** `Capture Audio` **and** `Capture Video` **buttons appear on application start-up. (b) The standard camera application in the device is invoked. (c) Recording video. (d) Alert dialog informing us that** `Video recorded successfully along with other information.` **(e) Recorded video appears in the Pictures Library.**

The `captureImageSuccess` callback is called if the image is captured successfully. An array of media file objects, each describing the captured image file(s), is passed to the callback. The media file array supports the same properties, `name`, `fullPath`, `type`, `lastModificationDate`, and `size` that we saw in the `captureAudio()` method.

The `captureImageError` callback is called if the capture process is canceled or some error occurs while capturing the image. The `captureOptions` object defines the parameters to configure image capturing—the same as we saw in the `captureVideo()` method.

The example given below captures an image using the device's default camera application:

```
<!DOCTYPE HTML>
<html>
    <head>
    <title>PhoneGap Application</title>
    <script type = "text/javascript" charset = "utf-8" src = "cordova-
    2.3.0.js"></script>
    <script type = "text/javascript">
    function onBodyLoad() {
        document.addEventListener("deviceready", PhonegapLoaded, false);
```

```
        }
    function PhonegapLoaded(){
        document.getElementById("captureImage").addEventListener("click",
        captureImage);
        }
    function captureImage() {
        navigator.device.capture.captureImage(captureImageSuccess,
        captureImageError, {limit: 1});
    }
function captureImageSuccess(mediaFiles) {
var len, i;
    len = mediaFiles.length;
    if(len > 0) {
        for(i = 0; i < len; i + = 1) {
            alert("Image captured successfully"+"\n"+
            "Image File: "+mediaFiles[i].name+ "\n"+
            "is stored at: "+mediaFiles[i].fullPath+"\n"+
            "Size of the image file is: "+mediaFiles[i].size);
        }
    }
}
function captureImageError(err) {
alert("Error occurred while capturing image:" +err);
}
    </script>
    </head>
    <body onload = "onBodyLoad()">
        <button id = "captureImage">Capture Image</button>
    </body>
</html>
```

The code above is self-explanatory and requires no further explanation.

# Using Geolocation API

Geolocation API can be used to fetch the location information of the device in terms of latitude and longitude. It is the global positioning system (GPS) that is usually used to determine a
device's location, including signals like the IP address, WiFi, and so on. Let us begin by finding
the device's current location.

## *Getting a Device's Current Location*

To determine the location of a smartphone, the getCurrentPosition() method is used as
shown below:

```
navigator.geolocation.getCurrentPosition(onSuccess, onError, geoOptions);
```

The onSuccess callback is executed when the device's location is successfully measured,
and the onError callback is called if some error occurs while measuring the device's location.

The optional `geoOptions` object can be passed to the `getCurrentPosition()` method to configure it. The `geoOptions` object supports the following properties:

- `enableHighAccuracy`—Boolean value that determines if the device's location has to be measured with a higher degree of accuracy. This option, if set to `true`, will give a more accurate value, but at the same time consumes more processing and battery power.
- `maximumAge`—Defines the maximum age in milliseconds of a cached location value. A smaller value for this property will make the `getCurrentPosition()` method update the device location more frequently.
- `timeout`—Defines the maximum amount of time in milliseconds that can be spent between the execution of the `getCurrentPosition()` method call and the `onSuccess` callback method before declaring a timeout.

The following `geoOptions` object configures the `getCurrentPosition()` method to measure the device location with higher accuracy and declare a timeout if a response is not received within 3000 milliseconds, that is, 3 seconds:

```
var geolocationOptions = {
    timeout : 3000,
    enableHighAccuracy : true
};
```

The `position` object is passed to the `onSuccess` callback method that includes the `Coordinates` object, which in turn contains the properties that can be used to display the device's location. The list of properties supported by the `Coordinates` object is provided below:

- `latitude`—Represents the latitude expressed in decimal degrees.
- `longitude`—Represents the longitude expressed in decimal degrees.
- `altitude`—Represents the height above sea level in meters.
- `accuracy`—Represents the accuracy of the latitude/longitude reading in meters.
- `altitudeAccuracy`—Represents the accuracy of the altitude coordinate in meters.
- `heading`—Represents the direction of travel relative to true north in degrees.
- `speed`—Represents the current ground speed in meters per second.

The following code shows how a position object passed to the `onSuccess` callback can be used to display the location information of the device:

```
function onSuccess(position) {
    var element = document.getElementById('geolocationinfo');
    element.innerHTML = 'Latitude: ' + position.coords.latitude + '<br/>' +
    'Longitude: ' + position.coords.longitude + '<br/>' +
    'Altitude: ' + position.coords.altitude +'<br/>' +
    'Accuracy: ' + position.coords.accuracy +'<br/>' +
    'Altitude Accuracy: ' + position.coords.altitudeAccuracy +'<br/>' +
    'Heading: ' + position.coords.heading +'<br/>' +
    'Speed: ' + position.coords.speed +'<br/>' +
    'Timestamp: ' + new Date(position.timestamp) + '<br/>';
}
```

As stated earlier, when an error occurs while measuring the device's location, the onError callback method is executed. An error object is passed to the onError callback whose code and message properties can be used to display the reason that caused the error. The error code can be one of the following constants:

- PositionError.PERMISSION _ DENIED
- PositionError.POSITION _ UNAVAILABLE
- PositionError.TIMEOUT

The message property of the error object defines the cause of the error in detail. An alert dialog can be used in the onError callback to display the error message as shown below:

```
function onError(error) {
    alert('code: ' + error.code + '\n' + 'message: ' + error.message + '\n');
}
```

## Watching a Device's Location

To watch a device's location periodically, geolocation watch is used. To create a geolocation watch, the watchPosition() method is used as shown below:

```
watchID = navigator.geolocation.watchPosition(onSuccess, onError,
geoOptions);
```

The newly created geolocation watch is assigned to the watchID variable. The onSuccess and onError callback methods are respectively called when the device's location is measured successfully and when some error occurs while measuring the device's location. The geoOptions object can be used to configure the watch.

The following geoOptions object configures the watch to ignore the cached values that are older than 5000 milliseconds (5 seconds), declares a timeout if a response is not received within 2000 milliseconds (2 seconds), and measures the location of the device with higher accuracy:

```
var geoOptions = {
    maximumAge : 5000,
    timeout : 2000,
    enableHighAccuracy : true
};
```

After defining the geoOptions object, the watchPosition() method can be called as shown below:

```
watchID = navigator.geolocation.watchPosition(onSuccess, onError, geoOp-
tions);
```

For example, we saw in the getCurrentPosition() method, as well as in the watch-Position() method, that a position object is passed to the onSuccess callback that contains the same geolocation properties that we discussed in the getCurrentPosition() method. The code below displays the location of the device through the position object passed to the onSuccess callback method:

```
function onSuccess(position) {
   var element = document.getElementById('geolocationinfo');
   element.innerHTML = 'Latitude: ' + position.coords.latitude + '<br/>' +
   'Longitude: ' + position.coords.longitude + '<br/>' +
   'Timestamp: ' + new Date(position.timestamp) + '<br/>';
}
```

In case of any error that might occur while finding the device's location, the `onError` callback is called that displays the reason that caused the error, as shown below:

```
function onError(error) {
   alert('code: ' + error.code + '\n' + 'message: ' + error.message + '\n');
}
```

### Canceling a Watch

To cancel the watch, the `clearWatch()` method is called, passing the `watchID` variable that is created through the `watchPosition()` method:

```
navigator.geolocation.clearWatch(watchID);
```

The resources allocated to `watchID` can be released along with a message informing us of the cancelation of the watch, as shown below:

```
function cancelWatch() {
   navigator.geolocation.clearWatch(watchID);
   watchID = null;
   alert("Location Watch Cancelled");
}
```

## Using Google Maps API

The Google Maps API is used to integrate the Google Maps service into our Web applications. We need to subscribe to the API's console Web site to obtain the API key. The API key is used in the applications so that the service can monitor the application's usage. The following are the main classes of the Google Maps API:

- `google.maps.Map` class—Defines a single map on a page. Any number of instances of this class can be created where each instance will define a separate map on the page.
- `google.maps.LatLng` class—Represents geographical coordinates in terms of latitude and longitude.
- `google.maps.Marker` class—Used to place markers on a map.
- `Geocoder` class—Used to convert an address to a `LatLng` object, and vice versa.

## Displaying Google Maps

Each instance of `google.maps.Map` class displays a simple Google map on a page. The `Map` class accepts the following two parameters:

- An HTML element that will contain the map. The preferred HTML element for displaying a map on a Web page is a `<div>` element. The code below shows a sample `<div>` element that can be used to display a map:

  ```
  <div id = "map_canvas" style = "width:100%; height:100%"></div>
  ```

  In the example above, we define a `<div>` element named `map-canvas` and set its size to 100%, which will expand it to fit the size on mobile devices.

- The second parameter used in the `Map` class is a `google.maps.MapOptions` object that is used to initialize the map. The `MapOptions` object defines map initialization variables as shown in Table 8.2.

The following example defines the map of type ROADMAP:

```
mapTypeId: google.maps.MapTypeId.ROADMAP
```

**Table 8.2  A Brief Description of the Initialization Variables Used in the `MapOptions` Object**

| Initialization Variables | Description |
|---|---|
| Latitudes and longitudes | To center the map on a specific point, we create a `LatLng` object and pass the desired location's coordinates to it in the order {latitude, longitude}. In the following example, we will center the map at 37.76944 latitude and –122.43444 longitude:<br><br>`center: new google.maps.LatLng(37.76944, -122.43444)` |
| Zoom levels | Determine the resolution to display the map. Value 0 for the zoom level will make the map fully zoomed out, and as we increase the value of this property, the map will zoom in at a higher resolution. In the following example, we will zoom in the map at the resolution value 8:<br><br>`zoom: 8` |
| Map types | Determine the map type. The following map types are supported:<br>• `ROADMAP`—Displays the normal, default road map view.<br>• `SATELLITE`—Displays Google Earth satellite images.<br>• `HYBRID`—Displays a mix of satellite views along with a layer for roads, city names, etc.<br>• `TERRAIN`—Displays physical map displaying terrain information like mountains, rivers, etc. |

A sample `MapOptions` object may look as given below:

```
var mapOptions = {
   center: new google.maps.LatLng(37.76944, -122.43444),
   zoom: 8,
   mapTypeId: google.maps.MapTypeId.ROADMAP
};
```

To create a new instance of the Map class, the JavaScript new operator is used as shown below:

```
var map = new google.maps.Map(document.getElementById("map_canvas"),
mapOptions);
```

We can see that a new `Map` instance called map is created. While creating a new map instance, we specify a `<div>` HTML element in the page that acts as a container for the map. The reference of the `<div>` element is obtained in JavaScript via the `document.getElementById()` method.

The Maps JavaScript API is written into a `<script>` tag as shown below:

```
<script type = "text/javascript" src = "http://maps.google.com/maps/api/
js?sensor = false"></script>
```

The `sensor` parameter of the URL must be included in the `<script>` tag, and it indicates whether the application uses a sensor (such as a GPS locator) to determine the user's location. The statement above indicates that no sensor will be used in the application.

The code given below sums up what we learned above. The code displays a Google map of ROADMAP type centered at 37.76944, –122.43444:

```
<!DOCTYPE HTML>
<html>
   <head>
   <title>PhoneGap Application</title>
   <script type = "text/javascript" charset = "utf-8" src = "cordova-
   2.3.0.js"></script>
   <script type = "text/javascript" src = "http://maps.google.com/maps/
   api/js?sensor = false"></script>
   <link href = "http://code.google.com/apis/maps/documentation/
   javascript/examples/default.css" rel = "stylesheet" type = "text/css"/>
   <script type = "text/javascript">
   function onBodyLoad() {
      document.addEventListener("deviceready", PhonegapLoaded, false);
   }
   function PhonegapLoaded(){
      var mapOptions = {
      center: new google.maps.LatLng(37.76944, -122.43444),
      zoom: 8,
      mapTypeId: google.maps.MapTypeId.ROADMAP
   };
   var map = new google.maps.Map(document.getElementById("map_canvas"),
   mapOptions);
   }
```

```
</script>
</head>
<body onload = "onBodyLoad()">
    <div id = "map_canvas" style = "width:100%; height:100%"></div>
</body>
```

In the code above, we ensure that the Maps API JavaScript code is loaded after PhoneGap is fully loaded. The `onBodyLoad()` function executes and loads PhoneGap. Once PhoneGap is loaded, the Maps API JavaScript code is loaded to perform the task of displaying the map.

## Combining the Geolocation and Google Maps API

We have learned about the Geolocation and Google Maps APIs, their classes, and methods that are used in finding the location of the device and displaying Google maps, respectively. How about combining the two APIs?

Let us create an application that displays Google maps as well as measures the location of the device. So, launch Eclipse and create a new Android project called `PGGoogleMapApp` and configure it for using PhoneGap. In the `assets/www` folder, open the `index.html` file and write the code as shown in Listing 8.6.

**Listing 8.6   Code Written in the `index.html` File**

```
<!DOCTYPE HTML>
<html>
    <head>
    <title>PhoneGap Application</title>
    <script type = "text/javascript" charset = "utf-8" src =
    "cordova-2.3.0.js"></script>
    <script type = "text/javascript" src = "http://maps.google.com/maps/api/
    js?sensor = false"></script>
    <link href = "http://code.google.com/apis/maps/documentation/javascript/
    examples/default.css" rel = "stylesheet" type = "text/css"/>
    <script type = "text/javascript">
    function onBodyLoad() {
        document.addEventListener("deviceready", PhonegapLoaded, false);
    }
    function PhonegapLoaded(){
        var mapOptions = {
        center: new google.maps.LatLng(37.76944, -122.43444),
        zoom: 8,
        mapTypeId: google.maps.MapTypeId.ROADMAP
    };
    var map = new google.maps.Map(document.getElementById("map_canvas"),
    mapOptions);
    navigator.geolocation.watchPosition(onSuccess, onError, {enableHighAccuracy:
    true});
    }
    function onSuccess(position) {
        var element = document.getElementById('geolocationinfo');
        element.innerHTML = 'Latitude: ' + position.coords.latitude + '<br/>' +
        'Longitude: ' + position.coords.longitude + '<br/>' +
        'Timestamp: ' + new Date(position.timestamp) + '<br/>';
    }
```

```
function onError(error) {
   alert('code: ' + error.code + '\n' + 'message: ' + error.message + '\n');
}
</script>
</head>
<body onload = "onBodyLoad()">
   <div id = "geolocationinfo">GeoLocation Information</div>
   <div id = "map_canvas" style = "width:100%; height:100%"></div>
</body>
</html>
```

In the code above, we see that two <div> elements are defined with the IDs geolocation-info and map _ canvas, respectively. The first <div> element will be used for displaying the geolocation information of the device, and the second <div> element will be used for displaying Google maps. The mapOptions object is defined to make the Google map centered at latitude 37.76944 and longitude -122.43444. Also, the Google map is set to display the default road map view that is zoomed in at level 8. An instance of the Map class is created to display the Google map in the <div> element of the ID map _ canvas. The watchPosition() method is called to measure the location of the device. The onSuccess callback method is called when the location of the device is successfully measured. In the onSuccess callback, the latitude and longitude of the device are displayed in the <div> element of the ID geolocationinfo, along with the time-stamp, that is, date and time of measuring the location of the device. The onError callback is set to display the error message if any error occurs while measuring the location of the device.

To display Google maps and to access the device location, we need to write permissions in the AndroidManifest.xml file as shown in Listing 8.7. Only the code in bold is new; the rest is the default code.

**Listing 8.7   Code in the AndroidManifest.xml File**

```
<?xml version = "1.0" encoding = "utf-8"?>
<manifest xmlns:android = "http://schemas.android.com/apk/res/android"
   package = "com.phonegap.pggooglemapapp"
   android:versionCode = "1"
   android:versionName = "1.0" >
   <uses-sdk
      android:minSdkVersion = "11"
      android:targetSdkVersion = "17"/>
   <uses-permission
      android:name = "android.permission.ACCESS_NETWORK_STATE"/>
      <uses-permission android:name = "android.permission.INTERNET"/>
      <uses-permission android:name = "android.permission.ACCESS_FINE_LOCATION"/>
      <uses-permission android:name = "android.permission.
      ACCESS_COARSE_LOCATION"/>
      <uses-permission android:name = "android.permission.
      ACCESS_LOCATION_EXTRA_COMMANDS"/>
   <application
      android:allowBackup = "true"
      android:icon = "@drawable/ic_launcher"
      android:label = "@string/app_name"
      android:theme = "@style/AppTheme" >
      <activity android:name = "com.phonegap.pggooglemapapp.
      PGGoogleMapAppActivity"
         android:label = "@string/app_name" >
         <intent-filter>
            <action android:name = "android.intent.action.MAIN"/>
```

```
        <category android:name = "android.intent.category.LAUNCHER"/>
      </intent-filter>
    </activity>
  </application>
</manifest>
```

Our application is ready to run. Start the `PhoneGapAVD` and run the application. Remember, your PC must be connected to the Internet. The Google map will appear in the emulator. To supply the location of the device, that is, to supply longitude and latitude values, we will make use of the Dalvik Debug Monitor Server (DDMS). To switch to the DDMS perspective, either click the DDMS icon in the toolbar or choose the `Window->Open Perspective->DDMS` option. In the DDMS perspective, we find our Android emulator, `PhoneGapAVD` running with ID `emulator-5554`. Select the emulator, `emulator-5554`, from the left pane and the `Emulator Control` button from the right pane. Under the `Location Controls` tab, we find two text boxes, `Longitude` and `Latitude`, that can be used for sending longitude and latitude values to the application. Let us supply the longitude and latitude values for the device as –122.43444 and 7.76944, respectively, followed by clicking the `Send` button, as shown in Figure 8.5.

Because the longitude and latitude values of San Francisco are supplied in the application above, the Google map will appear centered around San Francisco. Also, the geolocation information of the device that we supplied through the DDMS is displayed at the top (see Figure 8.6).

## *Displaying Google Map Centered at the Device Location*

In the application above, the Google map was displayed centered at the supplied longitude and latitude values. Now, let us modify the application so that the Google map is displayed centered at the device's location. That is, the application should first detect the location of the device and use that information in centering the Google map. To do so, open the `PGGoogleMapApp` that we created above. Open the `index.html` file in the `assets/www` folder and modify it to appear as shown in Listing 8.8. Observe the code in bold; the rest of the code is the same as we saw in Listing 8.6.

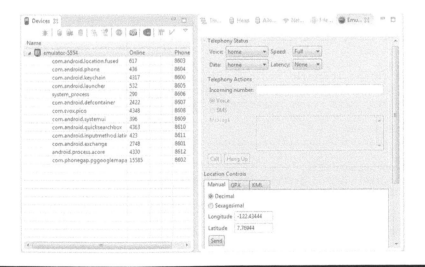

**Figure 8.5    Supplying longitude and latitude values of the device through the DDMS perspective.**

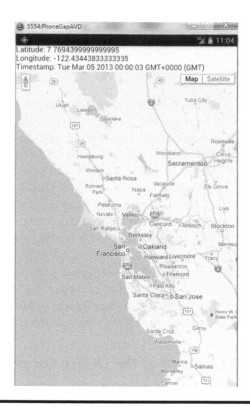

**Figure 8.6** A Google map is displayed centered at the specified location, along with the geolocation information displayed at the top.

**Listing 8.8** Code Written in the `index.html` File

```
<!DOCTYPE HTML>
<html>
    <head>
    <title>PhoneGap Application</title>
    <script type = "text/javascript" charset = "utf-8" src = "cordova-2.3.0.js">
    </script>
    <script type = "text/javascript" src = "http://maps.google.com/maps/api/
    js?sensor = false"></script>
    <link href = "http://code.google.com/apis/maps/documentation/javascript/
    examples/default.css" rel = "stylesheet" type = "text/css"/>
    <script type = "text/javascript">
    function onBodyLoad() {
        document.addEventListener("deviceready", PhonegapLoaded, false);
    }
    function PhonegapLoaded(){
        navigator.geolocation.getCurrentPosition(onSuccess, onError,
        {enableHighAccuracy: true});
    }
    function onSuccess(position) {
        var element = document.getElementById('geolocationinfo');
        element.innerHTML = 'Latitude: ' + position.coords.latitude + '<br/>' +
        'Longitude: ' + position.coords.longitude + '<br/>' +
        'Timestamp: ' + new Date(position.timestamp) + '<br/>';
        var mapOptions = {
```

```
        center: new google.maps.LatLng(position.coords.latitude, position.coords.
        longitude),
        zoom: 8,
        mapTypeId: google.maps.MapTypeId.ROADMAP
    };
    var map = new google.maps.Map(document.getElementById("map_canvas"),
    mapOptions);
}
function onError(error) {
    alert('code: ' + error.code + '\n' + 'message: ' + error.message + '\n');
}
</script>
</head>
<body onload = "onBodyLoad()">
    <div id = "geolocationinfo">GeoLocation Information</div>
    <div id = "map_canvas" style = "width:100%; height:100%"></div>
</body>
</html>
```

We can see that after the PhoneGap is loaded, the getCurrentPosition() method is called to find the device location. Upon measuring the device location, the onSuccess callback is called and the position object containing the geolocation information of the device is passed to it. In the onSuccess callback, the longitude and latitude of the device are displayed through the <div> element of the ID geolocationinfo. Also, the timestamp where the device location is measured is displayed. Thereafter, the mapOptions object is defined to center the Google map at the device location's latitude and longitude values. Finally, an instance of Map class is created called map to display the Google map in the <div> element of the ID map _ canvas.

If we run the application on the Android device, we might get an error, as shown in Figure 8.7a. The error occurs if Location services are not enabled on the device. To enable Location services on a device, open the Settings menu on it and select the Location services option (see Figure 8.7b) in it. From the Location services menu, enable both

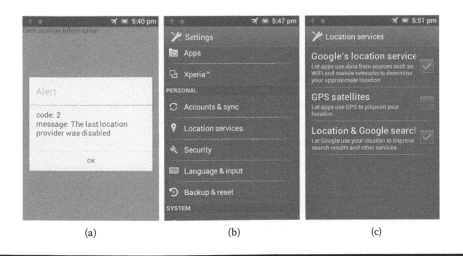

(a)                    (b)                    (c)

**Figure 8.7    (a) An error code is displayed if** Location **services are not enabled. (b) The setting menu on the device showing different options. (c) The location services menu showing different options.**

**Figure 8.8   A Google map is displayed centered at the device location.**

the `Google's location service` and `Location & Google search` options (see Figure 8.7c). Also, do not forget to switch on the WiFi on the device.

After enabling the `Location services` on the device, when we run the application, the Google map will appear centered at the device location, as shown in Figure 8.8. Also, the geolocation information of the device in terms of latitude and longitude is displayed along with the timestamp above the map.

## *Displaying Markers on the Map*

To display markers at the specified location coordinates on the map, the `google.maps.Marker` class is used. The instance of `google.maps.Marker` class is created and options are defined to indicate the location of the marker. Given below are the four options that are popularly used while creating markers:

- `position`—This is a required option and is used to indicate the location of the marker on the map. An instance of `google.maps.LatLng` class is created passing the desired latitude and longitude values to define the location of the marker.
- `title`—This is an optional option that is used to display text that appears hovering over the marker.
- `draggable`—A Boolean value that determines whether the marker can be dragged or not. The Boolean value `true`, if assigned to this option, will make the marker draggable.

■ raiseOnDrag—Boolean value when set to true makes the marker rise when dragged and lowers it when dropped.

To display markers in the Google map that we displayed above, open the PGGoogleMapApp and modify its index.html file to appear as shown in Listing 8.9. Only the code in bold is modified; the rest of the code is the same as we saw in Listing 8.8.

**Listing 8.9  Code Written in the `index.html` File**

```
<!DOCTYPE HTML>
<html>
   <head>
   <title>PhoneGap Application</title>
   <script type = "text/javascript" charset = "utf-8" src = "cordova-2.3.0.js">
   </script>
   <script type = "text/javascript" src = "http://maps.google.com/maps/api/
   js?sensor = false"></script>
   <link href = "http://code.google.com/apis/maps/documentation/javascript/
   examples/default.css" rel = "stylesheet" type = "text/css"/>
   <script type = "text/javascript">
   function onBodyLoad() {
       document.addEventListener("deviceready", PhonegapLoaded, false);
   }
   function PhonegapLoaded(){
       navigator.geolocation.getCurrentPosition(onSuccess, onError,
       {enableHighAccuracy: true});
   }
   function onSuccess(position) {
       var element = document.getElementById('geolocationinfo');
       element.innerHTML = 'Latitude: ' + position.coords.latitude + '<br/>' +
       'Longitude: ' + position.coords.longitude + '<br/>' +
       'Timestamp: ' + new Date(position.timestamp) + '<br/>';
       var mapOptions = {
          center: new google.maps.LatLng(position.coords.latitude, position.coords.
          longitude),
          zoom: 8,
          mapTypeId: google.maps.MapTypeId.ROADMAP
       };
       var map = new google.maps.Map(document.getElementById("map_canvas"),
       mapOptions);
       var marker = new google.maps.Marker({
          position: new google.maps.LatLng(position.coords.latitude, position.
          coords.longitude),
          title: "I am here"
          });
          marker.setMap(map);
   }
   function onError(error) {
       alert('code: ' + error.code + '\n' + 'message: ' + error.message + '\n');
   }
   </script>
   </head>
   <body onload = "onBodyLoad()">
      <div id = "geolocationinfo">GeoLocation Information</div>
      <div id = "map_canvas" style = "width:100%; height:100%"></div>
   </body>
</html>
```

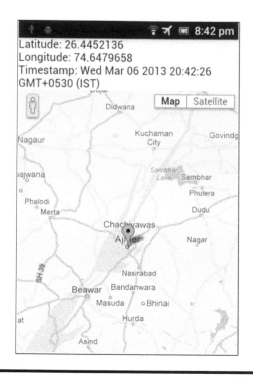

**Figure 8.9 A Google map is displayed centered at the device location and a marker is displayed at the device location.**

In the code above, we see that an instance of `Marker` class is created by the name `marker` and its `position` property is set equal to the longitude and latitude values of the device. The `title` of the marker is set to the text `I am here`. Upon running the application, the Google map will be displayed centered at the device location and the device location will be identified by a marker, as shown in Figure 8.9.

## Drawing Lines on the Map

To draw lines on the map, the `Polyline` class is used. The `Polyline` class supports lots of properties to set the color, opacity, path, map, and so forth, of the line. The following statements draw a red line between two positions, `p1` and `p2`:

```
var line = new google.maps.Polyline({
    p1: new google.maps.LatLng(latitude_value1, longitude_value1),
    p2: new google.maps.LatLng(latitude_value2, longitude_value2),
    path: [p1, p2],
    strokeColor: '#FF0000',
    strokeOpacity: 1.0,
    map: map
});
```

We can see that a line is drawn between two positions, `p1` and `p2`, where `p1` and `p2` are the `LatLng` instances defined by supplying the respective latitude and longitude values. Similarly, the following statements draw a red line between two markers, `marker1` and `marker2`:

```
var line = new google.maps.Polyline({
    path: [marker1.getPosition(), marker2.getPosition()],
    strokeColor: '#FF0000',
    strokeOpacity: 1.0,
    map: map
});
```

**Note:** The map property is essential in `Polyline` and other drawing classes because it defines the map object on which the line has to be drawn.

## *Finding the Distance between Two Positions*

To find out the distance between two position objects, the `computeDistanceBetween()` method is used, as shown in the statements below:

```
var p1 = new google.maps.LatLng(latitude_value1, longitude_value1);
var p2 = new google.maps.LatLng(latitude_value2, longitude_value2);
d = google.maps.geometry.spherical.computeDistanceBetween(p1, p2);
```

We can see that positions, that is, `LatLng` instances, `p1` and `p2` are defined by supplying the respective latitude and longitude values. The distance between the two positions is computed by the `computeDistanceBetween()` method and will be assigned to variable `d`. The distance computed will be in meters.

Let us modify the application `PGGoogleMapApp` to display a line between two markers in the Google map and display the distance between the two markers. We will be displaying the two markers at the following two locations:

■ The first marker will be displayed at the device's location.
■ The second marker will be displayed at the location near the device location. If the device location (or the first marker) is represented by `latitude` and `longitude` values, then the location of the second marker is computed by adding .5 to the `latitude` and longitude. That is, the second marker will be displayed at a location represented by latitude+.5 and longitude+.5 values.

So, open the `index.html` file in the `PGGoogleMapApp` application and modify it to appear as shown in Listing 8.10. Only the code in bold is modified; the rest of the code is the same as we saw in Listing 8.9.

**Listing 8.10   Code Written in the `index.html` File**

```
<!DOCTYPE HTML>
<html>
    <head>
    <title>PhoneGap Application</title>
    <script type = "text/javascript" charset = "utf-8" src = "cordova-2.3.0.js">
    </script>
    <script type = "text/javascript" src = "http://maps.google.com/maps/api/
    js?sensor = false"></script>
```

```html
<link href = "http://code.google.com/apis/maps/documentation/javascript/
examples/default.css" rel = "stylesheet" type = "text/css"/>
<script type = "text/javascript" src = "http://maps.google.com/maps/api/
js?sensor = false&libraries = geometry"> </script>
<script type = "text/javascript">
function onBodyLoad() {
   document.addEventListener("deviceready", PhonegapLoaded, false);
}
function PhonegapLoaded(){
   navigator.geolocation.getCurrentPosition(onSuccess, onError,
   {enableHighAccuracy: true});
}
function onSuccess(position) {
   var geolocationinfo1 = document.getElementById('geolocationinfo1');
   geolocationinfo1.innerHTML = 'Location 1: (Latitude: ' + position.coords.
   latitude + '<br/>' +
   'Longitude: ' + position.coords.longitude + '<br/>';
   var geolocationinfo2 = document.getElementById('geolocationinfo2');
   geolocationinfo2.innerHTML = 'Location 2: (Latitude: ' + position.coords.
   latitude +.5 + '<br/>' +
   'Longitude: ' + position.coords.longitude +.5+ '<br/>';
   var mapOptions = {
      center: new google.maps.LatLng(position.coords.latitude, position.coords.
      longitude),
      zoom: 8,
      mapTypeId: google.maps.MapTypeId.ROADMAP
   };
   var map = new google.maps.Map(document.getElementById("map_canvas"),
   mapOptions);
   var marker1 = new google.maps.Marker({
      position: new google.maps.LatLng(position.coords.latitude, position.
      coords.longitude),
      draggable: true,
      raiseOnDrag: false
   });
   marker1.setMap(map);
   var marker2 = new google.maps.Marker({
      position: new google.maps.LatLng(position.coords.latitude+.5, position.
      coords.longitude+.5),
      draggable: true,
      raiseOnDrag: false
   });
   marker2.setMap(map);
   var line = new google.maps.Polyline({
      path: [marker1.getPosition(), marker2.getPosition()],
      map: map
   });
   var p1 = new google.maps.LatLng(position.coords.latitude, position.coords.
   longitude);
   var p2 = new google.maps.LatLng(position.coords.latitude +.5, position.
   coords.longitude +.5);
   d = (google.maps.geometry.spherical.computeDistanceBetween(p1, p2)/1000).
   toFixed(2);
   document.getElementById('distance').innerHTML = "Distance between
   locations:" + d +" km";
}
function onError(error) {
   alert('code: ' + error.code + '\n' + 'message: ' + error.message + '\n');
}
</script>
</head>
```

```
<body onload = "onBodyLoad()">
    <div id = "geolocationinfo1">GeoLocation Information 1</div>
    <div id = "geolocationinfo2">GeoLocation Information 2</div>
    <div id = "distance">Distance</div>
    <div id = "map_canvas" style = "width:100%; height:100%"></div>
</body>
</html>
```

We can see that the `geometry` library is included in the application to compute the distance between two positions. Also, two `<div>` elements with IDs `geolocationinfo1` and `geolocationinfo2` are defined, where `geolocationinfo1` will be used to display the location information of the device and `geolocationinfo2` will be used to display the location information near the device. The `<div>` element with the ID `distance` will be used for displaying the distance between the two locations in kilometers. A `mapOptions` object is defined that centers the Google map at the device location. An instance of the `Map` class is created called `map` to display the Google map. Two markers, `marker1` and `marker2`, are displayed on the Google map. `marker1` is displayed at the device location, and `marker2` is displayed near the device location. An instance of `Polyline` is created to draw a line between the two markers. Two position objects, `p1` and `p2`, are defined where position object `p1` points at the latitude and longitude of the device and position object `p2` points at the location near the device (latitude + .5 and longitude + .5). Using the `computeDistanceBetween()` method, the distance between two position objects `p1` and `p2` is computed and is displayed through the `<div>` element, `distance`.

Upon running the application, two markers will be displayed on the Google map, one at the device location and the other near it. Also, a line is drawn between the two markers. In addition, the distance between the two markers is also computed and displayed (see Figure 8.10).

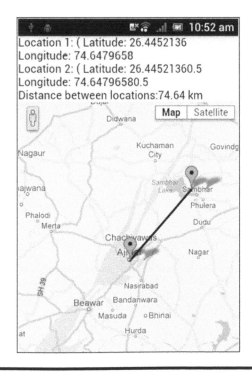

**Figure 8.10  A line is drawn between the two markers and the distance between them is computed.**

## Dragging Markers and Computing Distances

In the application above, we saw that the two markers are disabled; that is, we cannot move or drag them. Let us modify the application above so that we can drag either of the two markers. Also, when we drag either of the markers, their new geolocation information will be displayed and the new distance between the two markers will be computed and displayed.

So, open the application PGGoogleMapApp and modify the index.html file found in the assets/www folder to appear as shown in Listing 8.11. Only the code in bold is modified; the rest of the code is the same as we saw in Listing 8.10.

**Listing 8.11    Code Written in the index.html File**

```
<!DOCTYPE HTML>
<html>
    <head>
    <title>PhoneGap Application</title>
    <script type = "text/javascript" charset = "utf-8" src = "cordova-2.3.0.js">
    </script>
    <script type = "text/javascript" src = "http://maps.google.com/maps/api/
    js?sensor = false"></script>
    <link href = "http://code.google.com/apis/maps/documentation/javascript/
    examples/default.css" rel = "stylesheet" type = "text/css"/>
    <script type = "text/javascript" src = "http://maps.google.com/maps/api/
    js?sensor = false&libraries = geometry"></script>
    <script type = "text/javascript">
    function onBodyLoad() {
        document.addEventListener("deviceready", PhonegapLoaded, false);
    }
    function PhonegapLoaded(){
        navigator.geolocation.getCurrentPosition(onSuccess, onError,
        {enableHighAccuracy: true});
    }
    function onSuccess(position) {
        var geolocationinfo1 = document.getElementById('geolocationinfo1');
        geolocationinfo1.innerHTML = 'Location 1: (Latitude: ' + position.coords.
        latitude + '<br/>' +
        'Longitude: ' + position.coords.longitude + '<br/>';
        var geolocationinfo2 = document.getElementById('geolocationinfo2');
        geolocationinfo2.innerHTML = 'Location 2: (Latitude: ' + position.coords.
        latitude +.5 + '<br/>' +
        'Longitude: ' + position.coords.longitude +.5+ '<br/>';
        var mapOptions = {
            center: new google.maps.LatLng(position.coords.latitude, position.coords.
            longitude),
            zoom: 8,
            mapTypeId: google.maps.MapTypeId.ROADMAP
        };
        var map = new google.maps.Map(document.getElementById("map_canvas"),
        mapOptions);
        var marker1 = new google.maps.Marker({
            position: new google.maps.LatLng(position.coords.latitude, position.
            coords.longitude),
            draggable: true,
            raiseOnDrag: false
        });
        marker1.setMap(map);
        var marker2 = new google.maps.Marker({
```

```
        position: new google.maps.LatLng(position.coords.latitude+.5, position.
        coords.longitude+.5),
        draggable: true,
        raiseOnDrag: false
    });
    marker2.setMap(map);
    findDistance(marker1, marker2);
    google.maps.event.addListener(marker1, 'drag', function() {
        var geolocationinfo1 = document.getElementById('geolocationinfo1');
        geolocationinfo1.innerHTML = 'Location 1: (Latitude: ' + marker1.
        getPosition().lat() + '<br/>' +
        'Longitude: ' + marker1.getPosition().lng() + '<br/>';
        findDistance(marker1, marker2);
    });
    google.maps.event.addListener(marker2, 'drag', function() {
        var geolocationinfo2 = document.getElementById('geolocationinfo2');
        geolocationinfo2.innerHTML = 'Location 1: (Latitude: ' + marker2.
        getPosition().lat() + '<br/>' +
        'Longitude: ' + marker2.getPosition().lng() + '<br/>';
        findDistance(marker1, marker2);
    });
}
function findDistance(marker1, marker2){
    var p1 = new google.maps.LatLng(marker1.getPosition().lat(), marker1.
    getPosition().lng());
    var p2 = new google.maps.LatLng(marker2.getPosition().lat(), marker2.
    getPosition().lng());
    d = (google.maps.geometry.spherical.computeDistanceBetween(p1, p2)/1000).
    toFixed(2);
    document.getElementById('distance').innerHTML = "Distance between
    locations:" + d +" km";
}
function onError(error) {
    alert('code: ' + error.code + '\n' + 'message: ' + error.message + '\n');
}
</script>
</head>
<body onload = "onBodyLoad()">
    <div id = "geolocationinfo1">GeoLocation Information 1</div>
    <div id = "geolocationinfo2">GeoLocation Information 2</div>
    <div id = "distance">Distance</div>
    <div id = "map_canvas" style = "width:100%; height:100%"></div>
</body>
</html>
```

We can see that the function findDistance() is defined and uses two parameters, marker1 and marker2. Using the parameters marker1 and marker2, the findDistance() function retrieves the position objects, p1 and p2, that represent the positions of the two markers. Thereafter, the computeDistanceBetween() method is used to compute the distance between the two position objects, p1 and p2. The computed distance is converted into kilometers and displayed through the <div> element, distance.

Also, the drag event listeners are associated with the two markers so that whenever either of them is dragged, their new geolocation information is displayed through their respective <div> element and the findDistance() function is called to recompute the distance between the two markers.

Upon running the application, we see that the Google map is displayed with two markers. One marker will be displayed at the device's current location, and the other marker will be displayed

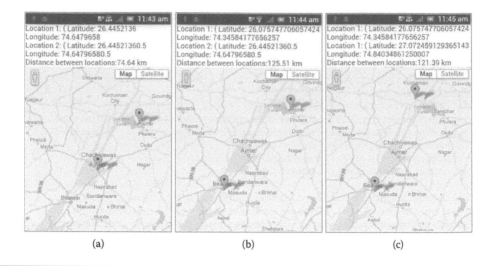

(a)                                (b)                                (c)

**Figure 8.11    (a) A Google map is displayed with two markers. (b) The geolocation information of `marker1` and updated distance. (c) The geolocation information of `marker2` along with the updated distance.**

near the device location. The geolocation information of the two markers will be displayed above the map. Also, the distance between the two markers will be computed and displayed in kilometers (see Figure 8.11a). Upon dragging the first marker on the Google map, that is, `marker1`, its geolocation information displayed above the map will change to reflect its current location. Also, the current distance between the two markers will be computed and displayed as shown in Figure 8.11b. Similarly, upon dragging the second marker, again, its geolocation information above the map will be updated along with the distance between the two markers (see Figure 8.11c).

Until now, we have been displaying the geolocation of the device in terms of latitude and longitude values. How about displaying addresses of the locations?

## Using the Geocoder Class

The `Geocoder` class is used to convert an address to a `LatLng` object, and vice versa. It includes a method, `geocode()`, that takes a `GeocoderRequest` object as a parameter, and a callback function that can be used to retrieve the device's complete address. The statements below show how the given latitude and longitude values can be converted into a formatted address using the `Geocoder` class:

```
var latlng = new google.maps.LatLng(37.76944, -122.43444);
var geocoder = new google.maps.Geocoder();
geocoder.geocode({'latLng': latlng}, function(resp, status) {
    if (resp[0]) {
        alert("Formatted address is "+ resp[0].formatted_address);
    }
}
```

We can see that a `LatLng` object called `latlng` is created, passing the specified longitude and latitude values. After creating the `latlng` object, the `geocode()` method is called on the

Geocoder instance, geocoder. If no error occurs while executing the geocode() method, the resp parameter in the callback function will contain the formatted address that represents the supplied latitude and longitude values. The alert dialog uses the first element in the resp array to display the formatted address.

Let us modify the application above so that instead of the latitude and longitude values, the formatted addresses of the markers are displayed. Also, when we drag either of the markers on the Google map, the formatted address must change to reflect the new location. In addition, whenever either of the two markers is dragged, we want the new distance between the two markers to be computed and displayed.

So, open the application PGGoogleMapApp and modify the index.html file found in the assets/www folder to appear as shown in Listing 8.12. Only the code in bold is modified; the rest of the code is the same as we saw in Listing 8.11.

**Listing 8.12   Code Written in the index.html File**

```
<!DOCTYPE HTML>
<html>
   <head>
   <title>PhoneGap Application</title>
   <script type = "text/javascript" charset = "utf-8" src = "cordova-2.3.0.js">
   </script>
   <script type = "text/javascript" src = "http://maps.google.com/maps/api/
   js?sensor = false"></script>
   <link href = "http://code.google.com/apis/maps/documentation/javascript/
   examples/default.css" rel = "stylesheet" type = "text/css"/>
   <script type = "text/javascript" src = "http://maps.google.com/maps/api/
   js?sensor = false&libraries = geometry"></script>
   <script type = "text/javascript">
   function onBodyLoad() {
      document.addEventListener("deviceready", PhonegapLoaded, false);
   }
   function PhonegapLoaded(){
      navigator.geolocation.getCurrentPosition(onSuccess, onError,
      {enableHighAccuracy: true});
   }
   function onSuccess(position) {
      var lat = parseFloat(position.coords.latitude);
      var lng = parseFloat(position.coords.longitude);
      var latlng = new google.maps.LatLng(lat, lng);
      var geocoder = new google.maps.Geocoder();
      geocoder.geocode({'latLng': latlng}, function(resp, status) {
         if (resp[0]) {
            var geolocationinfo1 = document.getElementById('geolocationinfo1');
            geolocationinfo1.innerHTML = 'Location 1: '+ resp[0].
            formatted_address;
         }
      });
      var lat2 = parseFloat(position.coords.latitude+.5);
      var lng2 = parseFloat(position.coords.longitude+.5);
      var latlng2 = new google.maps.LatLng(lat2, lng2);
      geocoder.geocode({'latLng': latlng2}, function(resp, status) {
         if (resp[0]) {
            var geolocationinfo2 = document.getElementById('geolocationinfo2');
            geolocationinfo2.innerHTML = 'Location 2: '+ resp[0].
            formatted_address;
         }
```

```
      });
      var mapOptions = {
        center: new google.maps.LatLng(position.coords.latitude, position.coords.
        longitude),
        zoom: 8,
        mapTypeId: google.maps.MapTypeId.ROADMAP
      };
      var map = new google.maps.Map(document.getElementById("map_canvas"),
      mapOptions);
      var marker1 = new google.maps.Marker({
        position: new google.maps.LatLng(position.coords.latitude, position.
        coords.longitude),
        draggable: true,
        raiseOnDrag: false
      });
      marker1.setMap(map);
      var marker2 = new google.maps.Marker({
        position: new google.maps.LatLng(position.coords.latitude+.5, position.
        coords.longitude+.5),
        draggable: true,
        raiseOnDrag: false
      });
      marker2.setMap(map);
      findDistance(marker1, marker2);
      google.maps.event.addListener(marker1, 'drag', function() {
        var geocoder = new google.maps.Geocoder();
        geocoder.geocode({'latLng': marker1.getPosition()}, function(resp,
        status) {
          if (resp[0]) {
            var geolocationinfo1 = document.getElementById('geolocationinfo1');
            geolocationinfo1.innerHTML = 'Location 1: '+ resp[0].
            formatted_address;
          }
        });
        findDistance(marker1, marker2);
      });
      google.maps.event.addListener(marker2, 'drag', function() {
        var geocoder = new google.maps.Geocoder();
        geocoder.geocode({'latLng': marker2.getPosition()}, function(resp,
        status) {
          if (resp[0]) {
            var geolocationinfo2 = document.getElementById('geolocationinfo2');
            geolocationinfo2.innerHTML = 'Location 2: '+ resp[0].
            formatted_address;
          }
        });
        findDistance(marker1, marker2);
      });
    }
    function findDistance(marker1, marker2) {
      var p1 = new google.maps.LatLng(marker1.getPosition().lat(), marker1.
      getPosition().lng());
      var p2 = new google.maps.LatLng(marker2.getPosition().lat(), marker2.
      getPosition().lng());
      d = (google.maps.geometry.spherical.computeDistanceBetween(p1, p2)/1000).
      toFixed(2);
      document.getElementById('distance').innerHTML = "Distance between
      locations:" + d +" km";
    }
    function onError(error) {
      alert('code: ' + error.code + '\n' + 'message: ' + error.message + '\n');
```

```
    }
    </script>
    </head>
    <body onload = "onBodyLoad()">
        <div id = "geolocationinfo1">GeoLocation Information 1</div>
        <div id = "geolocationinfo2">GeoLocation Information 2</div>
        <div id = "distance">Distance</div>
        <div id = "map_canvas" style = "width:100%; height:100%"></div>
    </body>
</html>
```

In the code above, we see that in the onSuccess callback method that is called on success-ful execution of the getCurrentPosition() method, the latitude and longitude values of the current device location are retrieved. Using the retrieved latitude and longitude values, the latlng instance of the LatLng class is defined. The latlng instance is passed to the geo-code() method of the Geocoder instance to convert the latitude and longitude values into the formatted address. The formatted address of the device is then displayed on the screen through the <div> element of the ID geolocationinfo1. Similarly, the location near the device is converted into a formatted address and displayed through the <div> element of the ID geolo-cationinfo2. The distance between the two markers is computed and displayed through the findDistance() function.

The drag event listeners are associated with the two markers marker1 and marker2. Whenever either of the markers is dragged, the geocode() method on the Geocoder class is called, supplying the new marker position to retrieve the formatted address representing the new marker location. The new formatted address is then displayed through the respective <div> ele-ments. Each time either of the markers is dragged, the findDistance() function is also called to compute the new distance between the markers.

Upon running the application, we see that the Google map is displayed with two markers. One marker will be displayed at the device current location, and the other marker will be dis-played near the device location. The geolocation information of the two markers will be displayed as a formatted address at the top of the map. Also, the distance between the two markers will be computed and displayed in kilometers (see Figure 8.12a). On dragging the first marker, that is, marker1 on the Google map, its formatted address will be changed to represent the new marker location. Also, the current distance between the two markers will be computed and displayed as shown in Figure 8.12b. Similarly, upon dragging the second marker, its formatted address will be modified to represent the new location of marker2. Again, the distance between the two markers will be updated (see Figure 8.12c).

## Using Compass API

The compass indicates the direction in which the device is pointing. It provides the device's head-ing in degrees from true north in a clockwise direction. Using the PhoneGap Compass API, when we turn the device in any direction, a number between 0 and 359.99 is displayed that corresponds to the direction in which the device is pointing. A value of 0 indicates the device is pointing north, 90 indicates it is pointing east, 180 refers to south, and 270 refers to west.

**Note:** Not all smartphones have a compass.

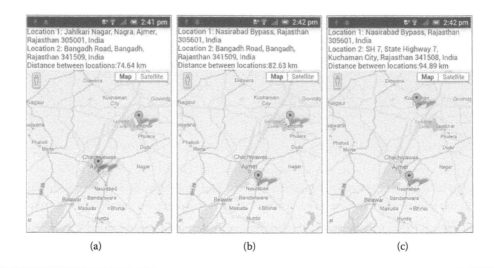

(a)                                    (b)                                    (c)

**Figure 8.12** **(a) A Google map is displayed with two markers and the formatted addresses of the markers are displayed at the top. (b) The new formatted address of `marker1` and the distance is updated. (c) The new formatted address of `marker2` along with the updated distance.**

To know the direction in which the device is heading or pointing, the `getCurrentHeading()` method is used as shown below:

```
navigator.compass.getCurrentHeading(onSuccess, onError);
```

The `onSuccess` callback method is called when the direction in which the device is pointing is successfully measured. The `onError` callback method is called when some error occurs while reading the compass. With the `onSuccess` callback, a `heading` object is passed as a parameter. The properties in the `heading` object can be used to display detailed information about the device's orientation. Below are the properties supported by the `heading` object:

- `magneticHeading`—Represents the device's current heading in degrees ranging from 0 to 359.99.
- `trueHeading`—Represents the device's current heading relative to the geographic North Pole in degrees ranging from 0 to 359.99. There are two North Poles; one is the geographic North Pole and the other is the magnetic North Pole, which keeps moving because of magnetic changes in the earth's core.
- `headingAccuracy`—Represents the deviation between the `magneticHeading` and `trueHeading` values in degrees.
- `timestamp`—Represents the time in milliseconds when the heading is measured since January 1, 1970.

In order to keep watching or monitoring the device heading at regular intervals, the `watchHeading()` method is called as shown below:

```
navigator.compass.watchHeading (onSuccess, onError,compassOptions);
```

The compassOptions object is used for defining the period or time interval in milliseconds to update the heading. For example, the code given below measures the direction in which the device is pointing every 3 milliseconds (3 seconds):

```
var compassOptions = {frequency: 3000};
var watchID = navigator.compass.watchHeading(onSuccess, onError,
compassOptions);
```

**Note:** If the compassOptions object is not provided, the default interval of 1000 milliseconds is used.

To stop measuring the device heading, the clearwatch() method is called and the reference of the watchID that we want to stop or cancel is passed to it as shown below:

```
navigator.compass.clearWatch(watchID);
```

Let us apply the knowledge gained so far to finding the direction in which a device is heading or pointing. So, create an Android project called PGCompassApp and configure it for using PhoneGap. In the assets/www folder, open the index.html file and write the code as shown in Listing 8.13.

**Listing 8.13  Code Written in the index.html File**

```
<!DOCTYPE HTML>
<html>
    <head>
    <title>PhoneGap Application</title>
    <script type = "text/javascript" charset = "utf-8" src = "cordova-2.3.0.js">
    </script>
    <script type = "text/javascript">
    function onBodyLoad() {
        document.addEventListener("deviceready", PhonegapLoaded, false);
    }
    function PhonegapLoaded(){
        navigator.compass.getCurrentHeading(onSuccess, onError);
    }
    function onSuccess(heading) {
    var date = new Date(heading.timestamp);
    alert("Timestamp: "+ date+"\n"+
    "Magnetic Heading: "+heading.magneticHeading+"\n"+
    "True Heading: "+heading.trueHeading+"\n"+
    "Heading Accuracy: "+heading.headingAccuracy+"\n");
}
    function onError(err) {
    if (err.code = = CompassError.COMPASS_NOT_SUPPORTED)
    alert("Compass not supported.");
    else if (err.code = = CompassError.COMPASS_INTERNAL_ERR)
    alert("Compass Internal Error");
    else
    alert("Unknown Error");
}
    </script>
    </head>
    <body onload = "onBodyLoad()">
    </body>
</html>
```

In the code above, we can see that after PhoneGap is loaded, the `getCurrentHeading()` method is called to find the direction in which the device is heading. If the direction of the device is measured successfully, the `onSuccess` callback method will be called. The properties supported by the heading object passed to the `onSuccess` callback are used to display the magnetic heading, true heading, and heading accuracy of the device. Also, the timestamp at which the heading is measured is also displayed. In case some error occurs, the `onError` callback will be called to display the reason that caused the error.

## Summary

In this chapter, we learned about different Phone APIs. We learned how to find acceleration of the device along the three axes using the Accelerometer API. We learned how to capture images using the Camera API. We saw the procedure for using the Capture API in capturing audio and video. We also saw how the Geolocation API can be used to find the device location. We looked at the methods used to watch the device's location at regular intervals. We also saw how Google map is displayed and how it can be centered at the device's current location. Finally, we saw how the Compass API is used to find the direction in which the device is pointing.

In Chapter 9, we will learn about Sencha Touch. We will learn how to download Sencha Touch and how it can be integrated with PhoneGap.

# Chapter 9

# Sencha Touch

In this chapter, we cover:

- Introducing Sencha Touch
- Model View Controller (MVC) architecture
- Enabling Web servers
- Installing Sencha Touch 2 Software Development Kit (SDK)
- Using the Sencha Cmd
- Folder Organization of the Sencha Touch App
- Understanding the component class, container classes, and layouts
- Creating views
- Understanding the `Index.html` file, using the `Ext.application` class
- Sencha Touch fields
- Using `xtype`
- Event handling
- Getting components
- Creating a welcome application
- Welcome application in the MVC format
- Creating a login form
- Creating a list application
- Navigating using tabs

## Introducing Sencha Touch

Sencha Touch is a powerful cross-platform framework that enables developers to develop HTML5-based mobile applications that are compatible with Android, iOS, and BlackBerry devices. Below are a few of the features of this mobile framework:

- Sencha Touch is built specifically for mobile devices. Developers can develop applications that appear like native applications.

- It is based on Web standards such as HTML5, CSS3, and JavaScript.
- It supports audio, video, animations, and local storage to develop dynamic, optimized, and fully featured applications.
- It enables the integration of GPS and device sensor data into applications.
- Excellent documentation makes it very easy to use.
- The Sencha Touch classes support the MVC architecture.

## Overview of the Sencha Touch Class Library

Sencha Touch comes bundled with several classes and components that can be readily used in developing applications rapidly. The following are the families of classes that are included in the Sencha Touch 2 class library:

- **Model classes**—Used to describe the business entities that are managed by the application. These classes basically help in defining the data to operate on.
- **Communication classes**—Used to describe storage and communication techniques used in the application. These classes help to consume data from different resources.
- **Views classes**—Used to describe the user interface of an application.
- **Controller classes**—Used to describe the business logic of an application. It defines the views to be displayed when a certain action is performed on the models.
- **Foundation utility classes**—Describes ready-to-use code. We can use different methods defined in the utility classes to perform lots of tasks straight away without writing a single line of code.

Before we continue, let us briefly review the MVC architecture.

## Model View Controller (MVC) Architecture

An application with all data and business logic in a single file makes it hard to not only manage but also debug. Such applications are also difficult to read. MVC architecture splits or organizes the application files into the following three parts based on their functionality:

- **Models**—All data and storage files are kept in this category.
- **Views**—User interface-related files are kept in this category.
- **Controllers**—Business logic files that handle the user interactions and determine the next views to be displayed are kept in this category.

Because long application files are split and categorized on the basis of their respective functions, the applications in MVC architecture are easy to manage and debug.

To develop and test Sencha Touch applications, we need a Web server to host and run our applications. Let us learn the procedure to enable Web servers on two major operating systems.

# Enabling Web Servers

The procedures below are given to enable Web servers on Mac OSX and Windows operating systems:

- The Mac OSX already comes with a Web server installed. To enable it, open `System Preferences` and choose the `Sharing` option followed by enabling `Web Sharing`. Thereafter, click on the `Create Personal Website` folder to set up a Web folder called `Sites` in our home directory. We can develop and test our Sencha Touch applications in this `Sites` folder.
- Microsoft Windows comes with Internet Information Server (IIS) installed. To ensure that IIS is running, open the `Control Panel`, choose `Program and Features`, followed by selecting `Turn Windows features on or off` (in Vista or Windows 7). A window as shown in Figure 9.1a will open up. Upon expanding the `Internet Information Services` node in the `Windows Features` dialog, additional categories of IIS features will be displayed (see Figure 9.1b). Select `Internet Information Services` to choose the default features for installation. We can always enable additional features, like `Web Management Tools` or `World Wide Web Services`, if desired. After checking the checkboxes of the IIS features that we want to enable, click the OK button to initiate the procedure to enable IIS.

To confirm that IIS is successfully enabled on our machine, open the browser and type the following URL: `http://localhost`. If we get the output shown in Figure 9.2, it means the IIS is successfully enabled on our machine. The output displayed in Figure 9.2 appears on execution of the default `index.html` file that exists in the Web folder.

To manage and configure IIS, open `IIS Manager` using either of the following ways:

- Open the `Control Panel`, select `Administrative Tools`, and double-click the Internet Information Services (IIS) Manager shortcut.

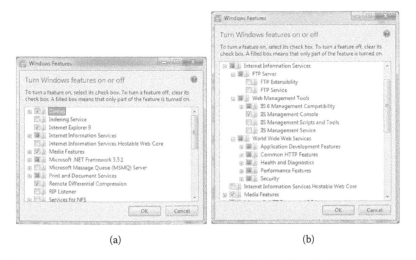

(a)                                          (b)

**Figure 9.1**  **(a) The Windows** Features **dialog which will enable/disable different features. (b) The available features in the Internet Information Services node.**

**Figure 9.2    The output displayed upon execution of the default** `index.html` **file in the Web folder.**

■ Click `Start`, type `inetmgr` in the `Search programs and files` box, followed by pressing the `Enter` key.

By default, IIS does not serve the Multipurpose Internet Mail Extension (MIME) type files. So, we need to add a MIME type to IIS to enable it to serve MIME type files. To do so, open the properties for the server in IIS Manager, click `MIME Types` (see Figure 9.3), and click the New button.

In the `File` name extension box, type `JSON` and `application/json` in the `MIME type` box, followed by clicking the `OK` button (see Figure 9.4).

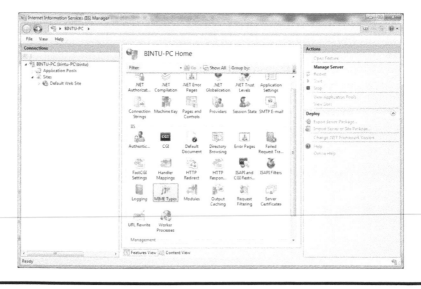

**Figure 9.3    Windows displaying IIS properties.**

**Figure 9.4   The dialog for adding MIME types to IIS.**

## Installing Sencha Touch 2 SDK

The steps below are given to install Sencha Touch 2 SDK:

■ To download the Sencha Touch framework, visit the http://www.sencha.com/products/touch/ URL and click the Download button. A zip file will be downloaded to our computer. The version of Sencha Touch available at the time of this writing is 2.1.1. Unzip the downloaded file and copy the directory containing the unzipped files to our Web folder. Open a Web browser and point at the directory containing the unzipped Sencha Touch files. For example, if the directory name in which the Sencha package is unzipped is sencha-touch-2.1.1, then point the browser to the http://localhost/sencha-touch-2.1.1 address. The Sencha Touch demo page will open, as shown in Figure 9.5, which confirms that Sencha Touch is successfully installed on our computer.

**Figure 9.5   Sencha Touch demo page.**

- The next step is to download the Sencha Touch Cmd from the URL `http://www.sencha.com/products/sencha-cmd/download`.
- Extract the SDK zip file to our Web folder, that is, in the `C:\inetpub\wwwroot` directory.
- To install the Sencha Touch Cmd installer, double-click the downloaded executable file of Sencha Cmd to invoke the `Sencha Cmd Setup Wizard`. The first screen is a welcome screen informing that Sencha Cmd utilities are used to package and deploy Sencha applications. Click the `Next` button to move further. The next dialog shows the license agreement and terms of using Sencha Cmd (see Figure 9.6a). Accept the agreement, followed by clicking the `Next` button to continue. The next dialog prompts us to specify the directory where we want to install Sencha Cmd. A default directory location will also be displayed. Keeping the default installation directory, click the `Next` button to continue. The next dialog informs us that the setup wizard is all set to install Sencha Cmd on our computer. Click the `Next` button to initiate the installation procedure. The Sencha Cmd files will be copied and installed on our computer. The final screen informs us that the Sencha Cmd has been successfully installed on our computer (see Figure 9.6b). Click the `Finish` button to exit the setup wizard. Sencha Cmd adds the Sencha command line tool to our path and enables us to generate new Sencha Touch application templates.

To confirm that Sencha Cmd is properly installed on our machine, change to the Sencha Touch directory, that is, `C:\inetpub\wwwroot\sencha-touch-2.1.1` directory, and type in the `sencha` command followed by the `Enter` key. If we get the output shown in Figure 9.7, it means that the Sencha Cmd has been correctly installed on our machine.

## Using the Sencha Cmd

The Sencha Cmd command line tool performs several tasks. It adds the Sencha command line tool to our path and generates a new application template. Let us learn the procedure to create a Sencha Touch application using the Sencha Cmd tool.

Open a Terminal window and change the directory to the Sencha Touch folder that exists in the Web folder. Recall, we unzipped the Sencha package in a folder called `sencha-touch-2.1.1` into the Web folder `\inetpub\wwwroot`. In the Terminal window, we will give the `sencha`

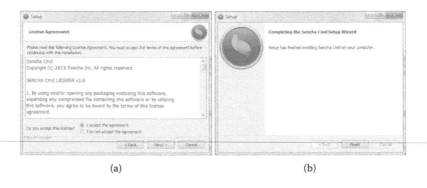

(a)                     (b)

**Figure 9.6 (a) The dialog displaying the License Agreement and terms of using Sencha Cmd. (b) The dialog confirming the successful installation of Sencha Cmd.**

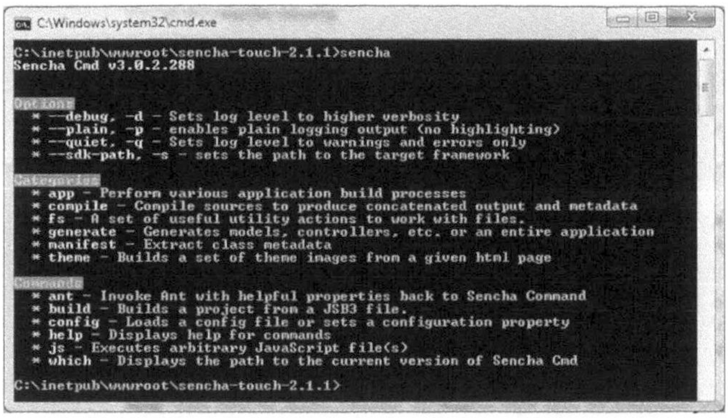

**Figure 9.7   The output confirming that Sencha Cmd is correctly installed.**

generate app command to create a new application. The sencha generate app command takes two parameters, the name of the application and its location, as shown below:

```
C:\inetpub\wwwroot\sencha-touch-2.1.1>sencha generate app MyApp.\MyApp
```

We can see that the name of our application is MyApp and the location defined for it is our Web folder. On giving the command above, the new application will be created and the Terminal window will show the output as shown in Figure 9.8.

The new application will be created and stored in the MyApp folder. Let us now look at different files and folders that are autogenerated for us.

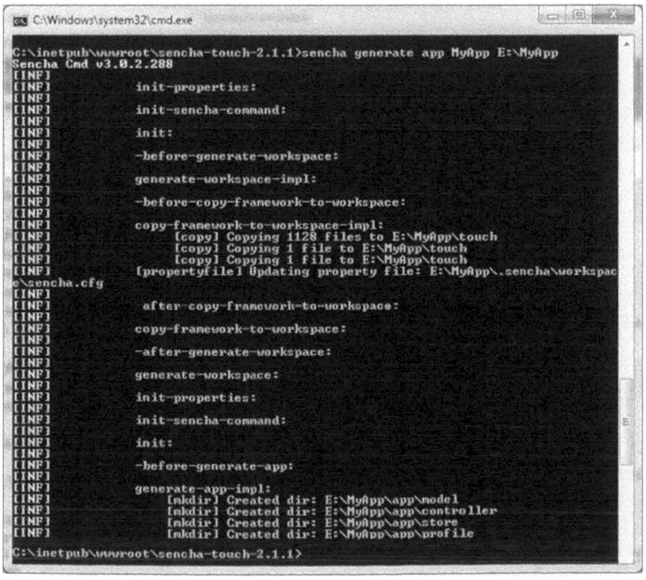

**Figure 9.8   The output displayed upon generating a new application.**

## Folder Organization of the Sencha Touch App

Recall, the Sencha Touch classes support the MVC architecture, and hence the Sencha Touch applications have a well-defined folder structure that is enforced throughout the framework. Upon opening the MyApp folder, we see the list of files and folders that are automatically created for us as shown in Figure 9.9.

- **App**—Contains the code of our application. The location of the code can be changed through the app.js file. Inside the app folder, the application code is categorized into different folders as explained below.
- **Controller**—Contains all the classes used to interrelate the model and views. The files that accept user input, process the input, store the processed information in storage, load the views in response to the user interaction, and so on, are kept in this folder.
- **Model**—Contains the data model definitions. That is, the files that define the data and storage of the application are stored in this folder.
- **Profile**—Contains application profiles to support the user interface (UI) for different platforms. Sencha Touch supports three different profiles for phones, tablets, and desktop browsers. Hence, we can define separate UIs for different devices.
- **View**—Contains the files that define the user interface in the application.

Let us run the application to see the default output. Open the browser and type http://localhost/MyApp, followed by the Enter key. The application MyApp will run showing the output seen in Figure 9.10.

The output above is because of the default content in the MyApp/app/view/Main.js file. The default code in the MyApp/app/view/Main.js file is shown in Listing 9.1.

| Name | Date modified | Type | Size |
|---|---|---|---|
| .sencha | 4/2/2013 8:06 AM | File folder | |
| app | 4/2/2013 8:06 AM | File folder | |
| resources | 4/2/2013 8:06 AM | File folder | |
| touch | 4/2/2013 8:06 AM | File folder | |
| app | 4/2/2013 8:06 AM | JS File | 2 KB |
| app | 4/2/2013 8:06 AM | JSON File | 5 KB |
| build | 4/2/2013 8:06 AM | XML Document | 2 KB |
| index | 4/2/2013 8:06 AM | HTML Document | 2 KB |
| packager | 4/2/2013 8:06 AM | JSON File | 4 KB |

**Figure 9.9   The list of files and folders that open in a typical Sencha Touch application.**

**Figure 9.10   The default output that is displayed upon running the** MyApp **application.**

**Listing 9.1** Default Code in `MyApp/app/view/Main.js` File

```
Ext.define('MyApp.view.Main', {
    extend: 'Ext.tab.Panel',
    xtype: 'main',
    requires: [
        'Ext.TitleBar',
        'Ext.Video'
    ],
    config: {
        tabBarPosition: 'bottom',
        items: [
        {
            title: 'Welcome',
            iconCls: 'home',
            styleHtmlContent: true,
            scrollable: true,
            items: {
                docked: 'top',
                xtype: 'titlebar',
                title: 'Welcome to Sencha Touch 2'
            },
            html: [
                "You've just generated a new Sencha Touch 2 project. What you're
                looking at right now is the ", "contents of <a target = '_blank' href
                = \"app/view/Main.js\">app/view/Main.js</a> - edit that file ", "and
                refresh to change what's rendered here."
            ].join("")
        },
        {
            title: 'Get Started',
            iconCls: 'action',
            items: [
            {
                docked: 'top',
                xtype: 'titlebar',
                title: 'Getting Started'
            },
            {
                xtype: 'video',
                url: 'http://av.vimeo.com/64284/137/87347327.mp4?token =
                1330978144_f9b698fea38cd408d52a2393240c896c',
                posterUrl: 'http://b.vimeocdn.com/ts/261/062/261062119_640.jpg'
            }
            ]
        }
        ]
    }
});
```

Before we begin with understanding the autogenerated Sencha Touch code, let us briefly introduce the Sencha Touch Component class that plays a major role in Sencha Touch applications.

# Understanding Component Class

All the visual components, like buttons, panels, sliders, toolbars, and so on, that are rendered on the screen are inherited from a base class called `Ext.Component`. This class acts as a building

**Table 9.1   Brief Description of the** Ext.Component **Class**

| Method | Description |
|---|---|
| addCls and removeCls | Adds or removes a CSS class from a component. |
| destroy | Removes the component from memory. |
| disable and enable | Disables or enables the component. |
| getHeight, getWidth, and getSize | Retrieves the current height, width, or size of the component, respectively. getSize returns both height and width. |
| setHeight, setWidth, and setSize | Changes the height, width, or size of a component. |
| show and hide | Shows or hides the component. |
| setPosition | Locates the component at the desired position. |
| update | Update the content of a component. |

block for all of the other components used in Sencha Touch applications and also provides configuration settings, methods, properties, and events to manipulate components as the application demands; that is, the components can be displayed, hidden, switched to an enabled or disabled state, resized as per the available screen space, and so on. Ext.Component also contains a number of useful methods that are used to get and set properties of any Sencha Touch component. Table 9.1 shows a few of the methods that are supported by the Ext.Component class.

Components are placed inside containers. Let us know more about Container classes.

## Container Classes

Container classes in Sencha Touch, as the name suggests, are the classes where other components, like buttons, input fields, toolbars, and so on, are kept. To render items or components in an application, they need to be placed in a container and arranged through a layout. The container controls height, width, margin, and so on, of the contained components. That is, the components or child objects in a container inherit all the attributes, like height, width, and so forth, of the container object. A few examples of containers include Panel, TabPanel, Toolbar, Carousel, and so on. All the container classes extend the Ext.Container class. That is, Ext.Container is the base class for all the containers. It provides the basic features that are required in different specific containers. Ext.Panel is the default container class used by Sencha Touch that supports docking.

To arrange components in a container, layouts are used. Let us now take a look at them.

## Layouts

Layouts are used to resize, arrange, and position the components in a container. The following are the types of layouts that determine how the components in a container have to be arranged:

- **Auto**—Renders one item after another. It is the default layout.
- **Hbox**—Arranges items horizontally in a container, that is, one item beside the other.

- **Vbox**—Arranges items vertically in a container, that is, one item below the other.
- **Card**—Renders items as a card; that is, only one item at the top will be visible and the others will be hidden behind it.
- **Dock**—Handles the docking for panels.
- **Fit**—Renders a single item and automatically expands it to fill the container.

Different configuration options are used in a layout. Table 9.2 shows a brief description of the configuration options used.

Every container in Sencha Touch has a `config` property named `layout` that accepts the type of layout we want to use to arrange and resize the items in a container.

The containers also support the following methods:

- **Query**—Searches for desired items within a container.
- **Update**—Updates the contents of the container.

The following are the two configuration options that are used in a container:

- `flex`—The flex configuration determines the space that a component can use in proportion to the overall layout. For example, if a container has a flex value of 2 and the other has a flex value of 1 in a vbox layout, it means that the container with the flex value of 2 will be taller; that is, it will be twice the size of the container with the flex value of 1.

**Table 9.2   A Brief Description of the Configuration Options Used in a Layout**

| Configuration Option | Description |
|---|---|
| `align` | Used to align the specified component in a layout. That is, the components can be aligned to the start, end, or center of the layout. This configuration option can also be used to stretch the specified component to occupy the complete container height or width. For example, the statements given below make the component occupy the complete container height:<br><br>`layout: {`<br>`type: 'vbox',`<br>`align: 'stretch'`<br>`}`<br><br>Valid values for the align configuration options are `center`, `start`, `end`, and `stretch`. |
| `direction` | Used to lay out items in reverse order. By default, the items are arranged from left to right. On assigning the `reverse` value to the `direction` option, the items will be arranged in reverse order, that is, from right to left. The statements given below lay out the items horizontally, from right to left:<br><br>`layout: {`<br>`type: 'hbox',`<br>`direction: 'reverse'`<br>`}` |

- cls—This configuration is used for applying the specified Cascading Style Sheets (CSS) class on the containers. For example, the following configuration option, when used in a container, will apply the styles mentioned in the redStyle class to the container:

```
cls: 'redStyle'
```

## Creating Views

The easiest way to create a view in a Sencha Touch application is to use the Ext.create class with an existing component. For example, the following code, when written in the MyApp/app/view/Main.js file (in the MyApp application), will create a simple panel with some HTML inside:

```
Ext.create('Ext.Panel', {
    html: 'Hello World!',
    fullscreen: true
});
```

The code above creates a panel with the HTML content showing the text Hello World! (see Figure 9.11). The configuration option fullscreen resizes the container (panel) to fill the entire screen irrelevant of the device used. Recall that the Ext.Panel is the default container which is usually used to render items on the screen.

A better way to use a container class is to create our custom class that extends the container class followed by instantiating our custom class, as shown in the statements below:

```
Ext.define('MyApp.view.Main', {
    extend: 'Ext.Panel',
    config: {
        html: 'Hello World!',
        fullscreen: true
    }
});
Ext.create('MyApp.view.Main');
```

In the code above, we create a view class named Main that extends the Ext.Panel class container. We use Ext.define for creating a new class. The view class is represented by the MyApp.view.Main convention, where MyApp represents the application name. The config object is defined to specify the config options for the new class. The view class is then instantiated using the Ext.create function. Upon running the application, we get the same text message, Hello World!, on the screen (see Figure 9.11).

To understand how Sencha Touch applications operate, we will begin with the index.html file.

**Figure 9.11  the output displayed upon running the** MyApp **application.**

# Understanding the `Index.html` File

The `index.html` file includes the JavaScript and CSS files provided in the Sencha Touch package. Even the content of our application is provided in the form of JavaScript. The default `index.html` file that is autogenerated by `Sencha Cmd` in the `MyApp` application is a bit complex to understand in the beginning, so we will create another HTML file called `index2.html` in the `MyApp` folder with simplified content, as shown in Listing 9.2.

**Listing 9.2   Code Written in the `index2.html` File**

```
<!DOCTYPE html>
<html>
   <head>
      <meta charset = "utf-8">
      <title>Hello World</title>
      <script src = "touch/sencha-touch-debug.js" type = "text/javascript">
      </script> #1
      <link href = "touch/resources/css/sencha-touch.css" rel = "stylesheet" type
      = "text/css"/> #2
      <script src = "my_app.js" type = "text/javascript"></script> #3
   </head>
   <body></body>
</html>
```

Statement 1 includes the debug version of the Sencha Touch JavaScript library in the HTML file. During development and testing, the debug version of the Sencha Touch library is used because it contains comments and documentation that are used in finding errors that occur. After the HTML file is developed and tested, `sencha-touch.js`, that is, the actual Sencha Touch JavaScript library, is included in the HTML file. That is, statement 1 will be replaced by the following line:

```
<script src = "touch/sencha-touch.js" type = "text/javascript"></script>
```

The `sencha-touch.js` library is optimized for production environments and consumes fewer resources, including bandwidth and memory.

**Note:** Never edit the `sencha-touch-debug.js` or `sencha-touch.js` files.

Statement 2 includes the default CSS file for the Sencha Touch library, `sencha-touch.css` in the HTML file. The Cascading Style Sheet files contain style information for different elements of the page. In statement 3, `my _ app.js` is the JavaScript file that will contain the source code of our application. We will soon create the `my _ app.js` file in the `MyApp` folder and define its code. The main thing to observe in the application above is the opening and closing set of `<body></body>` tags. The output of the code that we will be providing in our JavaScript file, `my _ app.js`, will be displayed through the empty `<body></body>` tag.

Almost all `index.html` files in a Sencha Touch application have the structure shown in Listing 9.2.

**Note:** To write comments, enclose the text between `<!--` and `-->` symbols. Anything enclosed between `<!--` and `-->` symbols will not be displayed in the browser. The comments are used for increasing the readability of an application.

The Ext object plays a major role in the Sencha Touch application that is created automatically when the Sencha Touch library is loaded. The Ext object provides methods to create an application and its components. Let us discuss the functions that will be used in the JavaScript file(s) of our application.

## Using the Ext.application Class

The Ext.application class creates and configures a new Sencha Touch application. This class also enables us to structure our application in the form of the Model View Controller, which is why every Sencha Touch application uses the Ext.application class. While using the Ext.application class, several configuration options are passed to it for configuring the application. The most commonly used configuration options are provided below:

- **Name**—A string that provides the namespace for all the objects contained inside the application. Sencha Touch creates this namespace automatically to define the scope for the application's objects. There should be no space in the name.
- **Launch**—This is a configuration option that specifies a function to be executed when the framework code is loaded and the application is ready to execute.

**Note:** Sencha Touch uses the namespace Ext for each of its functions to avoid conflict with the user's functions.

We will write the code shown in Listing 9.3 in our JavaScript file, my _ app.js, to display an alert dialog when the application starts.

**Listing 9.3   Code Written in the my _ app.js File**

```
Ext.require(['Ext.MessageBox']);
Ext.application({
   name: 'WelcomeApp',
   launch: function () {
      Ext.Msg.alert("Title","Hello World!");
   }
});
```

We can see that the alert() function has two parameters: one is the title of the dialog, and the other is the text to be displayed in the alert dialog. To run the index2.html file that we created in the MyApp folder, open the browser and point at the address http://localhost/MyApp/index2.html, followed by the Enter key. An alert dialog will appear displaying the text Hello World!, as shown in Figure 9.12.

We have already learned to use the Ext.Panel container (refer to the "Creating Views" section). Let us now learn how to use the base container class, Ext.Container, to display a HTML text, Hello World!. To do so, modify the JavaScript file my _ app.js to appear as shown in Listing 9.4.

**Figure 9.12   The alert dialog displaying the** Hello World! **message.**

**Listing 9.4   Code Written in the my _ app.js File**

```
Ext.application({
   name: 'WelcomeApp',
   launch: function () {
      var message = new Ext.Container({
         fullscreen: true,
         html: 'Hello World'
      });
      this.viewport = message;
   }
});
```

In the code above, an application is created called WelcomeApp. The application specifies a function that is launched or executed when the application is ready to execute. In the launched function an object of the Ext.Container class is created called message. The size of the container is set to fill up the entire screen. The items are a collection of Sencha Touch components that we want to be included in our container. The items list is enclosed in brackets, and the individual components within the items list are enclosed in curly brackets. An item in the form of HTML text Hello World! is rendered in the container. By default, a new application has a viewport that acts as a container to define the views of the application. The application's viewport is set to the Container object, and the message to display the item, that is, the HTML content, is defined in the container on the screen (see Figure 9.13).

There is one more class called Ext.setup that is used to set up an application and execute a function called onReady when the document is ready. To use the Ext.setup class, modify the JavaScript file my _ app.js to appear as shown in Listing 9.5.

**Figure 9.13   The** Hello World! **message is displayed upon running the** index2.html **file.**

**Listing 9.5   Code Written in the `my _ app.js` File**

```
Ext.setup({
   onReady: function() {
      var message = new Ext.Container({
         fullscreen: true,
         items: [{
            html: 'Hello World'
         }]
      });
   }
});
```

Upon running the application, the `Ext.setup` class will set up an application and will execute the `onReady` function, which in turn will display the `Hello World` message on the screen, as shown in Figure 9.13.

**Note:** The `Ext.application` class provides more features than the `Ext.setup` class while configuring a new application.

## Sencha Touch Fields

Sencha Touch supports the standard HTML field types given below:

- `checkboxfield`
- `fieldset`
- `hiddenfield`
- `passwordfield`
- `radiofield`
- `selectfield`
- `textfield`
- `textareafield`

Sencha Touch also supports the following specialized text fields that automatically validate the user's input:

- `emailfield`—Accepts only a valid e-mail address.
- `numberfield`—Accepts only numbers.
- `urlfield`—Accepts only a valid Web URL.

All the fields inherit their height, width, style, and so on, from the container configuration settings. We can optionally apply the following field-specific options to the fields:

- `label`—Used to display a text label with the field.
- `labelAlign`—Used to align the label with the field. That is, the label can be aligned to the `top` or `left` of the field. The default value of this option is `left`.
- `labelWidth`—Used to define the width of the label.
- `name`—Used to assign a name to the field.
- `maxLength`—Used to define the number of characters that can be used in the field.
- `required`—Compels the user to enter some data in the field to submit the form.

One method that is used to create components, containers, and so forth, in a Sencha application is to instantiate their respective classes. Another method is to use xtype. Let us learn more.

## Using xtype

xtype acts as shorthand for the class. It does not create the components immediately; instead, it creates them when they are actually required to be displayed on the screen. This technique not only simplifies the task of creating components, but also saves a lot of device memory.

For example, to display a text field, we need to instantiate the Ext.form.TextField class as shown below:

```
var nameField = new Ext.form.TextField({
    name: 'username',
    label: 'UserName'
});
```

A text field can also be created through xtype as shown below:

```
{
    xtype: 'textfield',
    name: 'username',
    label: 'UserName'
}
```

## Event Handling

To implement user interaction, we need to define various event handlers to respond to different events that might occur on different components of the application. The syntax of defining an event handler is as given below:

```
event: event_handler_function
```

### Example

The statements below handle the tap event on a button:

```
tap: function(button, e, eOpts) {
    ...........
    ...........
}
```

Different classes support different events. For example, the Ext.Component class supports initialize, hide, and show events; the Ext.Container class supports add and remove events; the Ext.Button class supports tap events; the Ext.field.Text class supports focus and blur events; and so on.

Most of the mobile frameworks, including Sencha Touch, support the following types of touch gestures:

- **Tap**—Represents a single touch on the screen.
- **Double-tap**—Represents two quick touches on the screen.
- **Swipe**—Represents moving of a single finger across the screen, from left to right or top to bottom.
- **Pinch or spread**—Represents touching the screen with two fingers and bringing them together or spreading them apart.
- **Rotate**—Represents placing two fingers on the screen and twisting them in a clockwise or counterclockwise direction.

To listen for the occurrence of different events, Sencha Touch uses listeners.

### *Listeners*

The term itself depicts that listeners listen or sense for the occurrence of different events in the components contained in a container and perform responsive actions. Like any configuration option, listeners can be associated with any component in Sencha Touch.

## Getting Components

In order to fetch the data entered by the user in different components, we need to get or access the components used in an application. To get components that exist in an application, Sencha Touch provides the following two functions:

- `Ext.getCmp()`—Gets the component with the supplied ID. For example, the statement given below gets the component with the ID `username`:

  ```
  var username = Ext.getCmp('username');
  ```

- `Ext.ComponentQuery()`—Gets single or multiple components that are related to the supplied component. For example, the statement given below gets all toolbars in an application:

  ```
  var toolbars = Ext.ComponentQuery.query('toolbar');
  ```

Let us apply the knowledge gained thus far in creating Sencha Touch applications.

## Creating a Welcome Application

Let us create a welcome application that prompts the user to enter a name. After entering a name, when the user clicks the button, a welcome message is displayed along with the user's name. The application will require a text field and a button, and to display them in our application, we will make use of `xtype`. Modify the my _ app.js in the MyApp folder to appear as shown in Listing 9.6.

**Listing 9.6   Code Written in the `my _ app.js` File**

```
Ext.require(['Ext.MessageBox']);
Ext.setup({
   onReady: function() {
      var message = new Ext.Container({
         fullscreen: true,
         items: [
         {
            xtype: 'textfield',
            name : 'username',
            label: 'UserName',
            id: 'username',
            placeHolder: 'Enter your name'
         },
         {
            xtype:'button',
            text:'Submit',
            listeners: {
               tap: function(button, e, eOpts) {
                  var name = Ext.ComponentQuery.query('#username')[0].getValue();
                  Ext.Msg.alert("Welcome "+ name);
               }
            }
         }
         ]
      });
   }
});
```

In the code above, we have used a placeholder in the text field. Placeholders are supported in most of the form fields and are used to display initial text in the fields to guide the user on what has to be entered in the respective fields. The initial text displayed through placeholders in the fields disappears when the fields are focused and some data are entered in them. We can see that a listener is associated with the button that listens or waits for the occurrence of a tap event on the button.

Upon running the `index2.html` file in the `MyApp` folder, we get a text field and a button control on start-up, as shown in Figure 9.14a. When the button is tapped, an event handler function is executed that retrieves the username entered in the text field of the ID `username` and displays it in the alert dialog with a welcome message (see Figure 9.14b).

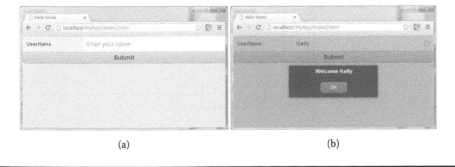

(a)                                                     (b)

**Figure 9.14   (a) A text field and button are displayed on application start-up. (b) A welcome message is displayed upon clicking the button.**

The welcome application above was created by using two files, `index2.html` and `my_app.js`. The application did not follow the MVC architecture format. What if we want to create the same welcome application in the MVC architecture format? Let us see how it can be done.

## Welcome Application in MVC Format

In MVC architecture, different JavaScript files have to be created that represent the `model`, `view`, and `controller` of the application, and these files have to be kept in the respective subfolders of the `app` folder of the application.

Let us name our welcome application `WelcomeApp`. So, in the Web folder (`C:\inetpub\wwwroot`), create a directory called `WelcomeApp`. In the `WelcomeApp` directory, copy the `touch` folder (refer to Figure 9.9) from the `MyApp` directory, as it contains all the Sencha Touch package files that will be required in the application. Also, create a folder named `app` in the `WelcomeApp` directory. Inside the `app` folder, create five subfolders named `controller`, `model`, `profile`, `store`, and `view`. Figure 9.15 shows the pattern of files and folders that we will be creating in this application.

Create a file `index.html` with the code as shown in Listing 9.7 in the root of the application, that is, in the `WelcomeApp` folder.

**Listing 9.7   Code Written in the `index.html` File**

```
<!DOCTYPE html>
<html>
<head>
    <title>Welcome App</title>
    <script src = "touch/sencha-touch-debug.js" type = "text/javascript"></script>
    <link href = "touch/resources/css/sencha-touch.css" rel = "stylesheet" type = "text/css"/>
    <script src = "app.js" type = "text/javascript"></script>
</head>
<body></body>
</html>
```

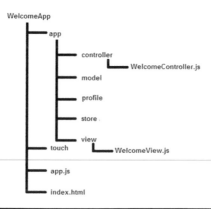

**Figure 9.15   The files and folders of the `WelcomeApp` application in the MVC architecture format.**

As expected, the `index.html` file includes the debug version of the Sencha Touch JavaScript library, the default CSS file for the Sencha Touch library, and our custom JavaScript file, `app.js`, that will contain our application code. The file includes a closing set of `<body></body>` tags that will be used to display the output of the application.

Create our custom JavaScript file called `app.js` in the root folder of the application and write the code as shown in Listing 9.8.

**Listing 9.8    Code Written in the `app.js` File**

```
Ext.application({
    name: "WelcomeApp",
    controllers: ["WelcomeController"],
    views: ['WelcomeView'],
    launch: function () {
        var welcomePanel = Ext.create('Ext.Panel', {
            layout: 'fit',
            items: [
            {
                xtype: 'welcomeform'
            }
            ]
        });
        Ext.Viewport.add(welcomePanel);
    }
});
```

In the code above, we can see that our application is named `WelcomeApp`. The application defines the controller file as `WelcomeController` and the view filename as `WelcomeView`. The application also specifies a function that is launched or executed when the application is ready to execute. In the launched function a container is created; that is, an object of the `Ext.Panel` class is created called `welcomePanel`. The size of the Panel container is set to automatically expand to fill up the entire screen. The item that is displayed in the Panel container is the `welcomeform` item. The details of the `welcomeform` item will be provided in the controller of the application. Finally, the application's viewport is set to the container object, `welcomePanel`, to display the item, that is, UI is defined in `welcomeform`.

## *Styling Buttons*

In this application, we will use a button that, when clicked, will perform the desired action. Buttons in Sencha Touch have a `ui` configuration setting that can be used to style buttons. The options used in the `ui` configuration setting are provided below:

- **Normal**—Displays the default button.
- **Back**—Displays a back button, that is, a button pointing to the left side.
- **Round**—Displays a rounded button.
- **Small**—Displays a smaller button than the default.
- **Action**—Displays a button that is brighter than the default button.
- **Forward**—Displays a button pointing to the right side.

In addition to text, we can also display icons in buttons. Let us take a look at this now.

## *Displaying Icons in Buttons*

To make it easier to remember, we can always display an icon along with the text in a button. The properties that can be used for defining an icon in a button are given below:

- icon—Used to define an image to be used as an icon.
- iconCls—Used to define an icon through a CSS class.
- iconAlign—Used to align the icon with respect to the button text. The valid values are top, bottom, right, and left, where left is the default value.

The following statements display a normal button with the text Home and with the icon defined in the home CSS class:

```
{
    xtype: 'button',
    ui : 'normal',
    text: 'Home',
    iconCls: 'home',
    iconAlign: 'right'
}
```

The icon will be aligned to the right of the button text. To define a text field and a button in the application's view, we will write the code as shown in Listing 9.9 in the app/view/ WelcomeView.js file. Recall, app.js file (refer to Listing 9.8) describes the view of the application as WelcomeView.js.

**Listing 9.9   Code Written in the `WelcomeView.js` File**

```
Ext.define("WelcomeApp.view.WelcomeView", {
    extend: "Ext.form.FormPanel",
    alias: "widget.welcomeform",
    itemId: 'welcomeForm',
    config: {
        title: 'Welcome Form',
        items: [
        {
            xtype: 'fieldset',
            itemId: 'NameFieldset',
            items: [
            {
                xtype: 'textfield',
                label: 'User Name',
                name: 'username',
                id: 'username',
                required: true,
                placeHolder: 'Enter your name'
            }
            ]
        },
        {
            xtype: 'button',
            id: 'submitButton',
            ui: 'action',
            text: 'Submit',
```

```
            action: 'submit'
        }
     ]
   }
 }
});
```

We can see that the `Ext.form.FormPanel` class is extended to create a form panel with the ID `welcomeForm`. The title assigned to the form is `Welcome Form`. In the form, a text field is defined with the ID `username`. The text field will be marked with an asterisk to indicate that it is a required field and cannot be left blank. A placeholder text, `Enter your name`, will be displayed in the text field to inform the user that a name has to be entered in the text field. A button with the text `Submit` is also defined. The ID assigned to the button is `submitButton`, and the `action` value is set to `submit`; that is, when the button is clicked, the `action` and its assigned value are passed to the controller to perform the desired task. Also, in the code above, we have used the `fieldset` xtype. Recall, from Chapter 6, the `fieldset` element is used to logically group together elements in a form.

Next, we need to define the controller of the application to do the following tasks:

■ Implement interaction with the form
■ Listen for the click or tap event on the button
■ Define the function to be executed to perform the task when the button is clicked

To do the tasks above, the code as shown in Listing 9.10 is written in the `app/controller/WelcomeController.js` file.

**Listing 9.10   Code Written in the `WelcomeController.js` File**

```
Ext.require(['Ext.MessageBox']);
Ext.define("WelcomeApp.controller.WelcomeController", {
    extend: "Ext.app.Controller",
    views: ['WelcomeView'],
    config: {
        refs: {
            welcomeForm: "#welcomeForm"
        },
        control: {
            'button[action = submit]': {
                tap: "displayMessage"
            }
        }
    },
    displayMessage: function (button) {
        var name = Ext.ComponentQuery.query('#username')[0].getValue();
        Ext.Msg.alert("Welcome "+ name);
    }
});
```

Upon running the application, a text field and a button will be displayed as shown in Figure 9.16a. After entering a name in the text field, when the user clicks the `Submit` button, a welcome message will be displayed along with the user's name, as shown in Figure 9.16b.

After creating a welcome application, let us create a login form application.

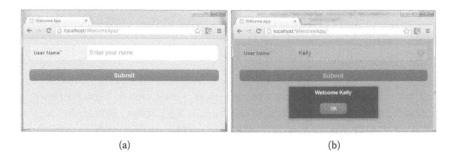

(a)                                   (b)

---

**Figure 9.16  (a) The text field and a button are displayed upon application start-up. (b) A welcome message along with the user's name are displayed.**

## Creating a Login Form

In the login form application, the user will be prompted to enter the username and password. If the username and password entered are guest and gold, respectively, then a welcome message will be displayed; otherwise, the Invalid username/password message will be displayed.

So, let us create a new directory called LoginApp in the Web folder (C:\inetpub\www-root). In the LoginApp directory, copy the touch folder that contains the Sencha Touch package files. Also, create a folder named app in the LoginApp directory. Inside the app folder create five subfolders by the names controller, model, profile, store, and view. Create a file index.html with the code as shown in Listing 9.11 in the root of the application, that is, in the LoginApp directory.

**Listing 9.11   Code Written in the index.html File**

```
<!DOCTYPE html>
<html>
<head>
    <title>Login Form</title>
    <script src = "touch/sencha-touch-debug.js" type = "text/javascript"></script>
    <link href = "touch/resources/css/sencha-touch.css" rel = "stylesheet" type =
    "text/css"/>
    <script src = "app.js" type = "text/javascript"></script>
</head>
<body></body>
</html>
```

The index.html file includes the debug version of the Sencha Touch JavaScript library, the default CSS file for the Sencha Touch library, and our custom JavaScript file, app.js, that will contain our application code. The file includes a closing set of <body></body> tags that will be used for displaying the output of the application. Create our custom JavaScript file called app.js in the root folder of the application and write the code as shown in Listing 9.12.

**Listing 9.12   Code Written in the app.js File**

```
Ext.application({
   name: "LoginApp",
   controllers: ["LoginController"],
```

```
      views: ['LoginView'],
      launch: function () {
         var loginPanel = Ext.create('Ext.Panel', {
            layout: 'fit',
            items: [
            {
               xtype: 'mylogin'
            }
            ]
         });
         Ext.Viewport.add(loginPanel);
      }
});
```

In the code above, we can see that the application is named `LoginApp`, the controller is defined by the name `LoginController`, and the view is defined by the name `LoginView`. In the function that is launched when the application is ready, a Panel container is created called `LoginPanel`. The size of the Panel container is set to automatically expand to fill up the entire screen. The item that is displayed in the Panel container is `mylogin`. The details of the `mylogin` item will be provided in the controller of the application. Finally, the application's viewport is set to the container object, `loginPanel`, to display the item, that is, login form.

To define a text field, a password field, and a button in the application's view, we will write the code as shown in Listing 9.13 in the `app/view/LoginView.js` file.

**Listing 9.13   Code Written in the `LoginView.js` File**

```
Ext.define("LoginApp.view.LoginView", {
   extend: "Ext.form.FormPanel",
   alias: "widget.mylogin",
   id: 'loginFormPanel',
   config: {
      margin: '0 auto',
      name: 'loginform',
      frame: true,
      url: 'authenticate.php',
      title: 'Login',
      items: [
      {
         xtype: 'fieldset',
         itemId: 'LoginFieldset',
         margin: '10 auto 0 auto ',
         title: '',
         items: [
         {
            xtype: 'textfield',
            label: 'User Name',
            name: 'username',
            required: true,
            placeHolder: 'Username'
         },
         {
            xtype: 'passwordfield',
            label: 'Password',
            name: 'password',
            required: true,
            placeHolder: 'Password'
         }
```

```
            ]
        },
        {
            xtype: 'button',
            id: 'loginButton',
            margin: '25 auto 0 auto ',
            style: '',
            maxWidth: 200,
            ui: 'action',
            width: '',
            iconCls: 'user',
            iconMask: true,
            text: 'Login',
            action: 'login'
        }
        ]
    }
});
```

We can see that the `Ext.form.FormPanel` class is extended to create a form panel with the ID `loginFormPanel`. The title assigned to the form is `loginFormPanel`. In the form, a text field is defined with the name `username`, a password field is defined with the name `password`, and a button is defined with the ID `loginButton`. The text displayed on the button is `Login`, and its action value is set to `login`. When the button is clicked, the action and its assigned value are passed to the controller to perform the desired task.

It is now time to define the controller of the application to do the following tasks:

- Implement interaction with the login form.
- Listen for the click or tap event on the button.
- Direct the data entered in the login form to the Hypertext Preprocessor (PHP) file for authentication.
- Observe the result returned by the PHP file. If the result returned by the PHP file is a `success`, that is, if the username and password match the desired texts, display a welcome message on the screen.
- Display the message `Invalid username/password` if the result returned by the PHP file is a `failure`; that is, the username or password entered by the user does not match the specified text.

To do the tasks above, the code as shown in Listing 9.14 is written in the `app/controller/ LoginController.js` file.

**Listing 9.14   Code Written in the `LoginController.js` File**

```
Ext.require(['Ext.MessageBox']);
Ext.define("LoginApp.controller.LoginController", {
    extend: "Ext.app.Controller",
    views: ['LoginView'],
    config: {
        refs: {
            loginForm: "#loginFormPanel"
        },
        control: {
            'button[action = login]': {
                tap: "authenticateUser"
```

```
            }
        }
    },
    authenticateUser: function (button) {
        this.getLoginForm().submit({
            url: 'authenticate.php',
            method: 'POST',
            success: function (form, result) {
                Ext.Msg.alert("Success", "Welcome ");
            },
            failure: function (form, result) {
                Ext.Msg.alert("Error", "Invalid username/password");
            }
        });
    }
});
```

We need to create a PHP file to perform the following tasks:

■ Access the username and password entered in the login form
■ Compare the entered name and password with the desired texts
■ Return the comparison results

To do the tasks above, write the code shown in Listing 9.15 in the `authenticate.php` file.

### Listing 9.15  Code Written in the `authenticate.php` File

```
<?php
    $usr = $_REQUEST['username'];
    $pw = $_REQUEST['password'];
    header('Content-Type: application/json');
    if($usr = = 'guest' && $pw = = 'gold'){
        echo '{"success":true, "msg":'.json_encode('This User is authorized').'}';
    }else{
        echo '{"success":false, "msg":'.json_encode('This User is NOT
        authorized').', "errors" : {"password" :'.json_encode('Password is
        required').'}'.', "pwd" :'.json_encode($pw).'}';
    }
?>
```

In the code above, we can see that the username and password entered in the login form are accessed and assigned to variables usr and pw, respectively. The data in the usr and pw variables are matched with the text guest and gold, respectively. If the user enters the username and password as guest and gold, then a success message is echoed; otherwise, a failure message is echoed. The result, that is, the success or failure message, is used in the controller file to inform the user whether or not the login was successful.

Upon running the application, a text field, a password field, and a button will be displayed. Upon entering the incorrect username or password, the message Invalid username/password will be displayed, as shown in Figure 9.17a. After entering the username as guest and the password as gold, when the button is clicked, a welcome message will be displayed, as shown in Figure 9.17b.

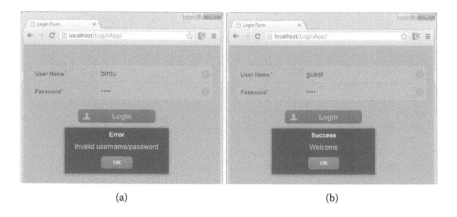

(a)                                                                              (b)

**Figure 9.17    (a) An invalid username/password message is displayed if an incorrect username or password are entered. (b) A welcome message is displayed if the correct username and password are entered.**

## Creating a List Application

In this application, we will learn how to display a few products through a list, and when any item from the list is chosen, the name of the selected item will be displayed through an alert dialog. The idea behind developing this application is to show you how certain options can be displayed via a list and how event handling is performed upon selecting an item from the list.

So, now we create a new directory called `ListApp` in the Web folder (`C:\inetpub\www-root`). Again, in the `ListApp` directory, copy the `touch` folder that contains the Sencha Touch package files. Also, create a folder named `app` in the `ListApp` directory. Inside the `app` folder create five subfolders by the name `controller`, `model`, `profile`, `store`, and `view`. Create a file called `index.html` with the code as shown in Listing 9.16 in the root folder of the application, that is, in the `ListApp` directory.

**Listing 9.16    Code Written in the `index.html` File**

```
<!DOCTYPE html>
<html>
<head>
   <title>List Application</title>
   <script src = "touch/sencha-touch-debug.js" type = "text/javascript"></script>
   <link href = "touch/resources/css/sencha-touch.css" rel = "stylesheet" type =
   "text/css"/>
   <script src = "app.js" type = "text/javascript"></script>
</head>
<body></body>
</html>
```

The `index.html` file includes the debug version of the Sencha Touch JavaScript library, the default CSS file for the Sencha Touch library, and our custom JavaScript file, `app.js`, which will contain our application code. The file includes a closing set of `<body></body>` tags to display the output of the application.

Create our custom JavaScript file called `app.js` in the root folder of the application and write the code as shown in Listing 9.17.

**Listing 9.17   Code Written in the `app.js` File**

```
Ext.application({
    name: 'ListApp',
    views : ['ProductsList'],
    controllers: ['ListController'],
    launch: function() {
        Ext.create('Ext.Container', {
            fullscreen: true,
            layout: 'fit',
            items: [{
                xtype: 'productsList'
            }]
        });
    }
});
```

In the code above, we can see that the application is named `ListApp`, the controller is defined by the name `ListController`, and the view is defined by the name `ProductsList`. In the function that is launched when the application is ready, a container is created. The size of the container is set to automatically expand to fill up the entire screen. The item that is displayed in the container is the `productsList` item. The details of the `productsList` item will be provided in the controller of the application.

To define a list we need to extend the `Ext.dataview.List` class. To define a list and the items to be displayed through it, the code shown in Listing 9.18 is written in the `app/view/ProductsList.js` file.

**Listing 9.18   Code Written in the `ProductsList.js` File**

```
Ext.define('ListApp.view.ProductsList', {
    extend: 'Ext.dataview.List',
    alias : 'widget.productsList',
    config: {
        data: [
            {text: 'Laptop'},
            {text: 'Camera'},
            {text: 'CellPhone'},
            {text: 'Tablet'}
        ],
        itemTpl: '{text}'
    }
});
```

We can see that the data are defined to keep the names of the products that we want to be displayed through the list. The list is assigned an alias, `productsList`. We want this when any product displayed through the list is selected, its name should be displayed through the alert dialog. To do so, write the code as shown in Listing 9.19 in the `app/controller/ListController.js` file.

**Listing 9.19   Code Written in the `ListController.js` File**

```
Ext.require(['Ext.MessageBox']);
Ext.define('ListApp.controller.ListController', {
   extend : 'Ext.app.Controller',
   config: {
      profile: Ext.os.deviceType.toLowerCase(),
      control: {
         'productsList': {
            itemtap: 'onSelectRow'
         }
      }
   },
   onSelectRow: function(view, index, target, record, event) {
      Ext.Msg.alert("You selected "+record.get('text'));
   }
});
```

We can see that when any item that is displayed through the list is clicked or tapped, the `onSelectRow` function will be invoked, which in turn displays the name of the selected product through the alert dialog. Upon running the application, a few product names will be displayed through a list, as shown in Figure 9.18a. Upon selecting any product from the list, its name will be displayed via the alert dialog, as shown in Figure 9.18b.

## Navigating Using Tabs

In this application, we will learn to create two panels called Home and Clients and will navigate between them using a tab panel. That is, we will create two tabs in the tab panel called Home and Clients, and when the Home tab is clicked, we will be navigated to the Home panel. Similarly, when the Clients tab is selected from the tab panel, the Clients panel will open up.

So, let us create a new directory called NavigationApp in the Web folder (C:\inetpub\ wwwroot). Again, in the NavigationApp directory, copy the touch folder that contains the Sencha Touch package files. Also, create a folder named app in the NavigationApp directory. Inside the app folder, create five subfolders by the names controller, model, profile,

(a)                                        (b)

**Figure 9.18   (a) A few products are displayed through a list. (b) A selected product is displayed through an alert dialog.**

store, and `view`. Create a file called `index.html` with the code as shown in Listing 9.20 in the root of the application, that is, in the `NavigationApp` directory.

**Listing 9.20  Code Written in the `index.html` File**

```
<!DOCTYPE html>
<html>
<head>
   <title>Navigation App</title>
   <script src = "touch/sencha-touch-debug.js" type = "text/javascript"></script>
   <link href = "touch/resources/css/sencha-touch.css" rel = "stylesheet" type =
   "text/css"/>
   <script src = "app.js" type = "text/javascript"></script>
</head>
<body></body>
</html>
```

As expected, the `index.html` file includes the debug version and default CSS file of the Sencha Touch JavaScript library and our custom JavaScript file, `app.js`, which will contain our application code. A closing set of `<body></body>` tags is defined to display output of the application. Create our custom JavaScript file called `app.js` in the root folder of the application and write the code as shown in Listing 9.21.

**Listing 9.21  Code Written in the `app.js` File**

```
Ext.application({
   name: 'NavigationApp',
   requires: ['NavigationApp.view.Viewport'],
   views: ['Home','Clients'],
   launch : function() {
      Ext.create('NavigationApp.view.Viewport');
   }
});
```

In the code above, we can see that the application is named `NavigationApp`, and the two views are defined by the names `Home` and `Clients`. In the function that is launched when the application is ready, an instance of the view, `Viewport`, is created. To define a `Home` panel, the code shown in Listing 9.22 is written in the `app/view/Home.js` file.

**Listing 9.22  Code Written in the `Home.js` File**

```
Ext.define('NavigationApp.view.Home', {
   extend: 'Ext.Panel',
   xtype: 'homepanel',
   config: {
      title: 'Home',
      iconCls: 'home',
      items: [
      {
         xtype: 'toolbar',
         title: 'Home'
      },
      {
```

```
        html: 'Home Panel'
      }
    ]
  }
});
```

We can see that the `Ext.Panel` class is extended to define the Home panel. A toolbar is displayed in the panel, the title Home is displayed in the panel, and an HTML text, `Home Panel`, is also set to be displayed in the panel. To define another panel, `Clients`, the code shown in Listing 9.23 is written in the `app/view/Clients.js` file.

**Listing 9.23  Code Written in the `Clients.js` File**

```
Ext.define('NavigationApp.view.Clients', {
    extend: 'Ext.Panel',
    xtype: 'clientpanel',
    config: {
        title: 'Clients',
        iconCls: 'user',
        items: [
        {
            xtype: 'toolbar',
            title: 'Clients'
        },
        {
            html: 'Clients Panel'
        }
        ]
    }
});
```

Like the Home panel, the Clients panel also displays a toolbar, a title, Clients, and an HTML text, `Clients Panel`.

Next, we need to define a view, `Viewport.js`. In the Viewport view, we will define a tab panel and position it at the bottom of the screen. In the tab panel, we will display two tabs, Home and Clients, which, when clicked, will open the respective panel. To do so, write the code as shown in Listing 9.24 in the `app/view/Viewport.js` file.

**Listing 9.24  Code Written in the `Viewport.js` File**

```
Ext.define('NavigationApp.view.Viewport',{
    extend: 'Ext.tab.Panel',
    config: {
        tabBarPosition: 'bottom',
        fullscreen: true,
        layout: 'card',
        items: [
        {
            xtype: 'homepanel'
        },
        {
            xtype: 'clientpanel'
        }
        ]
    }
});
```

(a)    (b)

**Figure 9.19   (a) The `Home` panel appears upon application start-up. (b) The `Clients` panel appears upon selecting the `Clients` tab.**

Upon running the application, the Home panel will open by default, showing the text Home Panel on the screen. At the bottom of the screen, a tab panel will appear showing two tabs, Home and Clients, as shown in Figure 9.19a. Upon selecting the Clients tab from the tab panel, the Clients panel will open showing the text Clients Panel on the screen, as shown in Figure 9.19b.

## Summary

In this chapter, we learned to use the Sencha Touch framework for developing mobile applications that are compatible with Android, iOS, and BlackBerry devices. We learned the Model View Controller (MVC) architecture format that is followed by the Sencha Touch applications. We also learned to enable Web servers, install Sencha Touch 2 SDK, and use the Sencha Cmd tool. We detailed the folder organization of the Sencha Touch applications. We also learned how to use the component class, container classes, layouts, xtypes, and event handling. We investigated the step-by-step procedure for creating different applications, including the welcome application, login form, list application, and navigating using tabs.

In this book, I have tried to keep things easy to understand. I hope you agree. You now have all the necessary information to solve different issues that you might come across while building and maintaining cross-platform mobile applications using PhoneGap Build.

Have fun creating your own applications, and thanks for reading!

# Appendix A: Setting Up an Android Environment

In this application, we will learn to set up an Android environment for developing PhoneGap applications.

## Setting Up an Android Environment

For setting up an Android environment for developing applications, we need to install the following software:

- Java SE Development Kit (JDK)—Can be downloaded from `http://oracle.com/technetwork/java/javase/downloads/index.html`.
- Eclipse Integrated Development Environment (IDE)—Can be downloaded from `http://www.eclipse.org/downloads/`.
- Android Platform Software Development Kit (SDK) Starter Package—Can be downloaded from `http://developer.android.com/sdk/index.html`.
- Android Developer Tools (ADT) plug-in—Can be downloaded from `http://developer.android.com/sdk/eclipse-adt.html`. The plug-in contains project templates and Eclipse tools that help in creating and managing Android projects.

**Note:** The Android application can also be developed through Android Studio—a new development environment. Android Studio can be downloaded from the following URL: http://developer.android.com/sdk/installing/studio.html. But because at the time of this writing, Android Studio is available as only an "early access preview" and few of its features are either incomplete or not yet implemented, I stick to using the Eclipse with ADT Plugin.

The Android SDK includes the core SDK tools, which are used to download the rest of the SDK components. This means that after installing the Android SDK Tools, we need to install Android platform tools and the other components that are required for developing Android applications. Go to `http://developer.android.com/sdk/index.html` and download the package by selecting the link for your operating system. For Windows users, the provided .exe file is named `installer _ r21-windows.exe`. After downloading the file, double-click it to initiate the installation process. The Android SDK Manager window will open. The dialog boxes that you will see now are from the Windows installer, and the screens may vary from other operating system installers.

The first screen is a welcome screen. Select the `Next` button to move to the next screen. Because Android SDK requires the Java SE Development Kit for its operation, it checks for the presence of JDK on your computer. If JDK is already installed, you will see the screen shown in Figure A.3 later. If JDK is not found, it will display a button with the caption `Visit java.oracle.com`, which you can use to download and install JDK. Upon selecting the button, you will be navigated to `http://www.oracle.com/technetwork/java/javase/downloads/index.html`, which shows links to download Java Platform, Standard Edition, Java SE Development Kit (JDK) bundles, and additional resources. The latest version of Java available at the time of this writing is JDK version 1.7. Select the JDK link that suits your platform (Windows, Linux, or Mac) and double-click the downloaded file to begin JDK installation. You will probably see a `Security Warning` dialog box asking whether you want to run or cancel the execution of the file. Select the `Run` button to initiate JDK installation. The first screen that you see is a Java setup wizard welcome screen. Select the `Next` button to see the `Custom Setup` dialog box for selecting optional JDK features that you want to install, as shown in Figure A.1.

Three categories of features (Development Tools, Source Code, and Public JRE) are displayed, and you can select from the respective drop-down lists to choose the list of features in each category you wish to install. The dialog box also asks for a drive location where you want to install the JDK. The default location displayed is `C:\Program Files\Java\jdk1.7.0 _ 09\`, but you can use the `Change` button to select another location. Let us keep the default settings and click the `Next` button to continue. The selected program features will be installed, followed by a dialog box that prompts for the destination folder to install the runtime environment (JRE), as shown in Figure A.2.

The dialog box displays the default location for installing JRE (`C:\Program Files\Java\jre7`). Use the `Change` button to place the program elsewhere. Let us keep the default location and select the `Next` button to continue. The Java files will be copied and installed on your

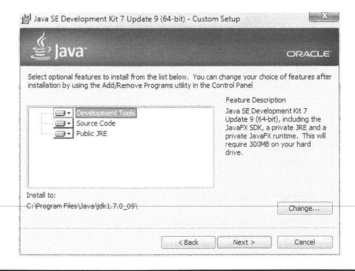

**Figure A.1** **The `Java Setup` dialog box.**

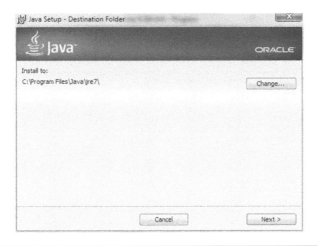

**Figure A.2   The dialog box prompting for the JRE installation location.**

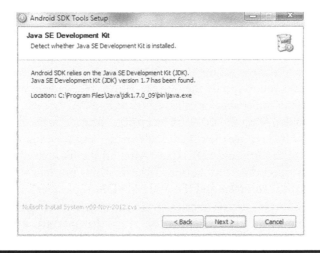

**Figure A.3   The dialog box informing you that JDK is already installed on the computer.**

machine. If the installation is successful, a confirming dialog box is displayed. Select the Finish button to exit the wizard. After Java installation, the Android SDK Tools setup wizard will automatically resume.

If Java is already installed on your computer before beginning with the Android SDK installation, the wizard will detect its presence and display the version number of the JDK found on the machine, as shown in Figure A.3.

Select the Next button. You will get a dialog box asking you to choose the users for which the Android SDK is being installed. The following two options will be displayed in the dialog box:

- Install for anyone using the computer
- Install just for me

Let us select the option Install for anyone using this computer, followed by clicking Next. The next dialog prompts us for the location to install the Android SDK Tools,

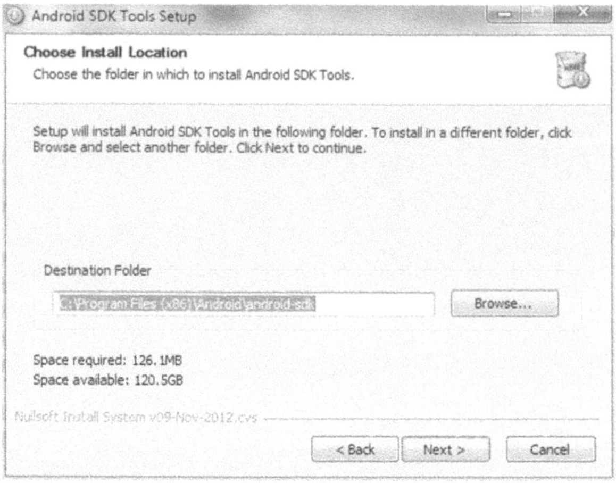

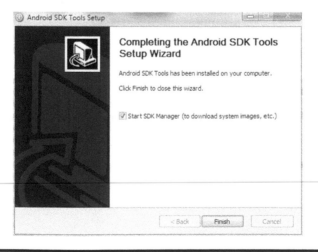

**Figure A.4  The dialog box to specify the Android SDK Tools installation location.**

as shown in Figure A.4. The dialog also displays the default directory location for installing the Android SDK Tools, C:\Program Files (x86)\Android\android-sdk, which you can change by selecting the Browse button. Keep the default directory for installing the Android SDK Tools unchanged, and then select the Next button to continue.

The next dialog box asks you to specify the Start Menu folder where you want the program's shortcuts to appear. A default folder appears called Android SDK Tools. If you do not want to make a Start Menu folder, select the Do not create shortcuts checkbox. Let us create the Start Menu folder by keeping the default folder name and selecting the Install button to begin the installation of the Android SDK Tools. After all the files have been downloaded and installed on the computer, select the Next button. The next dialog box tells you that the Android SDK Tools setup wizard is complete and the Android SDK Tools have successfully installed on the computer. Select the Finish button to exit the wizard, as shown in Figure A.5.

Note that the checkbox Start SDK Manager (to download system images) is checked by default. It means that after the Finish button is clicked, the Android SDK Manager,

**Figure A.5  The successful installation of the Android SDK Tools dialog box.**

one of the tools in the Android SDK Tools package, will be launched. The Android SDK is installed in two phases; the first phase is the installation of the SDK, which installs the Android SDK Tools, and the second phase is the installation of the Android platforms and other components.

## Adding Platforms and Other Components

In this step you will see how to use the Android SDK Manager to download and install the important SDK packages required for the development environment. The Android SDK Manager (Figure A.6) that opens up shows the list of all the packages and their installation status. The dialog box shows that the Android SDK Tools package is already installed on the machine. To install any other package, you just need to check its checkbox. The Android SDK Manager recommends a platform by checking the `Android 4.2 (API 17)` and `Google USB Driver` packages by default.

You can check more packages and uncheck existing packages to determine which application programming interfaces (APIs) you wish to install. Because you wish to work with the latest Android API, leave the default selected and choose the `Install 7 packages` button at the bottom to initiate installation. The next dialog box you see shows the list of the packages that you have selected to install, their descriptions, and license terms. You need to select the `Accept All` option, followed by the `Install` button to begin installation, as shown in Figure A.7.

An `Android SDK Manager Log` window appears showing the downloading and installation progress. It also shows the list of packages that have been loaded, the Android SDK platform tools that have been downloaded and installed on the machine, and the ones that are still being downloaded (see Figure A.8a). After selecting the `Close` button, the next dialog window is the `ADB Restart` window that provides information about updates and asks whether you wish to

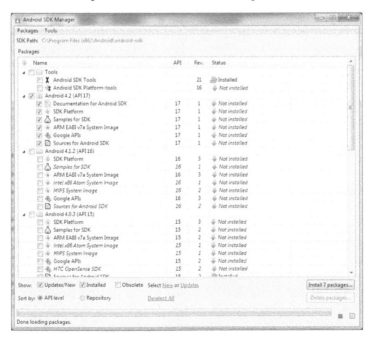

**Figure A.6   The Android SDK Manager showing the list of packages and their current status.**

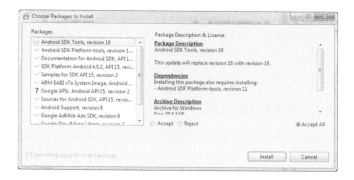

**Figure A.7** **The dialog box to accept the license terms for the selected packages and to begin installation.**

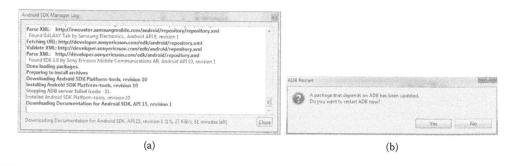

(a) (b)

**Figure A.8** **(a) The Android SDK Manager Log showing the status of different packages. (b) The** ADB Restart **dialog box, prompting you to Restart ADB.**

restart the Android Debug Bridge (ADB), as shown in Figure A.8b. Select the Yes button in the dialog to restart ADB.

The next dialog box is the Android SDK Manager, as shown in Figure A.9. The dialog box confirms that the Android SDK platform tools, Android 4.2 (API 17), and its components have been successfully installed on your machine.

You do not need the Android SDK Manager window for now, so you can go ahead and close it.

An Android application is a combination of several small components that includes Java files, Extensible Markup Language (XML) resource and layout files, manifest files, and much more. It will be very time-consuming to create all these components manually. So, you will be using the following two applications to help you:

■ **Eclipse IDE**—An integrated development environment (IDE) that makes the task of creating Java applications quite easy. It provides a complete platform for developing Java applications with compiling, debugging, and testing support.
■ **Android Development Tools (ADT) plug-in**—A plug-in that is added to the Eclipse IDE and automatically creates the necessary Android files so you can concentrate on the process of application development.

Before you begin the installation of Eclipse IDE, first set the path of the JDK that you installed, as it will be required for compiling the applications. To set the JDK path on Windows,

**Figure A.9  The Android SDK Manager showing that all the desired packages have been successfully installed on the machine.**

right-click on the My  Computer icon and select the Properties option. From the System  Properties dialog box that appears, select the Advanced tab, followed by the Environment  Variables button. A dialog box, Environment  Variables, pops up. In the System variables section, double-click on the Path variable. Add the full path of the JDK (C:\Program  Files\Java\jdk1.7.0 _ 09\bin\java.exe) to the path variable and select OK to close the windows.

## Installing Eclipse

Eclipse IDE is a multilanguage software development platform that is commonly used for developing Java applications. You can add plug-ins to extend its features for developing applications in other languages. Eclipse can be downloaded from the following URL: http://www. eclipse.org/downloads/. Eclipse  Classic and Eclipse  IDE  for  Java Developers are recommended. Just remember that both the JDK and Eclipse must be for the same version, either 32 bit or 64 bit. The latest version, Eclipse Classic 4.2.1, is available at the time of this writing.

Eclipse is a self-contained executable file; that is, all you need to do to install Eclipse is to unzip the downloaded file to any desired folder. To launch Eclipse, run the Eclipse.exe file. Eclipse IDE starts by displaying its logo, followed by a Workspace  Launcher dialog box, as shown in Figure A.10. The Workspace  Launcher dialog prompts for the location of the workspace folder where the Eclipse project files will be stored. A default location is displayed that you can change by selecting the Browse button.

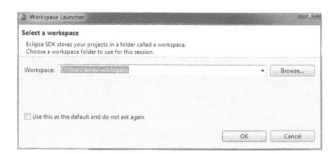

**Figure A.10** **The first screen you see after launching Eclipse IDE, asking for the workspace location to save applications.**

**Figure A.11** **The Eclipse welcome screen.**

The checkbox Use this as the default and do not ask again can be checked if you do not want Eclipse to prompt for the workspace every time it is launched. Select the OK button to continue. When Eclipse finishes loading, an Eclipse welcome screen is displayed, as shown in Figure A.11.

Select the curved-arrow icon at the top right of the screen to go to the Workbench, as shown in Figure A.12.

You can see that all the windows in the Workbench (Package Explorer, Editor window, Debug window, and Task List) are blank at the moment. These windows will update their content as you develop PhoneGap applications for Android. One more step is needed before you begin the Android application development—installing the ADT plug-in.

## Installing the Android Developer Tool (ADT) Plug-In

ADT is a plug-in for the Eclipse IDE that provides a powerful, integrated environment to build Android applications. It makes the task of developing Android applications quite easy. It integrates with Eclipse to add functionality for creating, testing, debugging, and deploying Android applications.

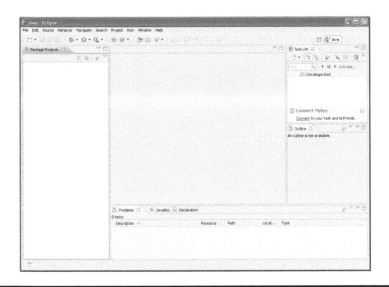

**Figure A.12   The Eclipse Workbench, showing windows and panels.**

To install the ADT plug-in, select the `Help->Install New Software....` option from the Eclipse IDE. You will see a dialog box asking for the location of the Web site from which you wish to install new software, as shown in Figure A.13a. Select the `Add` button to add a Web site or repository location. An `Add Repository` dialog box will appear, as shown in Figure A.13b. Enter the name of the repository in the `Name:` text box. Let us specify the name of the repository as `ADT Plugin`, although it can be any other address. In the `Location` box, specify the location of the repository as `https://dl-ssl.google.com/android/eclipse/`, followed by the OK button.

Eclipse will access the list of developer tools available at the specified site and display it, as shown in Figure A.14. In the figure, you can see that an entry named `Developer Tools` is

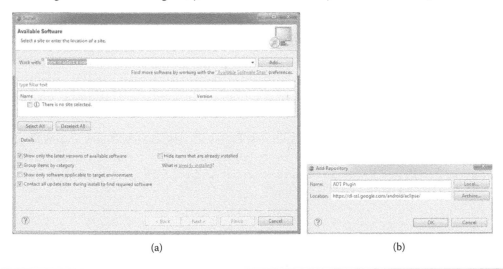

(a)                                    (b)

**Figure A.13   (a) The dialog box prompting for the location of the software installation Web site. (b) The dialog box to add the new repository information.**

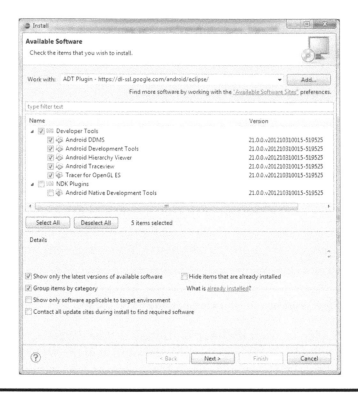

**Figure A.14   The dialog box displaying the list of developer tools available in the added repository.**

displayed, along with five child nodes: `Android DDMS`, `Android Development Tools`, `Android Hierarchy Viewer`, `Android Traceview`, and `Tracer for OpenGL ES`. We need to install all five tools, so select the parent node, `Developer Tools` (its child nodes will be autoselected), and select the `Next` button.

You will see a dialog box to review licenses for the ADT. Read the license agreement, check the radio button `I accept the terms of the license agreement` if you agree with the terms and conditions, and select the `Finish` button. The ADT plug-in will be downloaded and installed in Eclipse. After installation of the ADT plug-in, you get a `Software Updates` dialog box asking to restart Eclipse. To make the ADT plug-in show up in the IDE, you need to restart Eclipse. Select the `Restart Now` button from the `Software Updates` dialog box to make the installation changes take effect.

**Note:** If you do not want to take the time to install Eclipse, Android SDK Tools, and ADT plug-in, an ADT bundle is provided at: `http://developer.android.com/sdk/index.html`. Download the bundle and it will install all the essential Android SDK components and a version of the Eclipse IDE with built-in ADT for you.

## Making the ADT Plug-In Functional

To make the ADT plug-in functional inside of Eclipse, the plug-in needs to point to the Android SDK. Launch the Eclipse IDE and select the `Window->Preferences` option. In the

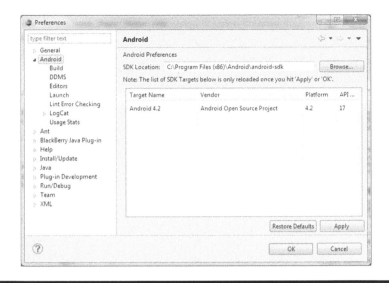

**Figure A.15** The Preference **window to specify the location of the Android SDK installation and the list of supportable platforms displayed after specifying the location of the Android SDK installation.**

Preferences dialog box, select the Android node and set the SDK Location box to specify the path where Android SDK is installed on your disk (see Figure A.15).

Upon specifying the path of the Android SDK, a list of SDK targets will be displayed. You can now develop and test the Android applications against any of the displayed targets. Select the Apply button, followed by the OK button, to reload the SDK targets and close the Preferences window. Eclipse now has the ADT plug-ins attached. That is, you can now develop and run the PhoneGap application for Android.

# Appendix B: Using Github

In this appendix, we will learn to:

- Create a Github account
- Create a local repository on our local machine
- Update the Github account with the local repository created on our machine

The first step is to create an account in Github. So, visit the `https://github.com/` URL to sign up for an account. Because we will be managing our Github repository through our Windows-based PC, let us download Github for Windows from `http://windows.github.com/`. Double-click the downloaded executable file and follow the wizard to install Github on our computer. Click the GitHub shortcut to launch it. The first screen that pops up is the login screen to the Github account. Enter the Github ID and password that we used when we created an account on the Github site (see Figure B.1a). Upon successful login, we get a screen as shown

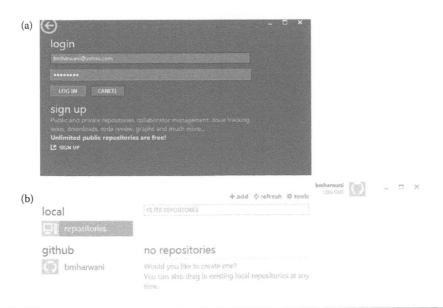

**Figure B.1** (a) Logging into a Github account. (b) The page showing information of the local and Github repository.

in Figure B.1b. We can see that the figure indicates that there is neither any local repository nor any repository on Github's account. So, let us create a local repository by clicking the +add link shown on the top.

We get a page that asks for the information for the new local repository. We enter the title and a small description of the new repository. The page will show the location on our disk drive where the newly created local repository will be stored. Check the Push to github checkbox because we will be pushing or uploading the local repository into our Github account later. The Github account to which the local repository is associated will also be displayed. Figure B.2a shows that the local repository will be pushed to the bmharwani account on Github. After entering the information of the new local repository, click the Create button to create the local repository at the specified location on the disk. The newly created local repository appears in the local section. The name bmharwani/PhoneGapApps that is assigned to the local repository indicates that PhoneGapApps is the repository created for the bmharwani account (see Figure B.2b).

In the repository titled bmharwani/PhoneGapApps, when we hover the mouse over the right arrow, the following text will appear, open this repo. Click on the right arrow to open the newly created local repository, PhoneGapApps. Upon opening the local repository, we find that two files, .gitattributes and .gitignore, are automatically created for us by default, as shown in Figure B.3.

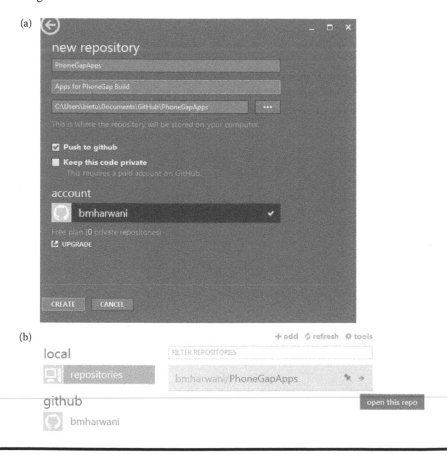

**Figure B.2** **(a) Entering information of a new local repository. (b) The newly created local repository appears in the local section.**

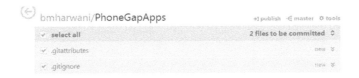

**Figure B.3   The new repository with two default files,** `.gitattributes` **and** `.gitignore`**.**

To copy files of our application into the local repository, we need to open the repository in the file explorer. So, select the `tools` icon at the top and select the `open in explorer` option from the drop-down menu that pops up. To the repository folder, copy the files of the application that we want to upload on the PhoneGap Build service, as shown in Figure B.4a. The figure shows that we copied three files in the local repository: `index.html`, `config.xml`, and `icon.png`. The three application files copied into the repository folder will then appear in our local repository, bmharwani/PhoneGapApps, as shown in Figure B.4b. All the files appear to be in the uncommitted state. In order to save the changes, the files need to be committed. In the dialog on the right side, we need to enter a title or small description to identify the commit action and click the `COMMIT` button at the bottom of the dialog. The title that is assigned to the commit action is used to identify it and cancel the commit operation, if required.

After clicking the `COMMIT` button, there is one more step to make the changes made to the local repository permanent. The commits made at the moment are entitled `unsynced commits`. Below the heading `unsynced commits`, we will see text showing some ID along with the text `Saving the three files`, as shown in Figure B.5. Click the text `Saving`

**Figure B.4   (a) Copying the files of an app into the local repository using file explorer. (b) The copied files appear in the local repository with "uncommitted changes."**

**Figure B.5   The page informing us that the commits made are in the "unsynced commits" state.**

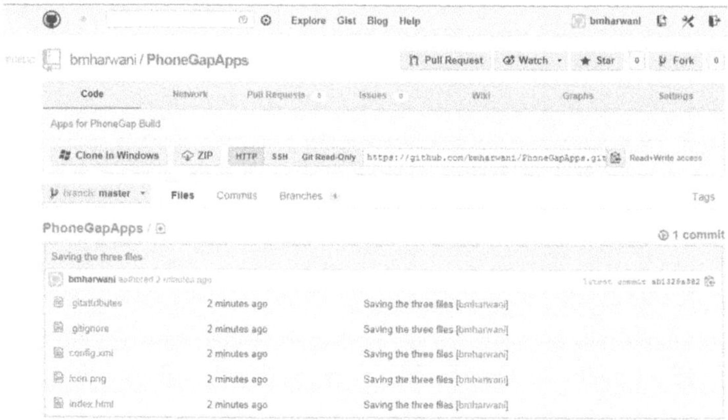

**Figure B.6** **The committed files of the application appear in the Github account.**

the three files to save the files that we added through the file explorer into the local repository.

To view the saved local repository files in the Github account, click the tools icon at the top and select the option view on github from the drop-down menu that pops up. The Github account will open, showing the files that we created in our local repository, PhoneGapApps, as shown in Figure B.6.

Now, our Git repository is ready by name, bmharwani/PhoneGapApps, to be uploaded on the PhoneGap Build service.

# Index

Milton Keynes UK
Ingram Content Group UK Ltd.
UKHW051932141024
449569UK00027B/1463